School and
the Social Order

School and the Social Order

Frank Musgrove
University of Manchester

JOHN WILEY & SONS
Chichester · New York · Brisbane · Toronto

Copyright © 1979, by John Wiley & Sons, Ltd.

British Library Cataloguing in Publication Data:

Musgrove, Frank, b.1922
  School and the social order.
  1. Educational sociology—Great Britain
  2. Social classes—Great Britain
  370.19,3   LC206.G7   79-40738
  ISBN 0 471 27651 0 (Cloth)
  ISBN 0 471 27653 7 (Paper)

Typeset by Computacomp (U.K.) Ltd.,
Fort William, Scotland
Page Bros (Norwich) Ltd.,
Mile Cross Lane, Norwich

Contents

CHAPTER 1

Personal Orientations

This book is a macrosociology of education. It will attempt to uncover the more significant connexions between schooling and the wider society. It is inevitably influenced by my personal perspectives and the nature of my experience.

I have been professionally engaged in education for more than thirty years, and for the last fifteen have occupied Chairs of Education in English universities. At a relatively early stage of my career as a schoolmaster, I reached four broad conclusions about education in highly developed industrial countries. The first was that universal schooling has arisen not from the complexities, but the simplicities, of advanced societies: its job has been to narrow curiosity (notably through early specialization) and not to enlarge it; its function must be understood not in relation to society's (largely illusory) needs for trained intellect but in relation to the stability of the social order (which includes orderly and indeed rapid change). The second conclusion was that most schools at the secondary stage should no longer exist except as entirely voluntary (and systematically demoralized) information centres. The third was that, nevertheless, access to a highly academic education is crucial for advancement in life: its importance is increased rather than diminished by the proliferation and devaluation of educational credentials. The fourth was that all these issues have been obscured and bedevilled since the War by examining them in simplistic terms of 'social class'.

These conclusions came directly from my work as a teacher in schools. I have written about all of them in some measure before.[1] I spent ten years (precisely) teaching in schools, from the late nineteen-forties to the late nineteen-fifties. This decade in schools embraced three phases: teaching as a member of the Colonial Education Service in the Government College in the remote territory of Western Uganda, an African boys' boarding school modelled on the English Public School (and with close personal links with Winchester College); teaching at the Secondary Modern School at Eastwood, on the Nottinghamshire coalfield, where D. H. Lawrence was born and spent his boyhood; teaching at Queen Elizabeth's Grammar School at Mansfield, also on the Nottinghamshire coalfield, a highly traditional selective grammar school whose pupils went in significant numbers into the major professions. (One became a notable Vice Chancellor of a new university in the nineteen-sixties.) This experience of teaching in schools has had a deep and abiding influence on my attitudes and perspectives, so that I still regard it as effrontery for 'educationists' with a shorter or less varied period to pronounce on the nature and problems of the educational process. I still find it difficult to take their writing seriously, however impressively backed by research. There is no more dangerous

1

man than the expert with one, or perhaps two, years of schoolteaching experience—except the legion who actually have none.

THE SIMPLICITIES OF COMPLEX SOCIETIES

My experience in East Africa underlies in a positive and creative way all subsequent developments in my professional career and intellectual life: the work that I did on education and the family in England[2] stemmed from my awareness of the importance of kinship ties (especially with the mother's brother) in the intellectual and social development of the African child; my work on the status of youth in England[3] was an extension and transposition of my interest in African 'age-sets'; and my work on 'migratory elites'[4] originated in an interest in melting-pot theories of culture contact and change and the connexion between migration and detribalization in Central Africa. But one circumstance above all impressed me as I tried systematically to uncover the nature of the tribal world in which I was now embedded: this was the sheer complexity of the knowledge (including the language) which an African child must learn. Western culture, by comparison, for any individual growing up in it, was relatively easy to master. The tribal knowledge required of any individual was not only complex, many-sided, and in widely diverse fields but was often highly abstract in character. The tribal African was commonly contemptuous of European culture for its intellectual inadequacy and inelegance.

My pupils had no difficulty in understanding the explanations of the social and physical world offered by European science, but they did not believe them. I examined these 'learning problems' as social rather than cognitive in character many years ago in studies of 'culture contact' as I experienced it.[5] Since that time Robin Horton has published influential work which makes substantially the same point.

Horton emphasizes the highly theoretical nature of African thought, treating '... African religious systems as theoretical models akin to those of the sciences'. (That magic and sorcery was 'wrong' is not the point.) He also says, quite rightly, that 'coincidence', 'chance', and 'probability' are concepts which find no place in the tribal African's explanation of events.[6] And it was my experience that it was precisely our use of such empty concepts that convicted us, in the eyes of Africans, of parading ignorance as explanation.

In my book, *Youth and the Social Order*, I drew attention to Margaret Read's anthropological studies in Nyasaland which accorded very closely with my own observations in the region of the Mountains of the Moon:

> Margaret Read has described (in her book, *Children of Their Fathers*) the learning required of a young Ngoni tribesman growing up to manhood: the reckoning of time and of the seasons; cosmology and the interpretation of the heavens; tribal history and customary law; veterinary knowledge and skills in the care of cattle; hunting techniques and the skills of building and other manual crafts. The girls undertook an elaborate training in the preparation of food, the arts of household management, bead and leather-work, the arts of speech, dancing and deportment. Formerly men married

in their late twenties; it was only with the advent of an allegedly more complex civilization and opportunities for employment in Western enterprises, that this prolonged preparation for adult life became unnecessary and the usual age at which men and women married steeply declined.[7]

I concluded that 'life in a "civilized" society is in many ways simpler and easier to learn than life in a non-literate tribe' and ' "civilization" makes the major content of our traditional education less necessary and not more'. This, indeed, is precisely what we should expect in a modern society characterized by Durkheim's organic social solidarity: complexity (for society) and simplicity (for the individual) are two sides of the same coin. The involved interconnectedness of the modern industrial world is achieved through specialization and the division of labour: the streamlining, rationalization, and simplification of the parts that individuals are called upon to play.

In industrial countries schools are more difficult than life (and industry, for 'sandwich course' students, far less demanding and problematical than college[8]). Intelligence levels tend to decline after young people leave their schools and colleges. Our schools do not make sense as a response to the very modest intellectual demands which, on average, 'complex Western societies' make. This is the conclusion of the French sociologist Pierre Bourdieu and (quite independently and by a different route) of the American economist Samuel Bowles. Therefore schooling must 'really' be about something else. And what it is 'really about', both conclude, is social order.

Pierre Bordieu's views are now fashionable in England and he is Director of Studies at the Ecole des Hautes Etudes in France. His argument and his prose (in his book *Reproduction*) are typically opaque, verbose, and redundant. He asserts that very little actually gets taught in schools and universities ('the informative efficiency of pedagogic communication is low'[9]). It is not the content but the form of the teaching—'the relation of pedagogic communication'—which is really important, as this relationship helps to perpetuate (in Bourdieu's term, 'reproduce') the traditional relationships of a class society.

Samuel Bowles and his coauthor Herbert Gintis are mercifully and refreshingly straightforward, and they actually produce evidence to support their argument. In an impeccable statistical analysis of American data on intelligence levels, education, social class origins, and occupational achievement, they conclude that intelligence in itself is relatively unimportant in explaining a person's economic success. It is true that extremely high or extremely low intelligence may have a decisive effect, but '... for the vast majority of workers and jobs, selection, assessed job adequacy, and promotion are based on attributes other than I.Q.'.[10]

Bowles and Gintis reach this important overall conclusion: that measured mental ability is in itself largely irrelevant to the occupational advancement of the individual and the efficiency of the economy, but it is vital (in America) in a less obvious, more indirect fashion, to the maintenance of the social order. Its 'true function' is to justify social inequality. As Bowles and Gintis put it: '... I.Q. clearly plays an important part in the U.S. stratification system ... the set of beliefs surrounding I.Q. betrays its true function—that of legitimating the social institutions underpinning the stratification system itself.' The I.Q. ideology, they maintain, 'serves to legitimate the hierarchical division of labor'. The educational system ostensibly identifies and certifies intellectual merit; in fact it is a device to legitimate fraud.

The basic argument of Bowles and Gintis regarding the relative unimportance of intelligence is in line with a large number of expert studies of the significance of 'human capital' in modern, highly developed economies. Ivar Berg's evidence is that American society is the victim of a 'great training robbery' and that employees are paid for their qualifications rather than their performance;[11] the Harvard economist, Richard Freeman, has advanced his very cogent 'over-educated American' thesis;[12] and in England there is strong evidence of a lack of fit (without undue consequences) between education and occupation in higher scientific work.[13]

Education impairs the performance of modern economies: they do not 'need' the vast and expensive educational apparatus of schools and colleges. What they do need is quite modest schemes of on-the-job training. But the top 10 per cent. of the ability range is crucial and must be identified and rigorously schooled. This is the unambiguous conclusion that emerges from Dael Wolfle's studies of the uses of human talent.[14]

The role of schools is neither simple, singular, nor self-evident. Bourdieu's 'reproduction' thesis will be examined later in this book; but my experience has been that the contribution of schools to the social order has been through promoting 'replacement' quite as much as 'reproduction'. (I devote Chapter 8 to this subject.) Certainly Government College in Western Uganda was reproducing neither the traditional tribal order nor the imperial order that had been imposed upon it.

Attendance at Government College was voluntary and fee-paying. Boys came from all the major tribes of Uganda (like the Baganda, Banyoro, Batoro, and Banyankole) and also from such relatively minor and backward non-Bantu tribes as the Lugbara, Teso, and even the pygmy Ba'amba of the Ituri Forest. The non-Bantu tribes in the north were remarkably egalitarian in their social and political structures; the great Bantu kingdoms of Toro and Buganda highly hierarchical. Bantu pupils had a high regard for social distinction and rank, and unabated respect for the high status clans (the Babito) which provided hereditary chiefs. They were deeply contemptuous of the egalitarian social policies that they believed the post-war British government was pursuing.[15]

The cattlemen (as distinct from the cultivators) were the people of high social status and power; in Ankole and neighbouring Ruanda they constituted a caste of quasi-feudal overlords.[16] And it was the proud cattlemen who were contemptuous of Western ways and relatively uninterested in sending their children to Western-type schools. These circumstances had the following long-term consequence: while the indigenous educational system (through kinship connexions and in particular apprenticeship to maternal uncles) 'reproduced' the traditional social order, the new system of European-type schooling replaced it. European-style schools were powerful means of promoting not the succession but the circulation of an indigenous elite.

Literacy did not help to reproduce the traditional order. Nor did it support the superimposed imperial order; it subverted it. It was certainly not sought by Africans for obtaining the quite small number of new, white-collar jobs thrown up by the 'modernizing' process. Schoolboys contemplated such jobs with horror: they would be endured for a few years to get cash for purchasing cattle, wives, and land. Western schooling cannot be explained as a response to the country's growing need for trained intelligence. The paradoxes of the situation in Uganda (as I examined them around 1950[17]) find a striking parallel in Philip J. Foster's well-known studies of Ghana around 1960: schoolboys wanted an abstract and literary education, but they did not want white-collar jobs; they wanted, in the main, to be farmers. They knew in fact that the chances were high that they would simply be unemployed.[18]

My Uganda pupils saw literacy quite explicitly as an important defence against imperial power. It was the only safeguard against the kind of trickery which they all believed had robbed them of their land and their rights in the Uganda Agreements of 1900. As Mulumba, the school-educated rebel leader said in his telegram to the Governor of Uganda in 1949: 'People of Uganda refuse one-sided Anglo–Uganda Agreements concluded in 1900 with illiterate peasants.' Literacy was a weapon against the imperial power which provided the schools and the teachers to promote it. The school was staffed by white officers of Her Majesty's Colonial Education Service; the 'pedagogic relationship' replicated and reinforced the imperial relationship. It was singularly ineffective in reproducing the imperial order.

THE WORLD OF D. H. LAWRENCE: THE REAL CASE FOR DE-SCHOOLING

The school at Eastwood in the nineteen-fifties was a classical secondary modern school of the post-war period. It had a firm if rather negative sense of its own identity. It was committed to not imitating or competing with the highly academic purposes of the grammar schools; none of its pupils took external examinations and in practice none was ever transferred to a grammar school as a late developer. It was 'streamed', and it ran in a well-ordered way between nine o'clock and four. There were no out-of-school activities. The staff were highly competent professionals (many with successful experience of teaching in pre-war elementary schools), and yet the school's central meaning for the children was as an arena in which you finally tested your manhood (or your womanhood) by 'telling the teacher off'.

It is often said nowadays that schools are 'middle-class institutions' and in consequence working-class children are apathetic, even alienated, and so fail to learn what the school tries to teach. This is a proposition which will be considered carefully in this book. Certainly the secondary modern school at Eastwood in the nineteen-fifties made no attempt at 'cultural relevance' through any kind of curricular orientation to the local world. There was certainly no celebration—indeed no recognition—of the miner's world of work and still less of the leisure culture of pigeons, allotment gardens, brass bands, and male voice choirs. And yet there was in fact cultural and moral solidarity between parents and teachers (many of whom in any event were local men and women with deep roots in the area). D. H.

Lawrence was as discreditable in the eyes of the teachers as of the parents—a 'mucky bogger', even 'an arsehole bandit'.[19] Only an Indian member of the teaching staff favoured, tentatively and apologetically, a (suitably expurgated) incorporation of D. H. Lawrence into the school curriculum.

Compared with the situation I had recently known in Uganda, 'cultural discontinuities' between the school and the local society were derisory. My pupils at Eastwood were not handicapped, like the ones I had recently taught, with the unshakeable belief that the earth was flat—unshakeable not from African stupidity but because it was buttressed at every turn by social custom and ritual and tied to respect for the fearful ancestors, the Bachwezi, light-skinned, one-armed, and one-legged creatures who had shaped the physical world, were still skilful as rain-makers and caused earth tremors, had made the crater lakes, and erected the mountains to rest the sky on. It was not self-evident to my Eastwood pupils that no accident was accidental and the fact that the intersection of two wholly un-connected series of events—like a man walking his dog and another man driving his car—was an obvious outcome of sorcery. I was never wholly persuaded that the apathy and 'under-achievement' of pupils at Eastwood Secondary Modern School could be ascribed to 'culture conflict', to major cultural discontinuities between the school as a 'middle-class institution' and the working-class world which it served.

The serious and unbridgable gap is not between (middle-class) teachers and (working-class) parents, but between teachers who are actually working in schools and 'educationists' who prescribe for them. Teachers in slum areas of big cities know that their 'middle-classness' is not part of the problem of educational failure and is in any event an invention of sociologists—a construction of reality imposed on them by experts. Certainly the headteachers of ten Liverpool schools which were (voluntarily) involved in the post-Plowden 'educational priority area' programme thought so. The attempt to mitigate their supposed middle-classness was ludicrous. One inquiry into the working of the scheme makes it clear that teachers regarded as irrelevant the middle-classness of teachers and 'argued that many of the downtown teachers were not middle class at all; the head of school X had been born and bred in the area, for example'.[20] This is a version of reality which fits precisely with my Eastwood experience.

Language differences have been picked out as the heart of the class–culture conflict problem in education; this is also a proposition I shall look at closely later in this book. But the boys I taught (in English) in Uganda spoke a dozen different languages: they were mainly Bantu languages—Lutoro, Luganda, and Lunyankole—but they also included the language of the Lugbara of the West Nile region and others marked by significant Hamitic influence. These languages are complex, subtle, and flexible. Some are essentially tonal (rather than intonational) in character and the pitch of entire utterances (as distinct from individual words or their prefixes) must be appreciated to grasp their meaning.[21] But these languages were nevertheless highly restricted for encompassing the concepts of Western physical and social science. The linguistic gap between a Mutoro pupil and his English schoolmaster is in fact immense. It did not seem to me that, compared with my

Batoro pupils, miners' children in Eastwood were the victims of serious linguistic deprivation. In relation to the curriculum of the school they were highly linguistically privileged.

In the notable Inglis Lecture delivered at Harvard University in 1948 Allison Davis drew heavily on the linguistic studies of anthropologists to make the same point. Lower-class English dialects were like many 'primitive' languages—vastly superior to Standard English in their complexity: 'It is very doubtful, in fact, that the refinements, as we consider them, of middle-class English indicate any higher degree of mental capacity than the complexities of lower-class dialects or of primitive languages.'[22] Since I taught African boys from the Semliki swamps, it has never seemed to me that minor variants of Standard English spoken by Englishmen—even in the backstreets of Bradford or Stepney—were a serious impediment to knowledge, even when it was presented with a flourish of adjectives, subordinate clauses, and finite verbs.

The conclusion I drew from teaching in the Secondary Modern School at Eastwood in the early nineteen-fifties—which was an excellent and very well run school of its kind—was not that it should have a more subculturally relevant curriculum with a reduced emphasis on writing Standard English but that it should not exist. This was not an argument from sociology or economics; it was an argument from humanity. Schooling for perhaps two-thirds of all adolescents is at best inefficient; it is commonly simply destructive and brutalizing for everyone involved. It is a gigantic absurdity. A straightforward test of a civilized country with any developed sensibility is that such institutions do not exist. There are almost certainly better (and cheaper) ways of graduating young people to manhood than maintaining a complex and costly educational apparatus in which pupils can eventually 'tell the teacher off'.

I have suggested elsewhere that there is today probably more violence in schools than out,[23] and schools are commonly an apprenticeship to vice. It is true, as I have also argued, that 'violence' can have many meanings for those involved, and at times violence in school is little more than an elaborate joke. A more subjective, 'phenomenological' sociology has taught us in recent years to get inside the skin of the 'actors' involved in a situation and to see it from their perspective. We should not conclude too readily that less successful pupils are 'alienated' and hate school (or that the successful ones love it and embody its values). Whatever the official version of schooling might be, or the picture obtained by a detached observer, pupils impose their own meanings and transform the reality of it. It is in the school's sheer boredom and pointlessness that they find high significance.

We now have some very good phenomenological studies of such transformations. Peter Woods has explored the significance of 'having a laugh'[24] and the high importance of a secondary school for young people as a place for 'mucking about', as well as the transformational properties of laughter for both pupil and staff. 'Doing nothing' is invested with almost as much meaning as 'acting silly', but 'Of course we don't act silly out of school. We wouldn't if we were anywhere important.'[25]

I shall return at the end of this book to the crucial issue of the patent absurdity of schools for most young people (and their teachers). At this point I must mention one further phenomenological study, not only because it confirms my own experience as a schoolmaster, but because it draws the right conclusions.

The significance of 'having a laugh' has been perceptively explored by Peter Woods; no less perceptively Elizabeth Rosser and Rom Harre have uncovered the meaning of 'trouble'.[26] They have shown that a deeper, rule-governed order underlies the apparent disorder of two comprehensive schools they have studied; the basic 'rule' which governs the behaviour of pupils is that you require the teacher to keep you in order and do everything you can to prevent him. The teacher's most grievous offence is weakness, and the unwritten rule which governs school life is that the soft teacher is shown no mercy. (These are similar rules to those which formerly governed bear-baiting, except that modern professional ethics and psychological theory proscribe for the teacher any effective measure of self-defence.)

But the underlying 'order', by any standard of civilized decency, is worse than the surface chaos of school life; and at least Rosser and Harre fully recognize this. Having found 'order' where no-one would suspect it, they do not proclaim that all is well. They see that the basic reality of school life is a triangle of personal and spiritual destruction based on 'contempt, depersonalization and reciprocal retaliation'. For pupils, 'The central issue ... seems to be the unseriousness of the institution and its practices and the depersonalization and contempt meted out to those who see it as such.' Rosser and Harre draw from their work a conclusion with which I wholly concur:

> Something has to give. Perhaps the 'school' should become a community resource, where those who *seek* knowledge and skill could find it, regardless of age and official attainments. And the apprenticeship to violence, which our schools now offer as a major part of the informal curriculum, particularly to those whose physical maturity is denied by the official theory of schooling, could be eliminated from the real curriculum, by letting those who will go free.

For teachers and pupils alike, school, in a majority of cases, is a barbarous sentence which a civilized society should not impose. Teaching at Eastwood in the nineteen-fifties was essentially the same as Lawrence's brilliantly truthful account (in *The Rainbow*) of Ursula Brangwen's experience at Brinsley Street School, Ilkeston, at the turn of the century; and this in turn is like the experience of teachers I interviewed in 1973 (who had joined the 'rank-and-file' or decided to teach in 'free schools') who felt brutalized and degraded—'forced to be bastards'—in order to survive.[27]

'Ursula Brangwen' did not put it precisely like that. After her violent showdown with the Standard Five pupil, Williams (who would be no more than thirteen years of age), she felt that 'she had paid a great price out of her soul to do this'. But it had to be so. 'She did not want to do it. Yet she had to. Oh, why had she leagued herself to this evil system where she must brutalize herself to live?' She watched the headmaster, Mr. Harby, who stood 'with strength and male power, and a certain blind, native beauty', reduced to petty and petulant bullying, to triviality and

9

ugliness, 'imprisoned in a task too small for him, which yet, in a servile acquiescence, he would fulfil, because he had to earn his living'.

There is an uncanny similarity between the words of 'Ursula Brangwen' and the teachers I interviewed exactly seventy years on, mainly in Manchester. Ursula had started with this intention: 'She would be so *personal*. Teachers were always so hard and impersonal. There was no vivid relationship.' My interviewees in 1973 said: 'I found the first term shattering. Discipline was such a problem. You had all these wonderful ideas on teaching, and discipline was so hard.' 'I had trouble early on because I had all sorts of ideals which just didn't work in practice. I refused to hit the kids, unlike all the other teachers, who were bumpers. ...' Ursula Brangwen had to learn to make herself a non-person and even to become a bumper. ('She did not want to be a person, to be herself any more, after such humiliation. She would assert herself for mastery. ...' However, 'It was agony ... to become distant and official, having no personal relationship with children.') And so it was with my interviewees: 'It was awful right from the start. I just couldn't be myself. I felt that I was acting a part.' And headmasters, however civilized, are driven to humiliate children and degrade themselves: 'I think that headmasters are on the lookout for scapegoats. They don't care as long as they can pin the blame on someone and be seen to assert their authority.'[28]

In *The Rainbow* D. H. Lawrence interpreted a teaching situation as he himself had experienced it in the Erewash Valley in 1903. Mass schooling had only recently been established, and it made sense as a gigantic sanitary operation in the conditions of industrial and urban growth at that time. A national network of compulsory schools was in effect a network of refugee camps to protect young people from the streets, from employers, and from their parents. By the early nineteen-fifties, when I was teaching at Eastwood, these refugee camps were already an anachronism, even in the Erewash Valley. Mass schooling, in a little less than a century, had accomplished its historic mission. In 1980 it amounts to national folly. 'Ursula Brangwen's' experience of entrapment, depersonalization, brutality and degradation, despair and guilt in a job with automatic, built-in failure is still quite normal (the tragedy is that the sheer professionalism of teachers prevents their saying so):

> Then followed a day of battle and hate and violence, when she went home raw, feeling the golden evening taken away from her, herself incarcerated in some dark, heavy place, and chained there with a consciousness of having done badly at work. What good was it that it was summer, that right till evening when the corncrakes called, the larks would mount up into the light, to sing once more before nightfall. What good was it all, when she was out of tune, when she must only remember the burden and shame of school that day.

AN ELIZABETHAN GRAMMAR SCHOOL AND THE PHILISTINE MIDDLE CLASS

Before the end of the century, it will be the mark of the civilized state that it has abolished compulsory schooling after the age of twelve or thirteen, and schoolteaching will no longer be a kind of charge or punishment imposed on working-class children in return for a higher education. Of course, to lower the age of compulsory school attendance will exacerbate the already serious problem of massive surpluses of human beings in post-industrial states. That is a social problem and must be found a social solution. We must not hand over to the schools all the inconvenient social dilemmas that are apparently insoluble.

That is not to say that schools 'don't matter'. On the contrary, they have an ever greater significance. Access to a demanding and rigorous education for all who both want it and can profit by it—whatever their age—is of ever greater importance both for social justice and national survival. The growing importance of access to high quality academic schooling (and prestigious credentials), the continuing difficulties experienced by working-class children, and the still greater disability of having a middle-class home, were among the conclusions I came to after teaching at Mansfield's Queen Elizabeth's Grammar School for boys.

In the nineteen-fifties this was a very traditional, highly selective school with a good sixth form, well-established links with the ancient universities, and a particularly good academic record in modern languages. A majority of its pupils came from miners' families, but there was, nevertheless, some middle-class 'over-representation', and the sons of both the 'new' (educated and professionally qualified) and the 'old' (propertied, business, and shop-keeping) middle-class were present in the school in large numbers. They were not noticeably scholastically superior—although scholastic performance was never informally discussed in the staffroom or in any way officially reported and categorized in social-class terms. (I have no detailed records in terms of 'social class'—indeed, they do not exist—but a notable surgeon of our times and a famous musician are both miners' sons whom I taught.) Only the parents, on Open Days and Parents' Evenings, exhibited noticeable social-class differences. The most striking gap was between the values of middle-class parents and the scholastic (and perhaps slightly other-worldly) traditions that the school stood for. (Twelfth-century monasticism was a long-hallowed 'Special Subject' in the Sixth.)

Middle-class parents, whatever their wealth, family, or Masonic connexions, knew that educational credentials mattered. They had no illusion that their sons could prosper without them. But they were confident that through their social position their sons' certificates could be handsomely converted into material rewards: they could augment, but they could not make good the lack of professional diplomas.

They wanted their sons crammed. The middle class of northern Nottinghamshire had scant regard for an 'invisible pedagogy'. Many of the 'new' middle class appeared to have obtained professional qualifications through correspondence courses, and the 'model answer' was an apparently foolproof pedagogical strategy which they insistently commended to their sons' teachers. Probably the deepest, most genuinely shared and abiding value that we held as a staff was that 'spoon-feeding' was bad for the intellect and worse for the soul. And more generally 'getting on' was really rather a discreditable preoccupation. The Senior Science Master was thought also to be the Careers Master, but undue concern about jobs was rather immoral. This was not, in fact, a 'middle-class culture'; it was a gentry culture. (Members of staff had been known to leave to become HMIs.)

There was no snug fit between the values of middle-class parents and those of the school; in fact, the middle-class parents were very much as Mathew Arnold (and the Schools Inquiry Commission) had described them a hundred or so years before. Two or three years later I was again forcibly struck by the gap between middle-class parents and school when I made more systematic inquiries into parental attitudes in the city of Leicester. That was in 1960. I carried out a planned study of parents' expectations of teachers on the New Parks slum-clearance estate and, for comparative purposes, the well-to-do upper-class district, Stoneygate.[29]

The inquiry was focused on the junior school. At this stage, educational credentials were not of particular concern in either area (but middle-class parents again tended to support a very traditional, highly 'visible' pedagogy). Social-class differences were most striking over the social training expected of the school. Stoneygate parents saw the school as a place that would help their children to 'mix'; New Parks parents saw the school as an ally to prevent it. In Stoneygate 'mixing' was the way to the boardroom; in the New Parks Estate it was the way to the juvenile court. But in Stoneygate there was no sense of the school as a place of intellectual culture or even moral values: it was the anteroom to organizational life with its fat rewards for 'fitting in'.

A great deal of this book on schools and the social order will necessarily and properly be about social class. It will figure prominently in chapters on social mobility, social control, equality, and elites. But my own experience both as a teacher in schools and as a researcher has taught me to be very cautious about its use to explain educational situations and outcomes.

I shall examine with particular interest, for example, the view of the French neo-Marxist, Louis Althusser, that it is now the school and not the workplace that is the site of class conflict in capitalist societies. This was never my sense of schools when I taught in them; it is not, by and large, my sense of schools now. And yet there is no doubt that class has got into some of our schools; in large measure it is sociologists and teachers who have been taught by them on in-service courses who have taken it there.

As educational systems become more sophisticated and self-conscious, it is important to be sensitive to their increasing autonomy; they move far from the original impulse which brought them into existence and straightforwardly determined their nature. Their developing and ever more complex practices become self-sustaining; they arise not from the 'needs of society' or even of children and their parents but from the needs of 'educationists'. Prominent among those needs is career advancement. The most spectacular output of the educational system in the past decade has been educational theorizing; it has greatly influenced the actual practice—even some of the basic structures—of education, especially, perhaps, in the field of curriculum reform. A number of people have done very well out of it. I shall be sensitive to social-class theories—as to all others—as inventions which get people soft jobs.

12

NOTES

1. For example, in *Youth and the Social Order* (Indiana University Press, Bloomington, 1965) is expressed scepticism about the 'complex learning' required in advanced compared with primitive societies (pp. 25–28), the role of schools in regulating the distribution of power between generations (pp. 154–158), and the need for a measure of de-schooling (pp. 161–163); the argument for a 'demoralized' and service-station role for teachers and schools is advanced in *Society and the Teacher's Role* (Routledge and Kegan Paul, London, 1969, pp. 1–8 and 79–89) and in 'The future of teacher training' in J. D. Turner and J. Rushton (Eds.), *The Teacher in a Changing Society* (Manchester University Press, 1974); and the problems of 'social class' are dealt with in 'Curriculum, culture and ideology', *Journal of Curriculum Studies*, **10** (1978).
2. See F. Musgrove, *The Family, Education and Society*, Routledge and Kegan Paul, London, 1966.
3. See F. Musgrove, *Youth and the Social Order*, Indiana University Press, Bloomington, 1965.
4. See F. Musgrove, *The Migratory Elite*, Heinemann, London, 1963.
5. See F. Musgrove, 'A Uganda school as a field of culture change', *Africa*, **22** (1952); 'Teaching geography to the peoples of Western Uganda', *African Studies*, **11** (1952); 'Education and the culture concept', *Africa*, **23** (1953); 'The sociology of African education', *African Studies*, **11** (1952); 'History teaching within a conflict of cultures', *History*, **40** (1955).
6. Robin Horton, 'African traditional thought and Western science', in M. F. D. Young (Ed.), *Knowledge and Control*, Collier-Macmillan, 1971.
7. F. Musgrove, *Youth and the Social Order*, Indiana University Press, Bloomington, 1965, p. 27.
8. See F. Musgrove, 'Personal problems in learning environments', *Educational Research*, **10** (1969).
9. Pierre Bourdieu and Jean-Claude Passeron, *Reproduction in Education, Society and Culture*, trans. by Richard Nice, Sage Publications, London and Beverly Hills, 1977, p. 107. It is also asserted that: 'In short, students and teachers have a duty—to themselves and to each other—to over-estimate that quantity of information which really circulates in pedagogic communication, because this is their duty to the institution' (p. 113). Bourdieu and Passeron claim that they are answering this question: 'Could the informative efficiency of pedagogic communication be so low if the pedagogic relation were reducible to a simple relation of communication? To put it another way, what are the particular conditions such that the relation of pedagogic communication can perpetuate itself when the information transmitted tends towards zero?' (pp. 107–108).
10. Samuel Bowles and Herbert Gintis, 'I.Q. in the U.S. class structure', in Jerome Karabel and A. H. Halsey (Eds.), *Power and Ideology in Education*, Oxford University Press, New York, 1977, p. 223. The correlation between IQ and economic success is indeed highly significant: 0.52 (see Table 1, p. 219); but the correlation between IQ and economic success when the educational level and class of origin are held constant is insignificant: 0.13 (see Table 4, p. 222).
11. Ivar Berg, *Education and Jobs: The Great Training Robbery*, Praeger Publishers, New York, 1970.
12. Richard B. Freeman, *The Over-Educated American*, Academic Press, New York, 1976.
13. P. R. G. Layard, J. D. Sargan, M. E. Ager, and D. J. Jones, *Qualified Manpower and Economic Performance*, Allen Lane Penguin Press, 1971.
14. Dael Wolfle, *The Uses of Talent*, Princeton University Press, Princeton, N.J., 1971.
15. See F. Musgrove, 'Education and the culture concept', *Africa*, **23** (1953):

> The Babito, the clan which supplied the Bakama of Toro and Banyoro, are clearly, to my Batoro and Banyoro pupils, people of superior station, though

economically and politically (they are not necessarily or even frequently, chiefs) the majority have no basis of social power. My Banyankole students who are Bairu, descendants of the indigenous Bantu peasant-cultivators, show a similar respect for the aristocratic, cattle-owning Bahima, even though the latter are not necessarily richer than themselves and are now failing to obtain the more important chieftainships in Ankole. My pupils are shocked to hear of modern British methods of redistributing national income. ...

16. For the changing social structure in Ruanda see E. C. Eggins, 'The disappearance of a feudal aristocracy', *Corona: The Journal of Her Majesty's Colonial Service*, **4** (1952).
17. See F. Musgrove, 'A Uganda school as a field of culture change', *Africa*, **22** (1952).
18. See Philip J. Foster, 'The vocational school fallacy in development planning', in Jerome Karabel and A. H. Halsey (Eds.), *Power and Ideology in Education*, Oxford University Press, New York, 1977. Forster gives evidence of schoolboys' strong interest in farming but realistic expection of low-level clerical work. See also *Education and Social Change in Ghana* (Routledge and Kegan Paul, London, 1965) which also emphasizes the African schoolboy's 'academic' and literary bias, the continuing high status of farming, and the remarkable realism of vocational expectations.
19. See Alan Read, 'Eastwood Ho!', *Observer Magazine*, 16 July 1978.
20. See P. S. A. Thomson, *Educational Priority Areas and the National E.P.A. Project 1968–71: A Study with Special Reference to Liverpool*, Unpublished M.A. thesis, University of Liverpool, 1978, pp. 293–295.
21. See William J. Samarin, 'Intonation in tone languages', *African Studies*, **11** (1952), and A. E. Meeussen, 'The tones of prefixes in common Bantu', *Africa*, **24** (1954).
22. Allison Davis, *Social-Class Influences upon Learning*, Harvard University Press, Cambridge, Mass., 1949, p. 82.
23. See F. Musgrove, 'The future of teaching training', in J. Rushton and J. D. Turner (Eds.), *The Teacher in a Changing Society*, Manchester University Press, 1974.
24. Peter Woods, 'Having a laugh: an antidote to schooling', in Martyn Hammersley and Peter Woods (Eds.), *The Process of Schooling*, Routledge and Kegan Paul, London, 1976.
25. Peter Woods, *Secondary School Realities*, Ph.D. thesis, Open University, 1978, pp. 252–253 and 519.
26. Elizabeth Rosser and Rom Harre, 'The meaning of "trouble" ', in Martyn Hammersley and Peter Woods (Eds.), *The Process of Schooling*, Routledge and Kegan Paul, London, 1976. See also Elizabeth Rosser and Rom Harre, *Rules of Disorder*, Routledge and Kegan Paul, London, 1978.
27. F. Musgrove, *Ecstasy and Holiness: Counter Culture and the Open Society*, Indiana University Press, Bloomington, 1974, pp. 163–173.
28. *Ibid.*, pp. 165–169.
29. See F. Musgrove, 'Parents' expections of the junior school', *Sociological Review*, **9** (1961).

Social Order

There are two powerful and contradictory notions of the social order which today influence the approach of sociologists to education: one view is hard, the other soft. The 'hard' view emphasizes the individual as the creature of the social order; the 'soft' view sees him essentially as its creator. The first looks at the social order from the outside, emphasizes its hard, thing-like nature, and perhaps sees it as a network of positions; the second looks at it from the inside and sees individual people trying to make sense of the world and order as a network of meanings. The first interpretation owes much to the Marxist tradition of social theory (although Emile Durkheim's influence is also very strong); the second owes much to Alfred Schutz and 'phenomenology'. The first leads to a rather despairing view of education; the second is more hopeful. Both are wrong. They have led at best to absurdity and at the worst to actual harm in the recent conduct of education.

The social order is quite simply how people ordinarily and customarily behave towards one another. It is the relatively stable relationships among people which remove from daily life any serious possibility of surprise. The way people behave may be set out quite explicitly in laws and rules; but the bedrock of order is everything that is 'self-evident', requiring no explanation.

Explicit rules are for new members (including young children) and for established members facing crisis; but a great deal of coded information is signalled to keep people routinely on course. Army officers, unlike privates, wear (soft-leather) gloves and so signal their non-manual, gentry standing. Notice of an important change in social status is commonly transmitted in code: widows less often wear 'weeds', but few girls conceal their engagement rings. More subtle messages may be sent when a person enters a new community and invades its boundary; the body's boundaries may also be modified—hair is cut, ears pierced, teeth drawn, and the foreskin removed.

The social order is the generally taken-for-granted character of social relationships (including the things people quarrel about) which only the stranger is likely to find problematical. It is buttressed not only or principally by explicit rules, but more tactfully, circuitously, and ambiguously through social symbols and metaphors. Social order is orderly, though not without 'normal' conflict;[1] it is a regular and recurrent form of human relationship.

It is not a 'structure', if by that is meant something substantial which social investigators will find if only they dig deep enough. It is a 'model' which we extract or generalize from all the social relationships that we experience and observe. It is a theory of what to expect. In this sense the social order is in the mind—subjective. On

14

this theory we base the practice of our daily lives. The model or theory predicts people's behaviour with remarkable accuracy: we are seldom entirely 'at a loss' and so ordered life is not only possible but usual. The social order is, in essence, as John Beattie has claimed, a working hypothesis.[2] It is a very serviceable hypothesis for practical action. It yields handsome profits for insurance companies and reasonable efficiency and sanity for ourselves.

This view of the social order is taken from the individual's point of view and the meaning and regularities that he finds in it: in that sense it is 'subjective'. But it is not solipsistic and magical, like some currently very popular views of the social order which have greatly influenced the theory and practice of education. Social order is not invented at the whim of individuals. Charles Horton Cooley's notion of the social order as he presented it to American students eighty years ago found a convincing middle ground between emphasis on society as a 'thing', on the one hand, and as an idea, on the other. Cooley's view, as he advanced it in his *Human Nature and the Social Order*, is in essence the view taken in this book.

The social order includes positions as well as people and their relationships. Indeed, the positions people occupy—age–sex positions, family and occupational positions, 'social-class' positions—greatly influence their relationships and help us to predict their behaviour. They do not enter into relationships as positionless beings. Cooley brought out well the two inseparable sides of the social order. On the one hand, he underlined society as 'a relation among personal ideas' and concluded that '... the imaginations which people have of one another are the solid facts of society';[3] nevertheless, there were positions which people occupied, some more snugly than others: 'We do not regard the individual as separable from the social order as a whole, but we do regard him as capable of occupying any one of an indefinite number of positions within that order, some of them more suitable to him than others.'[4]

There is currently much interest in the views of W. I. Thomas and his idea of the definition of a situation: 'If men define situations as real, they are real in their consequences.' But this does not mean that any individual can construct his own personal reality. That is the way to madness. Institutions as well as individuals define situations, and institutional definitions take priority. As Berger and Luckmann argue: 'The institutions must and do claim authority over the individual, independently of the subjective meanings he may attach to any particular situation. The priority of institutional definitions of situations must be consistently maintained over individual temptations at redefinitions.'[5] It is institutional definitions of reality, and not individual redefinitions, which constitute the social order and hold chaos at bay. .

A 'SOFT' VIEW OF THE SOCIAL ORDER

A very influential contemporary school of 'subjectivist' sociology has led educationists to a contrary view. Endless and unrestrained 'creativity' is now possible as pupils construct new knowledge and new worlds. The criteria of truth and falsehood are themselves 'socially constructed'. Pupils do not receive knowledge; rather melodramatically, they are condemned to impose their own personal meaning on the world.

Such views claim august ancestors (like Max Weber), but they derive immediately from the current vogue of subjective sociology. In marked contrast to this, sociologists (like historians) have usually played down or treated with great caution the individual's interpretation of his own life and times. They have often drawn a sharp distinction between the motives of individuals and the outcome of the activities in which they have been engaged. The soldier may enlist for glory or drink, but the war is to restore the balance of power; we marry for love, but marriage is for supporting, shaping, and moulding the young. A modern 'functionalist' has put this now old-fashioned view as follows: 'The subjective disposition may coincide with the objective consequences but again, it may not. The two vary independently.'[6] Karl Marx had expressed a similar view a century before (in his *Critique of Political Economy*) when he maintained that the individual can no more tell us the 'real' truth about his times than about himself and that even the relationships he enters into are independent of his will.

The current vogue of subjective sociology leads to the very opposite conclusion. What individuals involved in a particular situation 'make of it' is not, after all, largely irrelevant, misleading, or simply false; it is the only truth we can know. But the argument now goes much further than that: in 'making something of' our social world we actually make it. And so, says the American sociologist, Alan F. Blum, the social order was invented by sociologists.

It is very important to be quite clear about the nature of this bizarre proposition, because children are now being taught in schools as if it were true. (Blum's article, first published in America in 1970, was reprinted in England in 1971 in a very influential book on the sociology of education entitled *Knowledge and Control*.[7] Such views underlie arguments for non-directive teaching, the encouragement of 'spontaneity', and respect for the opinions of young children when 'apparently' false, accepting the 'validity' of the child's view of the world.) Blum says that 'order' in social life is uncovered by sociologists often when no-one would expect it to be there. That is perfectly true. That is their job. Durkheim discovered orderliness in such idiosyncratic behaviour as suicide. Marriages, births, and deaths are similarly not simply random and purely personal; there are regularities in their occurrence which sociologists and demographers reveal. But Blum concludes that the regularities do not 'really' exist; they have been constructed by the sociologist's methods of inquiry. It is difficult to find any other meaning in the following passage in which Blum summarizes his views:

> These regularities (of marriage, war and suicide) do not exist 'out there' in pristine form to which sociologists functionally respond, but rather, they acquire their character as regularities and their features as describable objects only through the grace of sociological imputation. Thus, it is not an objectively discernible, purely existing external world which accounts for sociology; it is the methods and procedures of sociology which create and sustain that world.

It is probably true that sociologists and demographers, through their statistical tables and frequency counts, make the social world seem rather more orderly than most people might take it to be; but all tabulations and classifications have a similar effect, and the anthropologist, Jack Goody, has examined the alphabet and its enormous potential for listing, ordering, and reordering reality, as a basic ingredient of the post-primitive social order.[8] But the social order is not thereby created, though it may be somewhat augmented and at times distorted: the orderly appearance of the world 'can be enhanced and expanded by the application of sociological methods of description'.[9] There is a large difference between saying that sociologists tend to exaggerate order and that they invented it.

Ethnomethodologists (like Aaron Cicourel) have very usefully refocused our attention on the more microscopic detail of social behaviour and have examined the social order as an 'ongoing accomplishment' of members. They do not see order as the acting out of socially given and agreed values, but arising from the way people minute by minute account for themselves and interpret one another's actions and intentions. The constantly recreated sense of a stable and orderly world is a 'reflexive accomplishment'.[10] Such a perspective is a useful corrective to more impersonal versions of order and in no way contradicts a broader view, from a distance, of the overall pattern of human affairs.

What is really doing the damage is the cliché (taken from the 'symbolic interactionists') about 'giving meaning to the world'. (It is reinforced by other clichés which refer to teachers, psychiatrists, parents, and magistrates as 'reality-definers'.) This potentially solipsistic view is quite clear in the essay by Alan F. Blum; it is just below the surface in the work of other writers who emphasize that social situations have no meaning in themselves, but only the meanings that people involved bring to them and perhaps 'negotiate' with fellow members.[11] This perspective found widespread support among educationists in the nineteen-seventies. It has brought discredit to 'objectivity' and made 'empirical' a term of abuse.

An American educationist, Maxine Greene, has powerfully exorcised objectivity in the school curriculum in her article in the influential American publication from Columbia University, *Teachers College Record*.[12] All pupils, apparently, even in their own country, are like Schutz's phenomenological stranger and their task is not to gain knowledge but to 'reconstitute meaning'. The school curriculum does not reflect the social order; it must create it, for 'disorder ... is continually breaking in; meaninglessness is recurrently overcoming landscapes which once were demarcated, meaningful'. In such circumstances the pupil has little choice but to '... generate structures of knowledge which may provide him unifying perspectives and thus enable him to restore order once again'.

It is extraordinarily difficult to see what, exactly, pupils will actually be doing in their schools all day long. But the curriculum is clearly conceived as a means of creating and sustaining social order by imposing meaning on an otherwise chaotic world. If he simply accepts 'structures of prescribed knowledge' the pupil will remain alienated from himself and his own possibilities. But in reality he has no choice: he is *condemned* to give meaning (to the world) and, in the process of doing so, recreating or generating the materials of a curriculum in terms of his own consciousness'. There is no body of knowledge 'out-there' for the pupil to receive: 'If the curriculum ... is seen as external to the search for meaning, it becomes an alien and an alienating edifice, a kind of "Crystal Palace" of ideas.'

In England, Esland goes further. He derides 'objectivism' (which is a way of writing 'objectivity' disparagingly) which is almost as bad as (or perhaps it is the same as) 'reification'. For Esland the teacher and his pupils form an 'epistemic community' and its job is to be a 'world-producer' and to resist being world-produced. Teaching and learning are conceived as 'the intersubjective construction of reality'. Esland concedes that these coproducers of reality experience some constraints; the realities they construct must have some support in the wider society. But the basic model is quite clear:

> The relationship between teachers and pupils is essentially a reality sharing, world-building enterprise. As participants in classroom interactions they intersubjectively typify and interpret the actions of one another through vocabularies which they take for granted as plausible. In this way, zones of knowledge are constructed and sustained in the transactional processes of school learning. ...[13]

This is a magical view. Reality is changed or even made by thinking about it. In the book *Knowledge and Control*, which carries Esland's article (as well as Blum's), there are two very impressive articles (first published in the journal *Africa*) by the anthropologist, Robin Horton. They were included because the editor thought that they supported the book's generally subjective and relativist approach to knowledge. They do not. In fact, Horton is at pains to show that the subjective ('idealist') undercurrents of post-Cartesian Western thought—in which mind is separated from matter but in some sense has power over it—is potentially magical. Reality is created by thinking about it: '... and a change of ideas means a change of things ... (This) means that the world is in the last analysis dependent on human whim, that the search for order is folly, and that human beings can expect to find no sort of anchor in reality.'[14] In his forthright strictures on *Knowledge and Control*, Antony Flew has made the same point: 'Whereas they (the editor and contributors) are infatuated by their "magical world-view", and endorse it as the new sociological revelation, Horton is appalled.'[15]

DURKHEIM'S 'HARD' VIEW

There is one 'hard' version of the social order which is no less influential today and no less preposterous. This is the view which is stated most clearly in a book written some eighty years ago by Emile Durkheim and Marcel Mauss called *Primitive Classification*. There are other 'hard' versions of the social order, derived principally from Karl Marx, which are more convincing and will be examined in the next section of this chapter. But Durkheim's view of the 'priority' of the social order and its 'replication' in men's thinking has been popularized by Basil Bernstein (abetted by Mary Douglas). It is the basic idea behind Bernstein's writing on integrated curricula and 'open' schools. If Durkheim's views are wrong, then the most powerful and successful advocacy of 'integration' and 'openness' in contemporary education is based on error.

It is not difficult to grasp the key idea of *Primitive Classification* and Durkheim's other major work in this field, *The Elementary Forms of the Religious Life*. It is not simply the platitude that social circumstances influence men's ideas and the way they think. If that were all, it would be as unobjectionable as it would be uninteresting. It is, however, a much tighter correspondence theory than that, claiming an exact, far less indeterminate connexion between the symbolic order and the social state. It is a theory of direct imprinting, replication, or modelling. Thus the circular camp of the Zuni Indians is the origin of the way they conceptualize space, the very source of the concept of circularity itself: 'Thus the social organization has been the model for the spatial organization and a reproduction of it.'[16]

In the 'soft' version of the social order, mind creates society; in Durkheim's 'hard' version, society creates mind. Social organization comes first and provides a model for concepts of time, space, and causality and for logic itself. Men did not arrange their camps in circular form because they had an idea of a circle; they gained the idea of 'circle' from the way they arranged their camps. Durkheim was very severe on Sir James Frazer for supposing the opposite.[17] The most succinct statement of this simple idea of reproduction is to be found in a famous passage in *Primitive Classification*:

> The first logical categories were social categories; the first classes of things were classes of men, into which these things were integrated. It was because men were grouped, and thought of themselves in the form of groups, that in their ideas they grouped other things, and in the beginning the two modes of grouping were merged to the point of being indistinguishable.[18]

The fundamental grouping of all human societies is a simple twofold division into those we can marry and those we can not; this basically binary form of social organization is seen by Durkheim's followers, right down to our own times, as the 'model' and source of all two-column forms of classification, and even for the distinction between the right hand and the left. The two halves of society are not in fact symmetrical: those we can marry are impure compared with those we can not; one half is sacred, the other profane; and the right hand is of greater worth than the left.[19] ('If organic asymmetry had not existed,' said Durkheim's disciple, Robert Hertz, 'it would have had to be invented.'[20]) The simple polarities and antitheses which we commonly use to organize our thinking—perhaps even the binary opposition on which we have constructed the digital computer—are 'models', reproductions or transformations of a basically binary social state.

These remarkable, simple, but elegant ideas are almost certainly wrong.[21] Many years ago Robert K. Merton criticized Durkheim's 'uncritical acceptance of a naive theory of correspondence';[22] more recently Raymond Firth has charged him not with naiveté but with unwarranted audacity which led to a 'staggeringly simplistic conclusion';[23] Rodney Needham observed (in his introduction to his own translation of *Primitive Classification*): 'There is no logical necessity to postulate a causal connexion between society and symbolic classification, and in the absence of factual indications to this effect there are no grounds for attempting to do so.'[24]

There were no adequate factual indications: as Raymond Firth has observed, the ethnographic basis of the 'highly debatable' Durkheim–Mauss argument was weak.[25] Durkheim made no attempt to test out his ideas over a range of societies. Needham concluded: 'In no single case is there any compulsion to believe that the society is the cause or even the model of the classification. ...'

The fact that these implausible and ill-supported ideas have found ready and uncritical acceptance in high quarters and have pervasively influenced the practice of social anthropology and the conduct of education is one of the most deeply disturbing and discreditable features of modern British intellectual life. Since the nineteen-forties, British anthropologists—especially those directed or inspired by Evans-Pritchard—have claimed to illustrate the way concepts are modelled on social states. Evans-Pritchard claimed to have done so in the nineteen-thirties when he concluded that for the Nuer of the Sudan time was a social relationship: the distance between events, he said, was not reckoned in time concepts, 'but in terms of structural distance, being the relations of groups of people to other groups of people'.[26]

Post-war Oxford scholars diligently replicated Evans-Pritchard's study of Nuer time concepts (and of Nuer spear symbolism). They found what they were looking for—correspondences between concepts and the formation of social groups. Middleton says of the Lugbara that '... events are related to each other not by their temporal relationships but by the social relationships of the personages whose activities compose myth and genealogical tradition'.[27] Peter Rigby begins a study of the Gogo of East Africa by announcing as a 'given' (bequeathed by Durkheim and Mauss) the 'structural relationship or "concordance" between the social and symbolic orders of any society'.[28] It would be too strong to speak of a conspiracy, but Needham has recently pointed to the social network which sustains these unproven ideas.[29] To understand their currency we must look not at their intrinsic merits but at the power of the people who have taken them up.

They include Basil Bernstein and the anthropologist, Mary Douglas. In her very popular (and intellectually elusive) book, *Natural Symbols*, Mary Douglas gives a blanket endorsement of Durkheim. Incredibly she asserts: 'As Durkheim himself has powerfully argued, any given classification system is itself a product of social relations.' Her deference to Durkheim is exceeded only by her tribute to Bernstein, who deserves the attention of anthropologists '... if only because he is sympathetic to a Durkheimian sociology of knowledge ...'. Of her book she says: 'The present book is an essay in applying Bernstein's approach to the analysis of ritual.' Bernstein in turn cites Mary Douglas to support an alleged replication of the social state in the school curriculum.[30] And so the circle of mutually supportive and reinforcing reference revolves endlessly around Durkheim and Mauss whose basic proposition has not even been questioned.[31]

It is the bedrock of Bernstein's view of the school curriculum. It is true that his slight, but widely quoted and extensively reprinted article, 'Open schools, open society?'[32] is framed as a question, which he never actually answers. His style, too, is elusive, so it is rarely possible to know what he is actually saying. But he is fairly obviously connecting up, in some way, two forms of society and two forms of school curriculum: one form of society is based on 'organic' and the other on 'mechanical' solidarity; one form of school curriculum is 'integrated' (in which the boundaries between subjects are weak) and the other is the 'collection curriculum' (in which the boundaries between subjects are strong).

Durkheim on the division of labour is the overt reference; Durkheim and Mauss on classification enter the argument covertly, via Mary Douglas. We now, it seems, have an 'open society' based on organic solidarity or extreme interdependence among its members and various elements. There has been a corresponding shift, we are told, in the secondary schools 'whose symbolic orders point up or celebrate the idea of mixture or diversity of categories'. Elsewhere the connexion is more straightforwardly stated: while nothing quite as blunt and crude as a 'cause' is referred to, there is a fairly unambiguous assertion that the integrated curriculum code is a 'realization' of organic social solidarity.[33] It is curious that it has taken at least two centuries for the social state to become replicated (or even realized) in the symbolic order of the school. We have had a very marked degree of specialization and division of labour at least since Adam Smith wrote about it two hundred years ago (Durkheim would say since the fourteenth-century medieval city[34]). It is odd that the procees of symbolic replication has been so slow. This is, perhaps, a tedious irrelevance.

There is doubtless some correspondence between the division of labour in society and change in the school curriculum. Sensible people who make educational policy see what is only too obvious, that modern life is a complicated affair of cooperation among specialists and that our schools should therefore make it clear how one branch of knowledge is connected with and perhaps dependent on another. That is a perfectly straightforward explanation of curriculum change and has the added advantage that it is probably true. There is no need to invoke Durkheim and Mauss (and Mary Douglas): this merely brings confusion, error, and intellectual pretentiousness into explanations which are quite cogent and sufficient without them. Highly abstract and largely unintelligible theorizing legitimates but does not explain. It makes the integrated curriculum seem not only inevitable but right. It is probably one of the educational disasters of our time.[35]

In later writing Bernstein himself pointed to an unbridged gap in Durkehim between society and symbol. Durkheim had failed to explain just how basic categories of thought were derived from the structuring of social relations. Bernstein now claimed that he had closed the gap with the socialization theory of G. H. Mead. This is to misunderstand Durkheim quite fundamentally. Durkheim is either right or he is wrong; the world is either like he says or it is not. He cannot be 'corrected' by this kind of tinkering, by filling gaps and providing missing links. Nevertheless, Bernstein claims to have done so in the form of Meadian socialization with its heavy reliance on the acquisition and use of language. Durkheim, Bernstein now complains, did not tell us just how it all works, but: 'Mead outlined in general terms the relationships between role, reflexiveness and speech and in so doing provided the basis of the solution to the *how*.'[36] But Mead is quite sufficient unto himself: he does not, he can not, correct or augment Durkheim. He can only make him redundant.

NEO-MARXISTS AND THE SOCIAL ORDER

The neo-Marxists have given the school a position of central importance in the maintenance and reproduction of the social order. They have assigned to it a remarkable and sinister potency in the perpetuation of inequality and injustice. The fact that it is wholly unaware that it is doing this—and even firmly believes that it is doing the opposite—merely underscores the depths of false consciousness and the deviousness of the capitalist order.

There are three key men and four key ideas in the Marxist revival. The three men are Gramsci, Althusser, and Bourdieu; the four (closely related) concepts are hegemony, legitimacy, ideology, and reproduction. Althusser and Bourdieu are living French intellectuals; Gramsci was an Italian who died in prison in 1937. His *Prison Notebooks* and his interpretation of hegemony have been of particular interest to social theorists and sociologists of education in recent years. Gramsci gave great significance to intellectuals in the distribution and maintenance of power and claimed that: 'Every relationship of "hegemony" is necessarily a pedagogic relationship.'[37]

The concept of hegemony is especially associated with Gramsci;[38] the concepts of ideology and legitimacy with Althusser;[39] and the concept of social reproduction with Bourdieu.[40] But all four ideas are closely connected in currently very popular neo-Marxist interpretations of education and the social order.

Hegemony is domination. It includes brute force. More importantly, it refers (as Gramsci interprets it) to the power of the ruling class to define the very limits of common sense. The dominant culture expresses and reinforces the hegemony of the ruling class. Hegemony is all-pervasive, deeply saturating the consciousness of a society. In Marxist analysis the school curriculum is (perhaps inevitably) part of the hegemonic 'superstructure' which reflects the power relations in society's economic base. Even the most counter-hegemonic or 'oppositional' curriculum innovation (like, say, the ill-fated William Tyndale school in the mid-nineteen-seventies) is destined to 'incorporation'.[41]

Hegemony is established in large measure through ideology. An ideology is a version of reality which gives the powerful their legitimacy. Hegemony, ideology, and legitimacy are closely connected ideas in contemporary analysis of schooling and the curriculum.[42] Child-centred progressive education, educational psychology (and especially mental-testing and 'measurement'), and courses of teacher training are among the 'legitimating ideologies' which, it is said, ensure the 'reproduction' of social inequality and the continued dominance of the ruling class. For Gramsci all hegemonic relationships are pedagogic relationships; for Bourdieu all pedagogic relationships are 'symbolic violence'.[43] In such terms of high melodrama schooling is now given a pivotal role in the subjection of the oppressed.

In Marx's writing ideology is interpreted as a distorted version of reality which serves the interests of a particular social group. Karl Mannheim uses the term in a similar sense.[44] Althusser is a Marxist revisionist because he sees ideology as less determined by the mode of economic production, and not as distortion or aberration.[45] It is the fabric and medium of all societies. It will not disappear, to be replaced by science, in a classless society. Nevertheless, ideology plays a different part in class and classless societies: in the latter, it ensures that the relations between men are for the benefit of all; but in the former it is the 'element' in which the relations between men are settled for the profit of the ruling class.[46]

Although ideology is not enough, and coercive power is in reserve to deal with times of crisis, it is 'normally' effective in maintaining order and reproducing unequal class (and sex) relationships. Neo-Marxists of today are revisionists precisely because they give a heightened prominence, a greater degree of independence, and a more 'idealist' emphasis to ideology than did Marx. Hegemony is not simply the unending and unproblematical exercise of class power by the ruling class; it needs the consent of the subordinate classes, and ideology secures it. It does so increasingly, and ever more effectively, through the educational system.

But the traditional legitimating ideology in Europe (and, indeed, America) has been the ideology of the family, and it is by no means dead. Only Althusser among contemporary theorists seems to have any real inkling of this. Although he gives education pride of place in today's Ideological State Apparatus and emphasizes its effective displacement of the Church, he recognizes that its power lies in its alliance with the family. It is the 'family–education couple' who are the key, in Althusser's analysis, to the transmission of the ruling ideology and the reproduction of the social relations of economic production.

Althusser is right. It is difficult to exaggerate the role of the family in making power legitimate throughout the past thousand years of Europe's history. The most extravagant and outrageous powers of kings, colonels, headmasters, and employers has been justified as a father's power. (Filmer's *Patriarcha* and Bodin's *Six Books of the Commonwealth* are among the more notable theoretical statements of this position.) Although this ideology began to wane in the seventeenth century, it remains remarkably potent.[47] Concepts of honour, which informally but effectively have regulated social behaviour, have always been closely tied to it; and they have been easily transposed to family-type groups like the 'House', the regiment, the Boy Scout troop, and the First Fifteen which have exacted deathless fealty. The family is far more important in the process of legitimation than 'culture', to which Bourdieu attaches crucial importance.

The affairs at the William Tyndale Junior School between January 1974 (when Terry Ellis became headmaster) and February 1976 (when the teachers were dismissed following disciplinary proceedings and the 'Auld' tribunal completed its inquiries) might have been a play written to illustrate Althusser's main theoretical argument. The curriculum and teaching methods were not only quite explicitly 'anti-middle class', they were hostile to parental power ('interference') and did not reproduce a family-style authority system in the school. The crisis situation that ensued (as children were withdrawn and parents complained) brought into action the Repressive State Apparatus in the shape of disciplinary action which led to the dismissal of teachers who had gone on strike and a quasi-judicial inquiry under Mr.

Robin Auld, Q.C. Patriarchal authority had been as much threatened as middle-class supremacy, and the revolt which led to the downfall of Ellis arose to a major extent because 'the middle class mothers became concerned that their own children would not learn their appropriate position in the social order'.[48]

Pierre Bourdieu, like Althusser, gives the school central importance in the transmission of power and inequality in modern capitalist societies. He is far less convincing. Nevertheless, his core proposition is scarcely remarkable. His extensive, involved, and highly abstract writing on this subject can be stated in one sentence: schools are very important, especially for upper-class families, because they convert a child's family advantages into cultural symbols and scholastic credentials, which are a legitimate basis for high social position, whereas today 'birth' is not. A voluminous output of books and articles has been necessary to make this point.

A person's social rank, position in his family, and his age were formerly the main determinants of social relationships and so of the social order. Property and occupation might also be of some importance, although formerly (and Walter Bagehot hoped rather forlornly that this might continue) a person's social rank was probably of much greater significance than either his wealth or his 'office'.[49] Today, we are told by Bourdieu that the crucial prop of the social order is education: it is '... one of the most effective means of perpetuating the existing social pattern'. It has this remarkable power because of its transformational properties: it can arrange for 'a social gift (to be) treated as a natural one'.[50]

The argument is conducted in an economic idiom of cultural 'capital', its 'investment', accumulation, and transmission. Upper-class families, the argument runs, are well endowed with cultural capital which they hand over to their children as they are growing up; this capital is invested in schooling which is organized to reward precisely the kind of literary and abstract culture that upper-class children have inherited. (Bourdieu calls this very useful family endowment the 'habitus'.) The educational system thus transforms a social into a scholastic heritage. This guarantees for the upper classes the superior and privileged position that formerly they might have enjoyed simply through naked power. But naked power and exploitation no longer work; they must be heavily concealed. The educational system is a very elaborate and effective form of camouflage. And Bourdieu claims that: 'The statistics showing the variations in academic success according to social class prove that culture is an accumulation of capital, the interest on which accrues to the bourgeoisie in the shape of diplomas, easily convertible into socio-economic advantages.'[51]

This is perfectly plausible. What is difficult is the related and necessary arguments, never fully developed, that the upper classes have a prior power to impose on the school the 'arbitrary curriculum' in which their sons feel entirely at home. They have the power to commit 'symbolic violence'—to define (in their own interests) what counts as knowledge. This is really quite interesting and would be very important if it were true. It has simply been taken as true by Bourdieu's English devotees.[52]

Bourdieu is advancing a new theory of rights. Power has to be seen as legitimate if it is to be acceptable (and therefore powerful); in the past theories of 'natural rights', safeguarded perhaps in a 'social contract', have given the powerful their legitimacy. Neither 'rights of nature' nor 'rights of birth' any longer suffice. What really makes you legitimate if you have power today, says Bourdieu, is also having culture: '... culture is for bourgeois society in its present phase, what other modes of legitimation of the social order and transmission of privilege ...' were for other dominant groups in the past. The 'worship of culture' by the ruling class is by no means disinterested: the profits of symbolic behaviour are not only symbolic.[53] This is at best a half-truth, and the evidence that Bourdieu assembles in its support actually refutes it.

This is the difficulty with Bourdieu: his contempt for evidence, his claim to be offering a transcendental view of the social order in terms of 'structuralism', and his recourse in practice to ramshackle statistics which do not bear examination.

For Bourdieu sociology is a form of geometry: the truths he is seeking are truths of reason, not truths of fact. He is concerned with the social order as a 'structure', and the structure is one of relationships (and especially of relationships among relationships).[54] He is dismissive of 'substance' and considers that both geometry and sociology deal with 'systems defined not by any substantial content but only by the laws of combination of their constitutive elements'.[55] The sociology of education must address itself to 'the laws that determine the tendency of structures to reproduce themselves' and his concern is with 'the science of the reproduction of structures'—which has nothing to do with observing relationships among actual people. He firmly rejects any such 'substantialist mode of thought'.[56] Truth in sociology does not come from assembling relevant facts. They are a tiresome distraction: 'Being built at the price of breaking away from phenomenal appearances, the system cannot receive the immediate and easy corroboration that facts at their face value or documents literally taken would provide.' (Even more: 'Methodological objectivism ... demands its own supersession.')[57] From these great heights we descend to an intellectual level that is paltry.

Bourdieu is quite explicit and emphatic that he is not merely showing yet again the tired half-truth that the social position of a child's family has a bearing on his academic performance. In the event he does precisely what he has disclaimed. It is all heavily disguised in a special opaque language, with much talk of capital, codes, deciphering, and the habitus. (Children get their 'codes' from their homes, which enable them not only to decipher but even 'appropriate' symbolic goods—in other words, they pick up at home a taste for museums and art galleries.) And the explanation he offers in terms of culture is almost certainly wrong, falsified by the very data he parades in its support.

This is what he claims: that his general argument (about culture as legitimation) is proved by the fact that the higher we go up the social scale (in France), the more culture is consumed. He says that the survey data he produced for France show that this is the case. They do not. There are eight social levels distinguished in the population at large, and when we examine the tables for ourselves we see that the richest and most powerful of these—the heads of industry and commerce—spend proportionately less on culture (in terms of a statistically adjusted or standardized expenditure) than 'intermediate office staff'. They are far behind 'professional and higher office staff', just about level with routine white-collar workers, and only a little ahead of 'workers' and small tradespeople. Bourdieu's table[58] simply does not show what he says it shows. It shows precisely the philistinism that can be expected at the top of commerce and industry, even in France.

This is confirmed in the supporting data, which lamentably fail to provide any support. The additional data take the form of surveys within the so-called 'dominant classes' themselves. This time seven levels are distinguished, the heads of commerce and industry being two of them. Evidence is provided that there is far more economic capital at these two levels than at any other (professionals, civil servants, managers, engineers, and teachers), but on nine cultural indicators (visiting art galleries, reading *Le Monde*, listening to classical music, and the like), they are consistently at the bottom.[59] They have the largest share of economic capital and the smallest share in the distribution of cultural capital among the dominant classes.

The reading habits of the leaders of French industry and commerce are deplorable. Further survey evidence shows that they come relatively high (fourth place out of seven) only with respect to reading adventure stories. They are bottom for history, philosophy, art, and political essays. Heads of industry come third for economics, but heads of commerce come bottom even here.[60] It is not the rich and the powerful (who are so efficiently 'reproduced') who consume culture and read philosophy and eighteenth-century novels. Culture in the main is consumed by people who are well educated but relatively poor and weak—notably by teachers.

What is astonishing, and itself in need of explanation, is the uncritical acclaim that Bourdieu has received in England in the past ten years (so that even a fairly critical essay concludes with a reaffirmation of his 'overall brilliance').[61] Durkheim has a majesty, boldness, and grandeur in his ideas; the fact that some of the most important ones are wrong is a relatively trivial matter. His daring thoughts are developed and expressed with crystal clarity. Bourdieu's are concealed in verbose language and a tedious and pretentious terminology. The only saving grace would be that he is sometimes right. He seldom is. Those English educationists who, so embarrassingly, have swallowed him whole, should be more alive to his rationalist's contempt for 'truths of fact' and to the pointlessness of looking for evidence that might prove him right.

CONCLUSION

The soft view of the social order carries little conviction; it is often simply absurd. The hard view is more plausible, but also verges on the absurd in its stronger forms. The soft view is part-and-parcel of a major movement in the thought and sensibility of Western intellectuals since the early nineteen-sixties. It is so far-reaching, fundamental, and pervasive that it perhaps merits Thomas Kuhn's now somewhat hackneyed term of 'paradigm-shift'.[62]

The soft view has arisen at the intersection of mid-twentieth-century idealist philosophy (as represented by Peter Winch[63] and some interpretations of Wittgenstein) and of a sociology which starts with the individual in his everyday world and the way he interprets his life with other people. (The 'phenomenology' of Alfred Schutz and the 'symbolic interactionism' of Herbert Blumer have been very influential here.) This more humanized sociology had the laudable intention of bringing the individual back into the picture, with his personal motives and need to make sense of his experiences. In the event it has made the world senseless, its meaning and nature being a matter of personal whim.[64]

In the soft view of the social order the individual does not get 'meaning' or truth from a world outside himself; he pours meaning on to it. There seemed to be support for this view in the influential writing of Peter Berger and Thomas Luckmann on 'the social construction of reality',[65] in the more esoteric pronouncements of Wittgenstein on 'forms of life',[66] and in Thomas Khun's views of the social origins of new scientific truths. Truth, it seemed, was what any group of consenting adults (or even children) agreed. No social group holds a version of truth superior to any other group's; any group claiming superiority is guilty of an epistemologically ethnocentric act.[67] This was rampant relativism, and today it pervades and rots the fabric of education. Everywhere—even (perhaps especially) in junior schools catering for disadvantaged areas—consenting persons construct their own realities. Cognitive sovereignty is claimed and conferred on every tiny parish in the world of the mind.

The hard versions of the social order are more convincing, but whereas the soft ones slide into solipsism the hard ones slide into determinism. They leave very little room for manoeuvre by individuals or institutions; everything is determined from 'outside'. But Durkheim's theory of the symbolic replication of the social state is so interesting, daring, and outrageous, that one wishes it were true.

Certainly two-column classification systems seem to be deeply embedded in a world-wide range of human societies (so much so that Rodney Needham concludes that they '... refer to constant tendencies of the human mind').[68] Perhaps these simple bipolar ways of organizing information and looking at the world merely indicate human laziness, nothing more exalted than recourse to what Jack Goody calls a 'folk taxonomy',[69] through which complex phenomena are ordered in a misleadingly crude and simple way. That is certainly the fate of contemporary education. Its complex realities are impaled on simple polar antitheses: restricted–elaborated (language); open–closed (curricula); visible–invisible (pedagogies); abstract–concrete (thought); divergent–convergent (thinking). For all its apparent sophistication, this mode of analysis makes its powerful impact on the mind, not because it offers truth but a slogan.

In this book considerable attention will be given to what seems to be the basically binary structure of English society. It pre-dates and in many ways still overrides the post-eighteenth-century rise of 'social classes'. It is the distinction between gentlemen and players. The deep structure of the English social order is the distinction between the gentry and aristocracy, on the one hand, and non-gentry, on the other. It is the distinction between grammar schools and Public Schools, on the one hand, and elementary (and secondary modern) schools, on the other; between graduate and non-graduate teachers; between Her Majesty's Inspectors and local authority advisers. It may not simply replicate the distinction between those we can marry and those we can not; between the right hand and the left; between the sacred and the profane; but it remains a powerful dualism in British society which perhaps does more than modern 'class' to explain the nature of English education.

B

The neo-Marxists are revisionists precisely because they have softened the more crudely deterministic forms of classical Marxist analysis. But their picture of education is still over-determined. In Bourdieu the school system is a kind of automatic reproductive mechanism which functions smoothly and efficiently precisely because it is an unconscious device which nobody has deliberately willed. A similar overdetermined view of the school system will be examined in the chapter (Chapter 4) on education and social control, for recent Marxist writing in America has assigned to schooling an apparently inexorable power to sustain the capitalist status quo.

This book will conclude that there is much more looseness of fit, a far greater indeterminacy, between education and the social order than is generally conceded in sociological studies. There is actually scope for human intelligence to change things in this way or that. And there is considerable—perhaps growing—autonomy within the system itself. Unlikely new degree courses are invented in polytechnics not because the capitalist system, society, or even students need them, but because their sponsors want promotion.[70] There are limits to such autonomy, but external constraints are less stringent than sociologists like to believe. There is a good deal of free play and room for manoeuvre, and the sociologist can do little more than bring a trained eye to bear on the interplay of the contingent and the unforeseen.

If he is wise he will also bring a mind well informed with facts and an eclectic range of theories and perspectives. He will be sensitized to his times not only by reading Marx and Durkheim; he may well see more relevance in Tonnies. The social order of our world shifts from community to association; there is no iron law which says that schools must reflect or support this shift. In fact they have been remarkably laggard in doing so. But this book will conclude that they should be deliberately pushed in that direction. No sociological law says this must happen, and sociology cannot tell us that it should. But an informed judgement based on experience as well as theory suggests that this is the wise way ahead.

NOTES

1. For the distinction between 'normal' and 'radical' opposition in societies see Monica and Godfrey Wilson, *Analysis of Social Change*, Cambridge University Press, 1945. 'Ordinary' opposition can be resolved within the existing order, but 'radical' opposition, which occurs in culture-contact situations in Africa, involved fundamental and irreconcilable conflict between law and law, logic and logic, and convention and convention.
2. See John Beattie, *Other Cultures*, Cohen and West, 1964, p. 58. Beattie warns against the fallacy of misplaced concreteness (p. 45), argues that 'the concept of society is a relational not a substantial one' (p. 34), and states that 'structure is built up by the analyst on the basis of data, but is itself not a datum but a construct' (p. 61).
3. Charles Horton Cooley, *Human Nature and the Social Order*, Chas. Scribner's Sons, New York, 1902, p. 87.
4. *Ibid.*, p. 394.
5. Peter L. Berger and Thomas Luckmann, *The Social Construction of Reality*, Penguin Books, Harmondsworth, 1967, p. 80.
6. Robert K. Merton, *Social Theory and Social Structure*, Free Press, New York, 1957, p. 25.

7. Alan F. Blum, 'The corpus of knowledge as a normative order: intellectual critiques of the social order of knowledge and commonsense features of bodies of knowledge', in M. F. D. Young (Ed.), *Knowledge and Control*, Collier-Macmillan, 1971.
8. See Jack Goody, *The Domestication of the Savage Mind*, Cambridge University Press, 1977. Lists, especially when arranged in two columns for contrastive or comparative purposes, may distort social reality to such an extent that the people concerned would never recognize it (see pp. 52–73).
9. Don H. Zimmerman and D. Lawrence Wieder, 'Ethnomethodology and the problem of order: comment on Denzin', in Jack D. Douglas (Ed.), *Understanding Everyday Life*, Routledge and Kegan Paul, London, 1971, p. 289.
10. See Thomas P. Wilson, 'Normative and interpretive paradigms in sociology', in Jack D. Douglas (Ed.), *Understanding Everyday Life*, Routledge and Kegan Paul, London, 1971.
11. See H. Blumer, 'The methodological position of symbolic interactionism', in Martyn Hammersley and Peter Woods (Eds.), *The Process of Schooling*, Routledge and Kegan Paul, London, 1976; and Norman K. Denzin, 'Symbolic interactionism and ethnomethodology', in Jack D. Douglas (Ed.), *Understanding Everyday Life*, Routledge and Kegan Paul, London, 1971: 'The meaning of an object resides in the meanings that are brought to it and hence must be located in the interaction process. ... The meanings given to objects typically derive from a group, or organized interactional, perspective' (p. 261).
12. Maxine Greene, 'Curriculum and consciousness', *Teachers College Record*, **73** (1971).
13. Geoffrey M. Esland, 'Teaching and learning as the organization of knowledge', in M. F. D. Young (Ed.), *Knowledge and Control*, Collier-Macmillan, 1971.
14. Robin Horton, 'African traditional thought and Western science', M. F. D. Young (Ed.), *Knowledge and Control*, Collier-Macmillan, 1971.
15. Antony Flew, *Sociology, Equality and Education*, The Macmillan Press, 1976, p. 37.
16. Emile Durkheim, *The Elementary Forms of the Religious Life*, trans. by J. W. Swain, Allen and Unwin, London, 1971, p. 12.
17. Emile Durkheim and Marcel Mauss, *Primitive Classification*, trans. by R. Needham, Cohen and West, 1963: 'Far from being the case, as Frazer seems to think, that the social relations of man are based on logical relations between things, in reality it is the former which have provided the prototype for the latter'.
18. *Ibid.*, p. 82.
19. Durkheim suggests that the distinction between right and left, 'far from being inherent in the nature of man in general', is a social product; see *The Elementary Forms of the Religious Life*, Allen and Unwin, London, p. 12. This theme is developed elsewhere by Robert Hertz.
20. Robert Hertz, 'The pre-eminence of the right hand: a study in religious polarity', in Rodney Needham (Ed.), *Right and Left. Essays in Dual Symbolic Classification*, University of Chicago Press, 1973.
21. The particular issue of dual symbolic classification has been long and vigorously disputed, especially at Oxford. Rodney Needham's papers on 'The left hand of the Mugwe: an analytical note on the structure of Meru symbolism' (*Africa*, **30,** 1960), 'Right and left in Nyoro symbolic classification' (*Africa*, **37,** 1967), and 'Nyoro symbolism: the ethnographic record' (*Africa*, **46,** 1976), are countered by John Beattie's 'Aspects of Nyoro symbolism' (*Africa*, **38,** 1968) and 'Right, left and the Banyoro' (*Africa*, **46,** 1976). Our tendency to organize our thinking into two columns of polar opposites (and even to incorporate logical categories like right and left into empirical categories like 'male and female' or 'cooked and raw' through analogical association) is obvious enough. Jack Goody has done something to de-fuse the 'grand dichotomy' by considering it simply as a 'folk taxonomy' (see *The Domestication of the Savage Mind*, Cambridge University Press, 1977). This book will be concerned with a very deep and abiding binary distinction in English society—between gentry and non-gentry—but does not see it as a transformation of any deeper, inherent social dualism.

22. R. K. Merton, *Social Theory and Society Structure*, Free Press, New York, 1957, p. 480.
23. Raymond Firth, *Symbols · Public and Private*, Allen and Unwin, London, 1973, p. 133.
24. Emile Durkheim and Marcel Mauss, *Primitive Classification*, trans. by R. Needham, Cohen and West, 1963, p. xxiv.
25. Raymond Firth, 'The right hand and the wrong', *Times Literary Supplement*, 21 February 1975.
26. E. E. Evans-Pritchard, 'Nuer time-reckoning', *Africa*, **12** (1939).
27. John Middleton, 'Some social aspects of Lugbara myth', *Africa*, **24** (1954).
28. Peter Rigby, 'Dual symbolic classification among the Gogo of Central Tanzania', in Rodney Needham (Ed.), *Right and Left*, University of Chicago Press, 1973.
29. Rodney Needham (Ed.), *Right and Left*, University of Chicago Press, 1973, pp. xvii, xxxi, and xxiv.
30. Basil Bernstein, 'Open schools, open society?', *New Society*, 14 September 1967. The reference is to Mary Douglas's earlier book, *Purity and Danger* (Routledge and Kegan Paul, London, 1966), which argues that the state of social boundaries is replicated in the symbolic sphere. A similar Durkheimian interpretation of the myth of virgin birth is advanced by Edmund Leach ('Virgin birth', in *Genesis as Myth and Other Essays*, Jonathan Cape, London, 1969). Mary Douglas refers approvingly to this in *Natural Symbols* (Barrie and Rockliff, 1970), along with her general endorsement of Durkheim and Bernstein.
31. Mary Douglas seems to be wholly unaware of the long history of cogent criticism of the Durkheim–Mauss thesis that social relations among men provide the prototype for logical relations among things. One of the best expositions and criticisms of Durkheim's 'sociologism' was made by Emile Benoit-Smullyan in his article, 'The Sociologism of Emile Durkheim and his School', which was reprinted shortly after the Second World War by Harry Elmer Barnes in his influential book, which has run through many editions, *An Introduction to the History of Sociology* (University of Chicago Press, 1948). Durkheim and Mauss conceded too many exceptions to their thesis—and the thesis breaks down if there are any exceptions at all. But systematic, comparative, empirical studies to test (and not merely 'illustrate') the Durkheim–Mauss thesis, based on evidence of concomitant variation, are few. Recently Vieda Skultans has used her data on spiritualist circles in Cardiff to test the alleged connexion between the tightness or looseness of social boundaries and the symbolic order, and can find no support (see *Intimacy and Ritual*, Routledge and Kegan Paul, London, 1974). The most ambitious correlational study is by Guy E. Swanson who examined fifty societies as 'models' for the concepts of supernature held by their members. The correlations are not impressive—and to 'prove' the case should really be unity (see *The Birth of the Gods*, The University of Michigan Press, Ann Arbor, 1960). As John Bowker has pointed out in a sympathetic approach to this and other Durkheimian studies, the social state must be replicated in *every* case if the thesis is valid. No doubt the form of society—the way people are grouped within it—has an influence on men's way of thinking, but 'structure is not a sole and exclusive cause of concept' (see John Bowker, *The Sense of God*, Oxford University Press, 1973, especially Chap. 2, 'Sociology and the social construction of reality').
32. Basil Bernstein, 'Open schools, open society?', *New Society*, 14 September 1967.
33. Basil Bernstein, 'On the classification and framing of educational knowledge', in M. F. D. Young (Ed.), *Knowledge and Control*, Collier-Macmillan, 1971. This article makes explicit reference to Durkheim and Mauss, and *Primitive Classification* is included in the bibliography.
34. Emile Durkheim, *The Division of Labor in Society*, trans. by George Simpson, Free Press, New York, 1964, pp. 186–189.
35. F. Musgrove, 'Power and the integrated curriculum', *Journal of Curriculum Studies*, **5** (1973).
36. Basil Bernstein, 'Social class, language and socialization', in B. R. Cosin (Ed.), *School and*

Society, Routledge and Kegan Paul, London, 1977.

37. For a discussion of Gramsci's 'idealist' conception of hegemony (compared with Marx's more coercive view) see Gwyn A. Williams, 'The concept of "egenomia" in the thought of Antonio Gramsci: some notes on interpretation', *Journal of the History of Ideas*, **21** (1960): 'He (Gramsci) implies strongly throughout and on occasions explicitly states that *egenomia* is the "normal" form of control, force and co-ercion becoming dominant only at times of crisis.' 'His emphasis on consciousness and the creative role of the intellect and the libertarian cast of his mind suffice, in themselves, to distinguish Gramsci among Marxists.'

38. See A. Gramsci, *Selections from the Prison Notebooks*, trans. by Q. Hoare and G. Nowell Smith, Lawrence and Wishart, 1971.

39. See Louis Althusser, *Lenin and Philosophy and Other Essays*, New Left Books, 1971; and *For Marx*, Allen Lane, 1969.

40. See Pierre Bourdieu and Jean-Claude Passeron, *Reproduction in Education, Society and Culture*, Sage, London, 1977.

41. For a discussion of 'base' and 'superstructure' and the incorporation of alternative and oppositional cultural forms, see Raymond Williams, 'Base and superstructure in marxist cultural theory', *New Left Review*, December 1973.

42. See F. Musgrove, 'Curriculum, culture and ideology', *Journal of Curriculum Studies*, **10** (1978).

43. See Pierre Bourdieu and Jean-Claude Passeron, *Reproduction in Education, Society and Culture*, Book I: 'Foundations of a theory of symbolic violence', Sage, 1977.

44. See Karl Mannheim, *Ideology and Utopia*, Routledge and Kegan Paul, London, 1936, p. 36.

45. For very good discussions of Althusser's revisionist position see Paul Q. Hirst, 'Althusser and the theory of ideology', (*Economy and Society*, **5** 1976) and Gregor McLennan, Victor Molina, and Roy Peters, 'Althusser's theory of ideology' (in *Cultural Studies*, No. 10: 'On ideology', Working Papers for Contemporary Cultural Studies, University of Birmingham, 1977).

46. Louis Althusser, *For Marx*, Allen Lane, 1969:

> In a class society ideology is the relay whereby, and the element in which, the relation between men and their conditions of existence is settled to the profit of the ruling class. In a classless society ideology is the relay whereby, and the element in which, the relation between men and their conditions of existence is lived to the profit of all men (pp. 235–236).

47. See F. Musgrove, 'The decline of the educative family', *Universities Quarterly*, **14** (1960).

48. Miriam B. David, 'The family–education couple: towards an analysis of the William Tyndale dispute', in G. Littlejohn, B. Smart, J. Wakeford, and N. Yuval-Davis (Eds.), *Power and the State*, Croome Helm, London, 1978. This paper presents a penetrating 'Althusserian' interpretation of the William Tyndale Junior School affair.

49. Walter Bagehot, *The English Constitution*, Kegan Paul, London, 1929: 'There is a third idolatry from which that of rank preserves us, and perhaps it is the worst of any—that of office' (p. 92).

50. Pierre Bourdieu, 'The school as a conservative force: scholastic and cultural inequalities', in J. Eggleston (Ed.), *Contemporary Research in the Sociology of Education*, Methuen, London, 1974.

51. Pierre Bourdieu, 'The thinkable and the unthinkable', *Times Literary Supplement*, 15 October 1971.

52. For example, Nell Keddie, 'Classroom knowledge', in M. F. D. Young (Ed.), *Knowledge and Control*, Collier-Macmillan, 1971.

53. Pierre Bourdieu, 'The thinkable and the unthinkable', *Times Literary Supplement*, 15 October 1971.

54. Pierre Bourdieu, *Outline a Theory of Practice*, trans. by Richard Nice, Cambridge University Press, 1977, p. 72.
55. Pierre Bourdieu, 'Structuralism and theory of sociological knowledge', *Social Research*, **35** (1968).
56. Pierre Bourdieu, 'Cultural reproduction and social reproduction', in Jerome Karabel and A. H. Halsey (Eds.), *Power and Ideology in Education*, Oxford University Press, New York, 1977.
57. Pierre Bourdieu, 'Structuralism and theory of sociological knowledge', *Social Research*, **35** (1968).
58. Pierre Bourdieu, 'Cultural reproduction and social reproduction', in Jerome Karabel and A. H. Halsey (Eds.), *Power and Ideology in Education*, Oxford University Press, New York, Table 1, p. 489.
59. *Ibid.*, Table 5, p. 498.
60. *Ibid.*, Table 6, p. 499.
61. John Kennett, 'The sociology of Pierre Bourdieu', *Educational Review*, **25** (1973).
62. Thomas S. Kuhn, *The Structure of Scientific Revolutions*, University of Chicago Press, 1962.
63. Peter Winch, *The Idea of a Social Science*, Routledge and Kegan Paul, London, 1958.
64. For a singularly unintelligent application of the 'soft' view to the practice of education, see B. A. Kaufman, 'Piaget, Marx and the political ideology of schooling', *Journal of Curriculum Studies*, **10** (1978): 'Objectivity is not an initial property but is invented by the subject. Therefore, objectivity is highly individualistic, not, as the materialists believe, a faithful copy of reality.'
65. Peter L. Berger and Thomas Luckmann, *The Social Construction of Reality*, Penguin Books, Harmondsworth, 1971.
66. See Kai Nielsen, 'Wittgensteinian fideism', *Philosophy*, **42** (1967); Patrick Sherry, 'Is religion a "form of life"?', *American Philosophical Quarterly*, **9** (1972); and J. F. M. Hunter, ' "Forms of Life" in Wittgenstein's *Philosophical Investigations*', *American Philosophical Quarterly*, **5** (1968).
67. See Peter Winch, 'Understanding a primitve society', *American Philosophical Quarterly*, **1** (1964); and J. D. Y. Peel, 'Understanding alien belief systems', *British Journal of Sociology*, **20** (1969).
68. Rodney Needham, *Right and Left*, University of Chicago Press, 1973, p. xxxi.
69. Jack Goody, *The Domestication of the Savage Mind*, Cambridge University Press, 1977, p. 36.
70. See B. F. A. Tipton, 'Some organizational aspects of a technical college', *Research in Education*, **1972,** No. 7.

CHAPTER 3

Social Class and the School

In the nineteen-seventies social class was brought to the very forefront of explanation of children's scholastic attainments and the relationship of schools to society. Social class has a bearing on education in two principal ways, which will be dealt with in this book in two separate chapters. In the first place, the social-class origins of children have some connexion with how well they do in their schools; in the second, social class influences the way schools operate as agencies of 'social control'. The two are in some measure related. The relative academic failure of working-class children in the school system may be brought about by the schools themselves to ensure the continued subjection of the working class. Of course, this is achieved in devious, hidden, and even unwitting ways, and quite contrary to the schools' avowed intentions. The argument is twofold: schools set tasks which working-class children find uncongenial and abnormally difficult, and they also teach them humility (their place in the system of 'authority relations'). The truth of the matter is almost certainly the opposite: working-class children often do badly at school precisely because they will not be docile and because they refuse, as a matter of honour, unquestioningly to give the teacher what he wants. But these are large and complex issues. The matter of social class and failure at school will be considered separately, as far as possible, in this chapter. The question of social control will be dealt with later in the book.

THE REINSTATEMENT OF CLASS

Class has been vigorously reinstated in sociological analysis since the early nineteen-seventies, especially by Marxists. It had seemed to many to be obsolescent: even Herbert Marcuse remarked its passing.[1] Survey work in sociology and education in the nineteen-fifties and -sixties had used class in a weak sense as a descriptive category (usually in terms of occupational status), and theorists (like Dahrendorf) had emasculated the concept, taking the bite out of class by emphasizing the divorce of ownership from the control of the means of production.[2]

Class in the strong sense, with all its connotations of power, was firmly rehabilitated in the world of education in 1972. This was the year in which Herbert Gintis published a notable critique of the school curriculum (and of Ivan Illich) in the *Harvard Educational Review*.[3] 'Schooling' has become now a term of abuse and 'school (or classroom) knowledge' is by definition unreal, irrelevant, distorted, or just plain fraudulent. The curriculum maintains, reproduces, or replicates the power structure of society either because its cultural discontinuities prevent working-class children from learning or because it8 ideological potency does not. To suggest that lower-class children fail at school from stupidity is not simply inadequate; it is immoral. It is to ignore the continuing but largely hidden disabilities of a class society.

We are now told that the ideology of affluence which prevailed in the nineteen-fifties hid the realities of class.[4] The working class had not disappeared; even affluent skilled workers had escaped 'embourgeoisement'.[5] Social class has become more rather than less important and ubiquitous in sociological analysis, and even post-war youth cultures like the 'Skinheads', in spite of their remarkable social conservatism,[6] are now reinterpreted as counter-hegemonic movements of class protest.[7] The school is a 'middle-class institution' in which the failure of working-class children is virtually guaranteed. And the selective English grammar school was the middle-class institution *par excellence*.

Thus it is really quite odd that more than half of the sons born to middle-class families fell below the social level of their fathers in the first half of this century. The outstanding feature of the school as a middle-class institution in twentieth-century England has been its inefficiency in safeguarding the interests of the middle-class. It has not been notable for its power of social reproduction, for what the middle-class has experienced is massive demotion. Fifty-four per cent. of sons born to professional and managerial fathers were, in 1949, at lower levels of social (occupational) status, but 33 per cent. of those born to working-class fathers (in manual and routine non-manual jobs) had risen to higher levels.

The grammar school—which for most of the earlier period had a large intake of middle-class fee-payers—has not been a signal success in sustaining middle-class children in the station to which they were born. Those middle-class sons who went to grammar schools (some 60 per cent. of the total) were not thereby saved from demotion: 40 per cent. (in 1949) were in jobs below the level of their fathers. Some of the younger ones would doubtless catch up. The actual numbers involved in this demotion were relatively small (compared with the numbers of working-class children who went up), but as proportion of all middle-class children, at more than 50 per cent. the magnitude is startling.[8]

There has been a highly significant shift from 'ascribed' to 'achieved' status in England since the end of the Second World War: a father's station in life is far less likely to determine his son's. (A study of status inheritance in 1949 found a correlation of 0.46; a roughly comparable study in 1972 found one of only 0.36.)[9] With regard to education, there has been a long-term, underlying trend throughout this century towards greater equality of access to its superior, more highly selective and prestigious forms.[10]

Nevertheless, this chapter does not deny that scholastic success is in some measure class-linked and that class gets into schools. But definition is crucially important. The irony is that the closer we get to a definition of class that a Marxist would recognize and accept (based on property and power over others as well as occupational prestige), the weaker is the connexion between class and success and failure at school. It is not a very close connexion whatever definition we use; and there is little connexion in selective, academic forms of education in England after the age of fourteen or fifteen. Class-linked aspirations and attainments disappear after that age; in our universities there is probably an inverse relationship between social class and class of degree. Class reasserts itself powerfully on job prospects and advancement after school and college; that is a different matter. This 'lagged effect' of class is something that anyone interested in social justice should have at the centre of his attention.

This chapter concedes that in some sense and to some degree class gets into schools. This is not only, or even principally, through class differences in inborn intellectual ability, although these indubitably exist. (In his famous book, *Inequality*, Christopher Jencks calculates that for white America innate differences account for only some 10 per cent. of the influence of class on educational attainment.) This chapter will try to establish just how class enters schools and what its consequences are, examining, for instance, theories of 'labelling' and 'self-fulfilling prophecy', and of the 'unfair' use of language and abstract, literary curricula. It will point to a singularly disturbing feature of our times: that one reason why class nowadays gets into some of our schools is that some teachers deliberately take it there. It is not only an instrument of revolution; it is the very latest in teaching aids.

THE MAKING OF SOCIAL CLASSES

It would be an exaggeration to say that 'social class' is an invention of sociologists. But it would not be a large exaggeration. Precisely as people throughout the Western world have found this a less useful category, sociologists have re-emphasized its importance: in the twenty-five years after 1945 a series of studies in both Britain and America showed an apparent decline in class consciousness.[11] Of course, people at large may have been capitalist dupes, their responses merely an expression of false consciousness. But it is the apparently unlimited number of classes that sociologists feel at liberty to distinguish according to the exigences of their research design that calls the meaning and credibility of 'class' into question.[12]

Joseph Schumpeter discussed the problem more than two decades ago: on the one hand, there was class which was clearly the creation of the researcher and, on the other, there were, perhaps, 'real' classes with an independent existence, 'which we observe but which are not of our making'.[13] Today sociologists' classes usually range from two to ten. Five is very popular (it is also the number of 'social classes' distinguished by the Registrar General). Runciman says that sociologists who use a 'class model' of society (as distinct from a 'status model' of prestige levels) 'seem seldom to envisage more than two or at the most three strata'.[14] That is untrue. His own study of social justice is based on what he perversely sees as still the great and basic class division between manual and non-manual workers, but sociologists are constantly inventing a 'new middle' or a 'new working' class in a desperate attempt to capture the complex and shifting realities of human inequality. The invention of new social classes has been the great growth point of sociology in the past decade.

Social classes are seen as the great building blocks of the social order in modern industrial societies. They are curiously insubstantial (and outside sociological circles unmentionable). In pre-industrial, aristocratic societies the scaffolding of the social order was rank and degree. They had firmness and precision; they were even given legitimacy and a sure anchorage in a pre-Copernican cosmology (and John Donne feared, in a famous poem, that in a heliocentric universe, 'Prince, subject, father, son, are things forgot'). Rank was signalled and reinforced in a multitude of overt ways, not least in apparel and forms of address. The new building blocks we are told are made up of jobs, and yet reference to jobs—certainly one's father's, increasingly one's own—is one of the great indelicacies of our time. It is a great new social silence, the new taboo on which the modern social order stands.

For Schumpeter, class was being at ease with one another; for most sociologists, it is doing the same sort of job. (If you are looking at classes you may emphasize the money or security of tenure that the job gives; if you are looking at status you will emphasize the prestige that it brings.)[15] What we get from looking at jobs may in fact be no more than 'learnt social noise',[16] and the problem of looking at working-class fishermen in Hull and miners in South Wales[17]—or even apparently homogeneous occupations like clerical workers[18]—in any unitary sense, is now increasingly and properly emphasized. 'Social class' loses its substance and robustness, and in the absence of any adequate definition is introduced into social analysis as 'a kind of shorthand' or as a 'summarizing variable'.

Marxists tend to invent new working classes, non-Marxists new middle-classes. The now rather tired thesis of the 'proletarianization' of white-collar, clerical workers was first advanced by Karl Marx (in *Capital*) on the basis of their weakening market position; it has found considerable support in post-war studies. There is no doubt that it is substantially true. More than twenty years ago Lockwood opposed it in his now classic book, *The Blackcoated Worker*: he recognized the decline of the office worker from his splendour and relative wealth in the Victorian counting house (though even then some of them did not wear gloves); and while the clerk was no longer, in the early nineteen-fifties, middle-class, he was not, apparently, working class either.[19] Runciman has taken a similar view, emphasizing, like Lockwood, the special and superior 'work situation' of clerks. Giddens broadly supports them, and he does not think that clerical workers have experienced the two-way split that some—not only Marxists—have predicted, merging to a limited extent with the bosses on the one hand and to a greater extent with 'workers' on the other.[20] (Dahrendorf[21] no less than Nicos Poulantzas[22] points to this two-way movement.) The truth by 1980 is the opposite of what Lockwood, Runciman, and Giddens have imagined. Affluent skilled manual workers may not have been taken into the middle-class, but as one very cautious research has recently reported: '... many of my data suggest that routine white-collar workers have, in past decades, experienced more significant and far reaching changes in their class situation than have affluent skilled craftsmen'.[23] It is yet another of the absurd inadequacies of class theory that, when clerks have been firmly dislodged from the middle-class, nobody knows where to put them.

Lines of demarcation are an unending problem. Indeed, it is a further great oddity of recent social class analysis that all the founder members of E. P. Thompson's working class, at the end of the eighteenth century, were capitalists. (Both Francis Place and Thomas Hardy, for example, owned their own workshops and means of production and employed apprentices, journeymen, and day-labourers. Both were the target of strikes: in 1793 the Journeymen Breeches-makers organized a strike against Place and in 1795 the Journeymen Boot and Shoemakers organized a strike against Hardy.)[24] The 'aristocracy of labour' in the later nineteenth century, like the affluent skilled worker today, has been especially difficult to locate: Hobsbawm places it unequivocally in the middle class.[25] There is general agreement that social classes were the creation of nineteenth-century industrialism (with some help from sectarian religion) and that the working class 'made itself' in responding to economic and social change between 1790 and 1832 and the middle class in opposing the Corn Laws until their repeal in 1846. But in retrospect the system of social classes is becoming highly complex: thus a 'forgotten middle class' (of fee-paid professionals) is now being distinguished from the other middle classes of the age.[26] Lines of demarcation depend on the criteria employed, and if form of income (fees, rents, profits, salary, wages) is taken as the basis of class (Marx's 'identity of revenues'), the picture differs from class based on occupation or even 'work situation'.

Among the new classes that are being identified today two are particularly relevant to the study of education. The 'new working class' in the sense of proletarianized white-collar workers means, as Gosta Carlsson warned us twenty years ago,[27] that many people who have left school and college with certificates and diplomas and have apparently gone 'up' into non-manual work have in fact gone 'down'; and the 'new middle class' in the sense of one based on education as distinct from property has apparently great potency through the informed pressure and even less tangible influence that it exerts on the educational system and even on curricula and teaching methods. Both these new class formations appear to be real and to have an existence which is independent of the social observer.

Great care is needed over terminology. Thirty years ago Wright Mills, in his notable book *White Collar*, called propertyless white-collar workers the 'new middle class';[28] but today Marxists are claiming very high levels of white-collar workers for a new *working* class. The old working class of the post-war era has been their despair; it has no revolutionary spark. The only serious signs of subversion are in the highly educated technocratic sectors of modern employment, and these are now claimed by Marxists for the working class. In France, Alain Touraine has written off the old working class as a revolutionary force; they have been replaced in the class struggle by high-ranking office workers, designers, and well-qualified technical workers.[29] In America, Gintis has taken a similar view and in a paper on the new working class argues that it includes engineers and professional workers who are now 'alienated' and have no real control over their work.[30]

In post-war England the working class has been an acute embarrassment to Marxist social theorists. We have had only the Campaign for Nuclear Disarmament, and that was solidly middle class. Parkin has analysed its origins and membership. On the march to Aldermaston they were largely actors, playwrights, and dons. Parkin, too, distinguishes 'educated workers' as a distinctive segment of the class structure; but more convincingly than Gintis he labels it a new *middle* class—not because it is proletarianized and debased, but because it is not. The welfare and 'creative' professions are its backbone; its power stems from intellectual achievements, professional qualifications, and a pivotal place in modern communications; and its superior morality is unquestioned.[31] Its weakness may be a fastidious distaste for power.

In summary: a new middle class has appeared based on high-level academic and professional qualifications and attainment in the world of the arts; a new working class has also appeared in the shape of proletarianized routine white-collar (and minor administrative) workers. As Westergaard says, 'It plainly makes no sense to label them "middle class" in the way that convention still does ...'[32] We have experienced in the middle of our class structure (in the words of Andreski) 'an inversion of pre-industrial grading (into lowly labourers and well-dressed men of the pen)'.[33] Canadians have always known that lumberjacks were in a class superior to clerks, and even thirty years ago paid cashiers no more than and ranked them below railway firemen.[34] If this inversion in the middle of the class structure of Western societies is not clearly recognized, educational systems will be grotesquely misinterpreted.

Grotesque misrepresentation has already occurred. It is clear that in many studies of education and society 'up' really means 'down'.[35] Institutions have been designated 'middle class' (in recent years pejoratively) because England's 10 per cent. of (male) clerical workers have been put 'above the line' and the 45 per cent. of skilled workers below. And so we have been guilty of the egregious folly of dismantling our educational system so that the sons and daughters of colliery clerks (middle class) would not steal some kind of unwarranted advantage over the sons and daughters of colliery fitters (working class). The folly is compounded by distracting attention, through concern with these puny distinctions in the middle, from the truly great issues of privilege at levels of society where inequality is of an altogether different order of magnitude.

DEFINITIONS OF CLASS AND ACADEMIC ATTAINMENT

The weight of the evidence for social-class influence on education rests on a small number of studies which were carried out in England in the early nineteen-fifties into two problems: the fairness and efficiency of 'eleven-plus' selection tests for grammar school places and the 'wastage' problem of early leaving (after the statutory leaving age at fourteen, but before taking public examinations at sixteen).[36] These studies showed that the children of unskilled and semi-skilled workers (some 20 per cent. of all adult male workers) fared relatively badly and that the children of professional and managerial fathers (some 15 per cent. of adult male workers) fared relatively well. For 65 per cent. of the population, including the 45 per cent. of skilled manual workers, the situation was much as it 'should' be: that is to say, their children were in the grammar schools at twelve and in the main still there at sixteen, in proportion to their numbers in the population. Largely because of undoubted distortion in the minorities at the extremes, the whole system was brought into disrepute and abandoned.

In these studies 'class' is nothing more subtle or sophisticated than the father's job placed on a prestige scale. There is no attempt to bring property or power over others into the picture, or otherwise to use a more classical notion of class, for which many sociologists are now arguing. This thin and inadequate conception of class is apologized for in some of the studies: Himmelweit thinks she is exonerated by conceding that this is 'a convenient shorthand description'.[37] It is not in fact shorthand. It is subterfuge.

The correlation between birth and death is unity and between social class and educational attainment around 0.3.[38] There is ample scope here for reprieve. Even this modest correlation coefficient needs to be treated with great caution. 'Educational attainment' often means (especially in American studies) age of leaving school or college, and it is still the case that often it is the dunces who take longest to finish the course.

The degree of indeterminacy in the relationship between social class and progress at school is perhaps best illustrated from the data of the report, *Early Leaving*. This very influential publication of the early nineteen-fifties by the Advisory Council for Education is a major landmark in establishing an apparently unacceptable degree of class bias in the operation of England's maintained and direct-grant grammar schools. The report is properly apologetic about the poor information, taken from admissions registers, on fathers' occupations for the 8,644 boys and girls included in the study.[39] It is admittedly far inferior to the classification of occupations undertaken by the Registrar General; but the report finally concludes that it is adequate. It is of particular importance to note that as far as possible the researchers unashamedly converted parents' occupational statuses into educational categories, claiming as a virtue their 'desire to separate those whose parents had either received a grammar school education themselves or followed occupations in which that tradition was strong'.

Thirteen per cent. of the children of unskilled labourers who were in the bottom third at the age of eleven had risen to the top third by the age of sixteen while 23 per cent. of the children of semi-skilled workers had done so. Of course, the net movement at these two occupational levels was downwards, but upward movement was significant. In the case of the largest occupational category, skilled manual workers' children (44 per cent. of the total), the net movement was comfortably upwards: 26 per cent. of these in the top third at the age of eleven were in the bottom third at the age of sixteen, but 33 per cent. of those in the bottom third at the age of eleven were at the top five years later.[40]

This degree of unpredictability, indeterminacy, or 'autonomy' in the system is roughly what might be expected from an overall correlation coefficient of 0.3. Lacey, in his book *Hightown Grammar*, gave a good illustration of intelligent middle-class boys moving downstream and working-class boys moving up; he described this as 'a degree of autonomy in the system of social relations in the classroom which can transcend external factors' such as social class. But he was quick to insist that 'this is not an attempt to disprove the established correlation between social class and academic achievement ...'[41]

It is impossible to know from a reading of Douglas's influential book, *The Home and the School*, how he arrived at parents' 'social class'. It is the key concept in the book. He gives a complicated and finally unintelligible account of his classification procedures,[42] and he does not hesitate to use the term 'social class'. This book, which was published ten years after *Early Leaving*, is one of those three or four enormously influential post-war studies which are generally thought to have demonstrated beyond reasonable doubt that England's maintained system of secondary education based on selection was massively and perhaps irretrievably class-biased.

The book is simply a report of how 5,000 children who were born in March 1946 (and who had been followed up in the meantime for medical research) fared in their eleven-plus examinations in 1957. In the earlier studies nine 'occupational classes' had been used for analysing the data on child health. These were now abandoned on the grounds that they were unstable. Importance would be given to 'the social origins and standard of education of mothers when devising a new social classification'. To an even greater extent than in *Early Leaving*, 'class' is given a heavy educational loading. In the event, the father's occupation is not wholly abandoned; it helped to distinguish some of the test scores. The 'classes' have every appearance of being invented after the event in a way that would reveal significant differences among children's test scores. This is disgraceful work, and to talk of 'social classes' is wholly unwarranted. Douglas does not place parents in class positions; they are not even status levels but are basically educational categories. 'Class' in this study has nothing whatsoever to do with property and power and position in the system of economic production. Douglas arrives at four 'social classes' (upper and lower middle and upper and lower working classes) and average test scores are different at these four levels.[43] When 'class' is defined in relation to education in this essentially circular fashion, in effect as a learning environment, it would be astonishing if it were otherwise.

There is precisely the same kind of circularity in King's study of one London grammar school, and just the same kind of quiet shift in the middle from class as an economic position to class as an educational category. King was not looking at academic progress and attainment, but at the commonly held view that middle-class children have the same values as those which prevail in grammar schools (and so are unfairly advantaged).

King analysed the 'social class' of pupils in the usual terms of the father's occupation, and gave extensive and very useful trend data in these terms for the fifty years between 1907 and 1957.[44] But he does not actually use class in this sense to answer the question about social class and values that he has set himself. This definition is quietly dropped for a very good reason: no value differences showed up. Differences appear (of a fairly trivial order) only when class is redefined as the education, and not the occupation, of parents. King says: 'Two important indices of cultural continuity were obtained; fathers' occupation and parents' educational experience. The latter proved to be the more powerful as a discriminator in the subsequent analysis.'[45]

In fact occupation is totally abandoned and we are never told how much more 'powerful' education was or whether occupation discriminated at all. But henceforth the analysis is conducted entirely in terms of whether parents went to a grammar school or not. (On this basis some differences in values appear, but none in 'involvement'.) In his conclusion King does not use the term 'class' at all, although it is embedded in the question he set out to answer: 'The survey of pupils confirmed that the holding of school-approved values was associated with the sons of parents who had been to grammar schools.'[46] Larger studies have sometimes produced results no more remarkable.

Educationists who have claimed excessive and distorting class influences on education have usually defined class as 'culture' or values, in effect as a learning environment. Allison Davis did so in America thirty years ago in a notable book on 'social-class' influences upon learning, arguing that the school made '... a narrow selection of a few highly traditional activities and skills, arbitrarily taken from middle-class culture ...'.[47] It is when class is defined in this weak cultural sense that it is found to be associated with children's progress and attainments at school; however, the more we remove the cultural and educational loading (and the in-built circularity) and move towards a 'classic' notion of class with strong economic connexions, the more the association tends to disappear.

Ainsworth and Batten found none. They followed the careers of the 1,500 'Plowden children' in the Greater Manchester area as they progressed through fifty-three Manchester schools (including three direct-grant and nine maintained grammar schools). Their inquiry focused on the year 1966–67 when the children were four-teen to fifteen years old. It is an outstandingly important, technically impressive, and methodologically impeccable study. It is unusual in its patent intellectual honesty.

They examined the relationship of seventy-nine 'environmental variables' to the children's attainments (as shown by the normalized and standardized scores obtained on a range of scholastic tests). The environmental variables included parents' attitudes to education and careers, and objective facts of social background which roughly approximated to 'class' in the classical sense: they included not only the father's occupation but also the standard of housing and other 'materialistic' indicators of socioeconomic position. Forty-two of the seventy-nine background variables were significantly correlated with the children's academic performance. They did not include the father's occupation or any other indicator of socioeconomic position.[48]

Variables relating to parents' attitudes, as distinct from their socioeconomic position, were related to scholastic performance. This is precisely what the Plowden study of a national sample of primary school children had found, and the Plowden report had been very careful but emphatic in distinguishing between parents' attitudes and their class position. The influence of parents' attitudes when assessed separately emerged as more important than occupation taken by itself: 'Our readers may be surprised that home circumstances at first sight seem less influential than previous inquiries suggested.'[49] Home is important; class is not: 'Parental attitudes appear as a separate influence because they are not monopolized by any one class.' Within-class differences are so great, as Wiseman argued, that between-class differences are swamped and rendered meaningless.[50]

Ainsworth and Batten likewise emphasize what they refer to as a syndrome of variables which pick up the crucial features of the 'education-orientated' home, and they likewise discount 'social class'. A complex of closely related variables correlate with attainment:

Immediately striking is the number of such variables concerned with parents' ambitions for their children in terms of education and careers, their awareness of school work and progress, the reading habits of the family, and the educational experience of the parents. No less striking is the absence from this list of the socio-economic measures—father's occupation, material needs, rateable value, housing standard, etc. This is in direct agreement with the results of the Plowden primary survey which stated—'although there is some slight association with social class, what matters is the degree of literacy in the home, and the attitudes of parents towards books and towards school. These correlations emphasize the existence of many good homes in the working class and many bad homes in the middle class.'

The 'home-centred' working-class family is one such 'good home', as Toomey found in the late nineteen-sixties in his important 'Medway' study. Working-class children who grow up in home-centred families—which are unsociable and spend a relatively high proportion of their income on the home—are good scholastic material.[51] Such parents do not only encourage; they help. What matters is having someone around who can actually do your quadratic equations when you're stuck, and skilled manual workers are often at least as well equipped in such matters as travelling salesmen.

CLASS CULTURE, YOUTH CULTURE, AND THE SCHOOL

The argument from class 'culture' or values in essence is this: middle-class children find school generally agreeable because it is like their homes; teachers have middle-class values and behave (and speak) in middle-class ways; middle-class pupils feel at home with them and can even accept their 'definition of the situation'. In consequence these pupils tend to do well at school. Working-class children, in contrast, find school strange and even hostile, they are not at home in it, may feel 'alienated', and so they do badly there. There is, moreover, a 'youth culture' which is essentially anti-school and tends to recruit and reinforce working-class dissidents. Polarized subcultures emerge in the school: one (basically middle-class) subculture is pro-school; one (basically working-class) subculture is anti-school. The anti-school, delinquescent subculture tidily intensifies as we go 'downstream'.

This now-classic picture[52] is almost certainly wrong in every essential. It is currently being refurbished with an implausible (but widely applauded) theory of cultural truce. In the secondary schools in the mining valleys of South Wales middle-class teachers stand arrayed against working-class pupils; but sometimes they call a truce and abate or even erase their middle-class characteristics. Both truancy and delinquency rates decline and academic attainments rise.[53] The evidence for this is among the very weakest in current educational research.

In an 'interactionist' study of two mainly working-class neighbourhood comprehensive schools in the Midlands, in which he was principally concerned 'to understand the way school appears to young people', Quine finally despaired of obtaining any anti-school quotes. He had set out to test the 'polarised cultures' thesis and found not an intensified anti-school culture as he moved 'downstream' but precisely the reverse. The point about streaming is that it is highly protective (like low rank generally: it saves you from impossible and indeed improper demands). The child of poor ability, when placed in the bottom stream, is not so exposed, constantly humiliated, and thoroughly demoralized as he would almost certainly be in an unstreamed school. The two schools were tough, the teachers even 'authoritarian': they talked child-centred rhetoric and used the cane.

Quine was perpetually surprised. The actions of the leading teachers belied their liberal theories: 'It was therefore all the more surprising that the pupils, far from generally resenting the schools, quite liked them. Generally this acceptance of the school regime was stronger in the bottom sets or streams.' A few older girls in the top stream showed some (very qualified) disapproval, but the bottom streams were almost euphoric: 'It was surprising that the children in the lower English and Maths sets in the fourth and fifth years were positively favourable to the schools—almost to the extent of becoming ritualists.'[54] It is conceivable, of course, that middle-class children would have liked these schools even more; this could not be tested since there were virtually no middle-class children in them.

In America, children from different social classes who have the same intelligence (as measured by orthodox intelligence tests) get the same school grades. As Christopher Jencks has pointed out, this is not consistent with the theory that middle-class children are better motivated and work harder because they find school more to their taste than do working-class children: 'But if this were the case, we would expect middle-class children to earn better grades than working-class children with similar test scores. Since they do not, the whole theory that school life is essentially middle class is called into question.'[55] English evidence calls it seriously into question, too.

In England, as in America, middle-class children hope to stay at school somewhat longer than do working-class children of the same intelligence and academic standing. This is the principal difference in their attitudes to education. When Eva Bene investigated attitudes to education among fourteen-year-old grammar school boys in London, she found overall quite trifling social-class differences. She made a statistical analysis of their responses to eleven statements relating to various aspects of school life and to five dealing with education-related leisure activities (like library membership). There were social class differences on only five of the sixteen items, and four of these were in the leisure sphere: 'These differences are, however, rather small, with the exception of the one which has to do with the age at which the boys want to leave school.'[56] Somewhat inconsistently (and at odds with American evidence), there was no social-class difference in the desire to proceed to a university. It would be rash to infer that working-class and middle-class boys differ in the strength of their academic motivation. As Bene points out:

> There seemed to be greater social class differences regarding the amount of schooling the boys wanted than regarding their desire to do well in their studies. The great majority of the boys of both social class groups stated

that one must try to be among the best in the school. ... No significant differences were found in any of the items concerned with the relative importance which boys attached to work and play. According to the obtained results, the majority of boys of both social classes would rather be good at schoolwork than at sports.

Incredibly, the author in conclusion sees her study as supporting those American social scientists who have highlighted social-class differences in children's academic and social motivation and attitudes to school, and her work is often cited in that sense.

A variety of terms has been used to describe the 'fit' between children and their schools from simple 'liking' to 'retreatism', 'ritualism', and the very popular 'alienation'. (We have even had 'needs' and 'presses' and rather complicated 'need–press analysis'.) In Los Angeles, Ralph Turner looked at it in terms of 'marginality'; in England I have looked at it in terms of 'role conflict'. In neither case did the confidently expected social-class differences appear.

Turner was interested in the causes and consequences of ambition and thought that working-class high school seniors, all set for social ascent, would experience in their schools a sense of displacement or 'marginality'; they would be ill at ease because they did not fit in. He investigated 3,000 high school seniors, expecting to find that those of working-class origin would subscribe to values which put them at odds with middle-class students and with their schools. He found no such thing— and was honest enough not to fudge the issue. He found no social-class differences in values and no working-class 'marginal men'.[57] Curiously he concluded that the youth culture brought working-class youths into the middle-class world, rather than keeping them out.[58] This is almost certainly the case in England, too.

My own study of 'role conflict' was an investigation of the different and perhaps irreconcilable pressures pupils felt they were under at school. (I tried to measure the gap between a pupil's notion of himself and the demands that other people—notably teachers and fellow pupils—made on him.) All the sociological literature led me to expect that working-class pupils in grammar schools would be under greater pressure (and so have higher discrepancy or conflict scores) and that perhaps the minority of middle-class pupils in secondary modern schools would be in similar difficulties. This was not the case. There were highly significant differences between grammar school and secondary modern school pupils. In the grammar schools pressures were greater and more discordant, and pupils' 'discrepancy scores' were high. Role conflict in secondary modern schools was low. There were no social-class differences at all.[59]

In 1954 Floud pointed to the English grammar school's 'distinctive middle-class tradition' and the 'fascinating problem' of assimilating working-class children.[60] In the following decade this theme became shrill in the sociological literature. It reached a crescendo in a book which had a remarkable influence: Jackson and Marsden's *Education and the Working Class*. Of course it had its critics: Wiseman wrote about it with contempt for its intellectual and methodological inadequacies.[61] But it is widely cited as evidence of pervasive 'class bias' in English education.

What is remarkable about Jackson and Marsden's study is that their conclusions are wholly belied by the evidence they provide. The basic study is of eighty-eight working-class boys and girls who successfully completed a grammar school course in Huddersfield in the late nineteen-forties and early nineteen-fifties. There are also subsidiary and much more fragmentary accounts of ten middle-class boys and girls and ten early leavers. The book gives a vivid account of interviews with parents and the way working-class homes were in almost every case galvanized into intellectual life through having a son or daughter at the grammar school: intellectual excitement ran through the home, and for two or three years, until fathers got out of their depth, 'they settled down to maths and physics homework alongside their sons and daughters'.[62] 'For some whose abilities had been particularly frustrated or under-developed, the grammar school was as rich an experience as for their sons and daughters.' By contrast the middle-class parents seem generally to have been at odds with the school, resisting and overriding its advice; and, indeed, the grammar schools of Huddersfield had a genius for misplacing, misjudging, and misunderstanding middle-class boys and girls (those they considered fit only for hotel catering ended up with Firsts and Ph.D.s, or anyway with Edinburgh degrees in brewing). And yet the authors conclude: 'Every custom, every turn of phrase, every movement of judgement, informs the working-class parent and the working-class child that the grammar schools do not "belong" to them.'[63] The book ends with a gigantic non-sequitor: 'selection' must cease, there must be 'open' schools which belong to the neighbourhood, and: 'The educational system we need is one which accepts and develops the best qualities of working-class living, and brings these to meet our central culture.'[64]

Of course, these working-class boys and girls were contemptuous of the absurd pretentions and juvenile attitudes of the schools: the school magazine, the corps, the scouts, and the First Fifteen. They were contemptuous of its absurdities and they added lustre to its dark oak honours boards. This working-class anti-school culture did not lead to delinquency, the C-stream, and early leaving, but to the Sixth Form, Open Scholarships, and Oxford and Cambridge. The 'alienated' working-class pupils who left early were not those who could not stand the 'ethos'; they were those who could not do the sums.[65] (The middle-class ten may have been just as contemptuous of the school's ritual and ceremonial pomposities: there are hints of this, but the account is too thin for the reader to judge.) What this study does make clear— unwittingly and, indeed, in spite of itself – is the total inadequacy of explanations in terms of values, ethos, and subcultures. It was middle-class 'Raymond Peters' who was 'intimidated by the masters'; these working-class boys simply refused to buy the school magazine; they relished the insults; and they stayed the full course and passed all their examinations with glory and éclat.

The disenchanted, bored middle-class grammar school pupil of good academic ability is now well attested in the literature. Since the late nineteen-sixties he has sometimes been lost to the counter-culture; more commonly he has been saved by the youth culture.

Lacey has given us a very convincing portrait of just such a highly intelligent middle-class low achiever at 'Hightown Grammar': 'Baker', who received every encouragement from his parents (his father was a senior lecturer at a technical college), and whose family ethos was exactly attuned to the school ('the socio-cultural resources of the family were extremely high ...'). But school was almost unendurably boring: 'Morning school crawled past at the usual depressing crab-like pace.' Only the dinner bell could save him from the intolerable tedium of English and French.[66]

Youth cultures (whether of the 'extra-mural' English variety as described by Sugarman[67] or of the American school-based variety as described by Coleman[68]) have gained a bad name for turning pupils from high academic endeavour. Coleman's highly sociable and athletic youth culture, as Bennett Berger points out,[69] is in fact a replica of the well-heeled adult suburban world and in no way subverts it; Sugarman's hedonistic youth culture is at odds with 'high quality' homes. But neither, it seems, helps pupils to do well at school. And so it is odd that 'Russell' of 'Hightown Grammar', from a family of dentists and physiotherapists, who was actually ill at the thought of going to school where his performance was poor, was eventually saved by the youth culture in which he was increasingly involved. He got from it self-confidence and a sense of belonging. He was 'integrated' into the school, settled steadily to his work, and finally did well.[70]

This formula seemed to be well established in England in the nineteen-sixties: an anti-school youth culture reinforces working-class culture and virtually ensures school failure. The evidence does not support it. Ian Birksted has illustrated the way in which a fifteen-year-old boy can be deeply 'into pop culture' and stand high in favour with both boys and teachers. To talk of being 'pro-school' or 'anti-school' is almost meaningless: the relationship is much more ambiguous. There is no inexorable link between pop culture and school failure; this boy likes having a laugh but is going to be sensible and do well in his O-levels (but he has residual misgivings because he knows that 'success' means being a right drip and spending the rest of your life just working and watching the telly).[71]

Lacey is finally unwilling to relinquish the link between youth culture and school failure, but he recognizes that by fourteen or fifteen years of age virtually all grammar school pupils are sophisticated in the ways of the youth 'scene'. The youth culture did not reinforce anti-school attitudes; it softened and brought together the pro-school and anti-school subcultures which are at the heart of Lacey's analysis of Hightown Grammar.[72] As in Turner's study of high school seniors in Los Angeles, the youth culture did not keep working-class boys out; it brought them in. And from the evidence we are given, it appears not to have diminished anyone's academic achievement, but to have enhanced it. The youth culture does not reflect and further class conflict, as Marxists now stridently insist;[73] it heals it.

David Reynolds has in recent years been publishing papers, based on his studies of nine overwhelmingly working-class secondary schools in mining valleys in South Wales, which have received a good deal of sympathetic notice. What these papers say in essence is this: schools are the site of social-class conflict between middle-class teachers and working-class pupils; but some teachers nowadays call a truce, class differences are greatly moderated if not actually erased, working-class pupils become more regular attenders at school, get into trouble less often with the police, and enjoy greater academic success. The simple hopefulness of this picture, rather than the subtlety of the analysis or the force of the evidence, perhaps helps to account for the attention it has received.

Curiously, what first surprised Reynolds about his nine schools was 'not that there is so much conflict, but that there is so little'.[74] In some, it seems, where a truce reigns, there is virtually none. 'Truce' is simply a pretentious term for teachers not bothering any more. Even Reynolds, at times, accords it no greater dignity: 'A truce situation means, simply, that the teachers will go easy on the pupils and that the pupils will go easy with the teacher.' What we have in fact is a perfect recipe for educational disaster and a quiet life. Pupils doubtless do not mind being there: such devitalized and trivialized schools provide a tolerably comfortable waiting room in which to spend the years before life really starts.[75] The solution is not a truce; it is closure.

These superficial papers would not merit serious attention if it were not for the claim that in truce schools academic performance improves. 'Academic attainment' means the proportion of school leavers who go on to take courses at the local 'tech'. As a 'measure' it is almost meaningless. But in any event, the non-truce school B has been getting 26 per cent. of its leavers into the tech; three other schools out of the remaining eight, even under truce conditions, have got 21 per cent., 18 per cent., and 8 per cent. respectively. Even if these figures mean anything at all, they do not mean what Reynolds says.

When there is no truce, says Reynolds, 'the conflict between middle class teachers and working class pupils is played out with entirely predictable results'. By this he means that the famous working-class 'anti-school sub-culture' appears (school B is cited as evidence). And so academic research is trapped in the rhetoric of current fashion. This would be a matter of no great importance if it were not for clear evidence that such research actually influences policy-makers and politicians. It has done incalculable damage not only to education but to the English working class.

Arguments from the matching of school culture and social-class culture are still widely supported. In spite of his protestations to the contrary and his claim to be offering something much more exalted, all that Bourdieu is advancing is a very simple, even naive theory of cultural continuity, match or fit between the school and the middle-class family. It is '... the habitus acquired in the family which underlies the structuring of school experiences (in particular the reception and assimilation of the specifically pedagogic message)'.[76] Elsewhere he states his matching theory even more simply:

> The culture of the elite is so near to that of the school that children from the lower middle class (and *a fortiori* from the industrial and working class) can acquire only with great effort something which is *given* to the children of the cultivated classes—style, taste, wit − in short, those attitudes and aptitudes which seem natural in members of the cultivated classes. ...[77]

'Cultivation' in the family is not enough. What matters is actual help with ng programmes of study (even if it has to be provided by stealth to avoid the ...ool's wrath). Lacey is absolutely right to conclude his study of Hightown Grammar not with the emphasis on 'culture' which pervades the book but on the family as a pedagogical resource. The 'good home' provides not values but skills. Lacey finally—and correctly—portrays the school not so much as a collection of pupils bearing enabling or disabling class cultures but as a collection of competing family units.[78] The middle-class family, as a pedagogical resources base, will usually be quite well placed in this competition while the small proportion of families of unskilled workers will not; but the families of skilled manual workers—in fact the largest 'class' of all—will more than hold their own.

LANGUAGE

Language, it is commonly said, is at the very heart of social-class differences in academic attainment. In its very simplest form the argument is that middle-class children are brought up to speak Standard English and find this a great help in their school work; working-class children are not and in consequence are considerably handicapped. This simple proposition is now advanced in very complex ways, and Basil Bernstein distinguishes what are, perhaps, these same two forms of language as two linguistic 'codes': the 'elaborated' (which he previously called a 'formal language') and the 'restricted' (previously a 'public language').[79] It is not always clear whether 'code' means secret signs (as in Morse code) or a set of rules (as in the Highway Code).

The confident linking of social class and code which marked the earlier papers was considerably hedged about in the following twenty years; but the notion that working-class children are seriously disadvantaged because they grow up to speak a less developed, more restricted form of language than middle-class children is now firmly embedded in the minds of teachers and educationists. The truth is almost certainly the opposite: middle-class children succeed in spite of their 'elaborated' and empty language, which is a serious impediment to clear thinking and effective learning. It has proved to be an especially serious affliction for sociologists.

The easy and fluent use of language is under heavy attack because of its apparently upper-class connotations, and it is now almost immoral for schools to encourage it. We are witnessing a remarkable disparagement of linguistic ability, even of words themselves: they are a sorry substitute for experience. The invention of the printing press and the production of vernacular Bibles are now seen as a very mixed blessing;[80] anthropologists regret the introduction of literacy into tribal societies because it 'distances' personal relationships and communication is reduced to a few marks on paper instead of taking place 'in the more concrete ambience of the face-to-face situation'. The whole quality of social life is inevitably thinned.[81]

Literacy is now becoming so discreditable—because it is a substitute for 'real' experience and because (it is quite erroneously said) it has strong upper-class connexions—that conscientious schoolteachers hesitate to promote it. At the William Tyndale School in the mid-nineteen-seventies experience was given precedence over writing about it[82] and working-class parents were seen as subversive because they wanted their children to have 'middle-class' skills. This may be the extreme case, but the headmaster of the perfectly orthodox 'progressive' 'Mapledene Lane Junior School' also had deep reservations about verbal abilities. His school has quite recently been very perceptively described. He explained in a tape-recorded interview how he came into conflict with working-class, slum-clearance parents not because they attached too little importance to literate and verbal skills, but because they attached too much. The following is an extract from the headmaster's recorded views on the subject:

> I think that they feel that they all want to help their children, don't they?
> ... I think a lot of them would like their children to do what you and I do
> with a certain amount of ease ... which is talk. This is what they would
> really love. They think doing what you're told in school ... getting your
> sums or your spelling right helps towards this end. I feel sorry for parents,
> I really do.[83]

Here I shall make three main points: that the distinction between the two 'codes' and their social-class connexions is largely illusory; that the relationship of language to 'real' or 'underlying' ability is in any case exaggerated; and that the 'restricted code' does not in any event cut working-class children off from school—it is what teachers talk in classrooms anyway.

The 'restricted' form of language is characterized by unfinished sentences, a dearth of subordinate clauses, and a poverty of adverbs and adjectives. It is a language of the concrete, whereas 'elaborated' language is fashioned to express abstract thought. It is a language of the implicit rather than the explicit: it is elliptical—it does not spell things out. But above all it is a language of 'particularistic meanings', and whereas elaborated language easily expresses ideas which have a general, even universal, application, the ideas most easily expressed in the restricted code are context-bound. And the school, says Bernstein, is necessarily concerned with the transmission of 'universalistic orders of meaning' to which the middle-class child has commonly, though not invariably, been pre-sensitized.[84]

This thesis is nowhere supported by inquiries into the 'linguistic codes' that are actually used in schools. The alleged social-class linkages are now admittedly weak; very interesting work is being done by American anthropologists who have some interest in linguistics, which brings into question the basic distinction between concrete and abstract language and thought.

All meaningful speech involves a high level of abstraction, and even formal logic is not devoid of concrete reference. 'Strictly speaking,' says the American anthropologist, Eleanor Leacock, 'there is no such thing as "concrete" speech or language.'[85] The real distinction is between profound thinking and superficial thinking. The abstract nouns which embellish middle-class speech are actually dead metaphors; the elaborated code is loaded with inert images. In striking contrast, Leacock maintains, American negroes use metaphors which are still alive: concrete and vivid, in which the relevant characteristics of a situation are abstracted and stated in the form of analogy.

William Labov reaches a very similar conclusion regarding middle-class speech handicaps from his comparative studies of the street language of black urban-ghetto children in America. For him, too, middle-class speech is a graveyard of dead metaphors. He concludes that: 'The concept of (lower class) verbal deprivation has no basis in social reality.'[86]

The picture Labov paints is of the negro 'speech community' in which the use of language is vital, subtle, effective, complex, and socially important:

> We see a child bathed in verbal stimulation from morning to night. We see many speech events which depend upon the competitive exhibition of verbal skills: sounding, singing, toasts, rifting, louding—a whole range of activities in which the individual gains status through his use of language.

Labov does not hesitate to compare this use of language favourably, from the point of view of effective thinking and communication, with Standard English and the elaborated code. These, he claims, are 'turgid and redundant', characterized above all by verbosity; they confuse naming with knowing, and 'words take the place of thought, and nothing can be found behind them'. This severely 'dysfunctional' linguistic code is a serious handicap for white, middle-class Americans:

> Our work in the speech community makes it painfully obvious that in many ways working-class speakers are more effective narrators, reasoners and debaters than many middle-class speakers who temporize, qualify, and lose their argument in a mass of irrelevant detail. Many academic writers try to rid themselves of that part of the middle-class style that is empty pretension, and keep that part that is needed for precision. But the average middle-class speaker that we encounter makes no such effort: he is enmeshed in verbiage, the victim of sociolinguistic factors beyond his control.

In his book, *East is a Big Bird*, Thomas Gladwin reveals the remarkably abstract, but efficiently pragmatic, conceptual world of a Puluwat canoe navigator and the intellectual accomplishment which routinely ensures the survival of a primitive people on long voyages across the Pacific. The navigator must classify and process a great amount of specific information: 'In other words, Puluwat navigation is a system which simultaneously employs fairly high orders of abstraction and yet is pervaded by concrete thinking.' Like Eleanor Leacock, Gladwin is forced to conclude that the abstract–concrete dichotomy is false, and its application to remedial education for poor children in America damaging; like Labov he is driven to question the 'superiority' of the thinking involved in middle-class speech and work and to cite a lower-class activity as a supreme example of abstract thinking—the work of the big-city taxi-driver. The driver must work with a complex map of the city in his mind on which he superimposes the flux of traffic and from which he must make rapid and accurate inferences: 'Can one call this image of the city with which the driver must work anything but an abstraction?'[87] It is a job which not uncommonly is done by dropouts and school failures.

So alien to the working-class child, said Bernstein, was the abstract, 'formal language' of the school that it did not merely confuse him: it was an assault upon his identity. In highly melodramatic language Bernstein described this school situation as 'persecutory', in which the lower-class child was exposed to 'a persistent attack on his language and so his mode of orientation. He is bewildered and defenceless in this situation of linguistic change.' But the socialization of the middle-class child has made him 'predisposed to the ordering of symbolic relationships' and he finds himself, at school, in a situation which he can not only accept and respond to but exploit.[88]

There is no substance in this hysterical analysis which has done so much damage to English education and helped to create a false and altogether exaggerated consciousness of class in English society. It rests on an uncritical acceptance of G. H. Mead's view of the crucial role of language in 'socialization'. Certainly Witkin found no evidence that working-class children were in any sense assaulted or persecuted by the English language in the thirty-six schools (involving 3,400 fourth-year pupils) in which he conducted his inquiry into children's evaluation of the English lesson.

Throughout the ten grammar schools, eighteen secondary modern schools, and eight comprehensive schools, fourth-year pupils were generally well disposed to the study of English, and the overall picture is that a higher proportion of working-class than middle-class children thought that: 'In my English lessons I feel that I have learnt something important to me.' Sixty-four per cent. of the working-class pupils thought that this was so, but only 57 per cent. of the middle-class children. (This difference is statistically significant.) However, there was no social-class difference in the grammar schools, where working-class pupils were reduced to the same level as middle-class pupils.

Witkin was forced to conclude from his extensive survey that there was no evidence that working-class pupils felt persecuted because their language was under attack and so made a negative evaluation of the English lesson: 'The reverse seems to be the case.' More generally Witkin concluded that the 'class culture conflict model' of education was useless: 'The precise nature of the influence of school structure on the experience of the child is obscured rather than revealed by such a view.'[89]

It remains curious that middle-class children generally do very well at school although they suffer from the severe disability of having learnt the formal, abstract, and empty language of the elaborated code. We have almost certainly overemphasized in recent years the significance of language both in 'socialization', in a general way, and in intellectual functioning, more particularly. Thirty years ago Allison Davis was saying substantially what Bernstein and his followers are saying today: school curricula reflect the highly verbal culture of the middle class—'we have been led by scholastic culture to overrate reading as a means of developing mental processes'[90]—and if only intelligence tests could be stripped of words and made 'culture-fair', the true intellectual abilities of lower-class children would stand revealed.

The history of the invention and application of 'culture-fair' tests is deeply

embarrassing. In the Inglis Lecture at Harvard in 1948, Allison Davis gave some highly confusing and ambiguous preliminary results; subsequent work with the Davis–Eells test (which removed the linguistic loading of normal tests) did not yield the hoped-for results. Lower-class children did no better in it than on a traditional (Kuhlmann–Finch) test; middle-class children did much better than lower-class children on both.[91] Comparable data in England obtained from the use of non-verbal (picture) tests of ability gave similar results.[92] These are rather technical matters, but we should not let that frighten us. Whatever else these results mean, they indicate strongly that language has been exaggerated in the study of social-class differences.

The argument in terms of socialization in the home and cultural continuity with the school is being made today in precisely the terms in which Bernstein first advanced it more than twenty years ago. The allegedly different ways in which working-class and middle-class mothers talk to their young children is perhaps now more at the centre of attention, and evidence is produced that the latter use more abstract language and talk more about principles.[93] If this is so, what really requires explanation is that their children learn anything at all. Any competent teacher knows that, whatever the background of his pupils, he must do precisely the opposite.

The language of the classroom is not continuous with the language of the middle-class home, if that is in fact abstract and oriented to universalistic orders of meaning; the language of the classroom is a highly restricted code. Teacher training is largely about getting young graduates to use it: to stop talking like a book, to prune their subordinate clauses, and even their finite verbs, and to translate all the abstract nouns that first come to their minds into concrete form. (Young journalists usually need a similar training.) Douglas Barnes has illustrated just such an effective teacher in action; but his language would never do in a book.[94]

If Bernstein's two codes exist—if they are anything more than 'bastard poetry masquerading as science'[95]—then the language exchanges of experienced teachers and their pupils are pure 'restricted code'. One ethnomethodologist's account of 'making a lesson happen' illustrates this perfectly: the teacher's short, incomplete sentences; his short commands and questions (which are not really questions but statements); his simple and repetitive use of conjunctions; the implicitness of meanings; the concrete and specific character of the interchange which is heavily context-bound.[96]

In his attempt to uncover the underlying 'rules' of the interchange between teachers and pupils in classrooms, Hargreaves reveals a flow of talk which is almost wholly unintelligible without a knowledge of the context—and of which particular context has been 'switched on'. This is a small-scale, intimate, face-to-face world of implicit meanings in which very little needs to be spelled out. 'Stop talking' has five different meanings according to context. 'To understand the different meanings of the same words required us (the researchers) to make explicit the differences in the contexts of utterance.'[97] The middle-class child, socialized to a universe of transcendant meanings, can find school only persecutory, a sustained assault upon his essential self.

LABELS, HALOES, AND SELF-FULFILLING PROPHECIES

Class, it is said, is taken into schools by the language teachers use and by the labels they apply to their pupils. Both these propositions are false. There is doubtless some limited truth in the old adage: 'Give a dog a bad name ...', but what has become known as 'labelling theory' is among the more pretentious and ill-supported branches of current social science. It is almost as pretentious as the theories of 'halo effect' and 'self-fulfilling prophecy' from which it is, in fact, indistinguishable. The 'label', 'halo', or 'prophecy' is simply a misjudgement (by someone of importance) that people live up to. Even the famous haloes in Elton Mayo's Hawthorne studies have now been re-examined and judged nugatory.[98]

There is no evidence that teachers deliberately or consciously discriminate against working-class children, although there is evidence that they avoid too much 'interaction' with pupils who actually smell. (Discrimination against the middle classes, as at the William Tyndale School, is justified on the grounds that they can take care of themselves.) Jencks (in *Inequality*) concluded that in America: '... high school teachers reward a set of traits which, with the exception of academic aptitude, are not very class-related. This clearly contradicts most people's preconceptions.'[99] Lacey makes the following comment on 'Hightown Grammar': 'I did not record a single instance of a child being discriminated against because he was from a working-class background. In fact, I have recorded incidents where working-class children were given special treatment because of their difficulties at home.'[100]

Labelling theorists would not necessarily deny this, but some would say that through the application of labels the effect is the same. Labelling theory has been most vigorously applied to education in England by Hargreaves, and he does not link labels and social class; it has been quite passionately applied to education in America by Rist, and he maintains that it is through teachers' labelling activities that American education sustains the very class barriers that it is 'ideologically committed to eradicate'.[101]

Hargreaves was much influenced by an American study of 'late bloomers' which is reported in *Pygmalion in the Classroom*.[102] (Children who had been quite randomly selected were labelled as 'late spurters'; they exceeded themselves subsequently in their school work. This was apparently a case of 'Give a dog a good name ...'.) His own research in a secondary modern school had also impressed on him the dangers of 'the categorization process'.[103] He is alive to the powerful criticisms that have been levelled against the 'pygmalion' study,[104] and illustrates from his own experience as a schoolboy who was weak at Latin how labels may be falsified; but he nevertheless warns against premature categorization and is especially wary of 'streaming'.[105] At a common-sense level this is unexceptionable.

Rist far exceeds common sense. His study of labelling and 'social class' was made in a school in a black ghetto, 'a blighted urban area' where most families needed help from public welfare agencies. It is not clear what 'social class' means in this context, although some parents were poorer and had less education than others. Rist observed thirty children in their kindergarten and the eighteen who proceeded to the first grade and the ten who went on to the second.

After their first week in the kindergarten the teacher sorted them into three groups and seated them at three separate tables. This arrangement was made for organizational reasons. The first table in fact received more of the teacher's time and attention than the other two; although the groups were not 'ability groups', the teacher referred to the first table as 'fast learners'. Children at this table did not (often) smell of urine, they were mostly of lighter skin colour, and their hair was shorter and tidier. Their parents were somewhat better educated and not quite as poor as the rest.

These initial groupings tended to persist into the next two years (although the picture is rather confused because a high proportion of the original pupils—in fact eventually two-thirds—went off to other schools). In the second grade the three tables were made fully aware of their differences because the teacher actually called them 'Tigers', 'Cardinals', and 'Clowns'. It would be astounding, in the light of such outrageously unprofessional conduct, if the 'Clowns' had even tried to do as well as the rest.

This study tells us something about the professionalism or otherwise of teachers; it also shows how much more dangerous than explicit 'streaming' is the pretence that you are not streaming at all; it tells us nothing whatsoever about the influence of labels. Rist does not hesitate to conclude from this highly impressionistic study that the American school system buttresses class: 'The picture that emerges from this study is that school strongly shares in the complicity of maintaining the organizational perpetuation of poverty and unequal opportunity.'

At 'Mapledene Lane' primary school teachers talk disparingly about the 'clueless', allegedly disorganized lives of their pupils' working-class parents, and especially about the incompetence of mothers and their succession of 'fancy men': in short, they see their pupils as the product of a particular social-class background. But they do not take class into the classroom: the labels they freely apply to their pupils— 'thick', 'dim', 'bright', and 'really peculiar'—are psychological and not social labels. It is true that mixed-ability classrooms become informally 'stratified', with the 'problem children' at the bottom of an informal status system, comparatively neglected. Sharp and Green, the authors of this notable and generally convincing study, are very much concerned with teachers' 'typifications' of their pupils, but they are very doubtful indeed about the fulfilment of self-fulfilling prophecies, and whether labelling pupils and having particular expectations of them have determinate results. The authors have much to say about 'the social construction of pupils' classroom identities', but they are also alive to the significant part that pupils play in their own identity construction; the final emphasis is not on any inexorable outcome of labelling but on revision and reversal, on the ongoing 'accommodation' and 'transaction' that take place as the teacher copes with her management dilemmas.[106]

Labels, even when applied by very powerful 'reality-definers' and 'significant others' have a way of coming unstuck—as I found when I made a study of disabled people in a Cheshire Home[107] and another of adults who had gone blind.[108] The same has been found of long-term prisoners;[109] even Rist in a recent paper has backtracked appreciably from the position he assumed when he wrote about the ghetto school. He is much more tentative about labels and now asks: 'How strong is the label and can it be made to stick?' He is now more fully aware that '... there is a social process involved where individuals are negotiating, rejecting, accepting, modifying, and reinterpreting the attempts at labelling.'[110]

Another recent study in this area in England broadly confirms the picture at Mapledene Lane. Of course teachers 'typify' and attach labels in order to manage their lives effectively, but the labelling is not class-linked. James Murphy, like Sharp and Green, found primary school teachers using not social labels but psychological labels relevant to their teaching of children: '... the teachers saw the children as in some "contextless" sense as "having it" or "not having it"—they were "bright" to "dull".' When pushed (by the researcher) teachers could usually locate a pupil in a 'social class' ('she's from a middle-class home; she had a horse for her birthday'), but this was a very latent or dormant form of classification and seemed not to enter into daily interaction with the pupils.

Teachers could produce endless 'factors' which they thought influenced children's academic performance: 'What was particularly significant about such a list, however, was that such "factors" were not described in term of "class".' The labels they used were 'brassy', 'hard as nails', and 'a right little madame'. Teachers were well able to maintain a clear distinction between the social attributes and the academic attainments of pupils. The form order (based on attainment) at the end of the year was not related to teachers' pupil 'preferences', class-linked or otherwise. The only prophet who would have found himself fulfilled would have based his predictions on IQ.[111]

SOCIAL CLASS AND TEACHING METHODS

There is no doubt that working-class parents feel let down by child-centred, 'progressive' teaching methods, but usually they can do little about it. If school populations are falling they may be able to 'vote with their feet' by withdrawing their children and finding a school more to their taste. Middle-class parents likewise find child-centred, 'progressive' education not to their liking; they are often more vocal and may have some political leverage. But what is really surprising is the degree of insulation that the educational system enjoys from all social classes. Class is now to some extent in the schools like a Trojan Horse—because some teachers have taken it there. But it is not true that middle-class parents—even 'new middle-class' parents—have engendered, or even support, an 'invisible pedagogy'. It is only lecturers in teacher training colleges and Professors of Education who do so.

When he writes about language and socialization Bernstein says the school is an extension of the middle-class home; when he writes about teaching methods he says it is an extension of the working-class home: 'From the point of view of working-class parents, the visible pedagogy of the collection code at the primary level is immediately understandable.'[112] Certainly the traditional, respectable working class has always been keen on classification and framing: the parlour separate and highly polished for 'company' on Sundays; strong fences round gardens; everything tidy, sorted, scrubbed, and in its proper place. And Bernstein is quite perceptive when he recognizes that reading, writing, and counting are what working-class mothers want for their children; that if the invisible pedagogy of the open-plan school is to proceed unchallenged, working-class mothers must be 'resocialized or kept out of the way'; and that there is 'symbolic continuity (or extension) between the working class home and the school'. The school is a working-class institution after all.

Just as Bernstein has two language codes, so he has two pedagogies. The codes are elaborated and restricted; the pedagogies are invisible and visible. The class alignment is now different. The old-style 'visible pedagogy' which involved the teaching of separate subjects in a phased and organized way is strongly supported by both the working class and the old middle class; the new pedagogy of 'exploration' and teaching which waits patiently on 'learning readiness', and is neither phased, bounded, nor organized, is sustained by a new middle class. The old middle class tolerate it in the primary schools because they can teach their children to read and write themselves or hire someone who can.[113] The invisible pedagogy reflects (perhaps even replicates) the 'personalized organic social solidarity' which, Bernstein tells us, has arisen with the new middle class. But the new middle class would like their children to be able to hold down jobs eventually, so even they want a visible pedagogy at the secondary stage.

Working-class parents are commonly in despair, but to keep the good opinion of teachers they may learn the progressive rhetoric and secretly try to teach their children themselves. This was the position with slum-clearance parents at Mapledene Lane.[114] Working-class parents whose children are rather borderline are especially penalized; as one distraught mother recently told a researcher: 'I hear if they don't want to do anything they don't do it. ... The school's all right for those who are clever, but they don't do enough for those who need an extra shove. Linda needed pushing—me and her had great battles. It's been a struggle, but she's grateful now.'[115] The invisible pedagogy exacerbates social-class differences and tragically subverts the social and educational progress of a hundred years.

Bernstein's argument is still basically a continuity-between-home-and-school argument. There are two aspects of the 'new' middle-class home which are extended to schools to constitute the new, invisible pedagogy: the first is that mothers are nowadays swamped by their children (and so teachers, apparently, should be swamped likewise); the second is the astonishing claim that the new middle class do not distinguish between work and play (and neither, by extension, must the curriculum).

The 'new' middle-class mother can not get away from her child: she is no longer a distant, domestic manager flanked by governesses and nannies. As Bernstein puts it: 'For such a mother interaction and surveillance are totally demanding. ...' In short, she is now reduced to precisely the position that working-class mothers have always been in—and that 'old' middle-class mothers are in nowadays, too.

The new middle class is swamped by work as much as it is swamped by children; and deeply do they resent it. Certainly their wives resent it, as the Pahls made clear in their study of managers and their wives.[116] The old middle class—doctors and parsons—are also swamped, and their wives resent it, too, as I have recently shown in my study of Anglican clergymen.[117] Dentists are able to separate work and play more easily, and do not hesitate to do so. But 'class', whatever its use in looking at education, is almost useless when looking at work–play relationships.[118] But more to the point in relation to Bernstein's correspondence theory, adult play, as Giddens points out, 'is not psychologically identical with the play of children'.[119] Erikson had emphasized the same point in *Childhood and Society*, highlighting the child's use of play for understanding reality and the adult's use of play for taking a holiday from it.

It is this erroneous and misleading class-linked notion of play that Terry Ellis had picked up and placed at the centre of the invisible pedagogy of the William Tyndale School. And it was precisely the 'new' middle class that rose up against this invisible pedagogy and destroyed it.

Ellis and his colleagues claimed to represent and champion the oppressed and disadvantaged working class; and indeed middle-class children were systematically neglected on principle. The headmaster 'felt the need to discriminate in favour of the disadvantaged child, who lacks the family and social support most middle-class children enjoy'.[120] What the teachers seemed to find unpardonable was that 'aspiring working-class parents' (the teachers' own pejorative term) wanted precisely what middle-class parents wanted (including the will and ability to compete). It was children from these families who were most severely castigated: 'They saw school as a place to work, and had a very narrow concept of what work was. Anything that seemed like play was a waste of time.'[121]

But it was not only, or even principally, the 'aspiring working class' that made the attack on the William Tyndale School; it was exactly the 'new' middle class as Bernstein conceives it—university graduates employed in social work and the 'media', left-wing in their political stance, supporters of all great humanitarian causes—who actively, adroitly, and effectively campaigned against the school. They had been moving into Islington and buying up run-down, low-cost houses and turning them into ideal Habitat homes; they became school managers; they had useful contacts and were on the phone. 'The cabal-like telephone politics of the new activists—the "highly-educated" ones as they were called—were something new.'[122] They seemed to be wholly unaware that they were the harbingers of a new personalized organic social solidarity.

The teachers at William Tyndale quite deliberately took class into the school; in their own account of their policy and actions their basic categories are class categories.[123] The school is conceived as Althusser conceives it: as the site of the class struggle. It had never before occurred to the social classes concerned to see the school in these terms. As the circumspect and judicious Auld Report observed: 'On the evidence of some of those who had known the school for some years, this was the first time that any element of class consciousness was introduced to the school.'[124]

The relationship between social class and pedagogy is now being stood on its head: class does not create pedagogy; pedagogy creates class. Class becomes a pedagogic device for enlisting the interest of an apathetic working class. Paulo Freire has pointed the way.

When we have cut through the quite incredible verbiage of Freire (in works such as *The Pedagogy of the Oppressed*) we find that he is saying one thing of note, which any competent teacher knows anyway: you do not teach by making difficult things easy, but by making easy things hard (Freire would say 'problematical'). You make the obvious into a problem by showing it in a strange context. That basically is what teaching is. All Freire's talk of 'praxis' and 'conscientization' means only this: if we make an oppressed and illiterate peasant realize that a spade is not simply a tool for digging the ground—it makes profits for the landowner and it can also be used for hitting him over the head—he is more likely to learn the word 'spade'. An analysis and deepened awareness of class conflict as a preliminary to an adult literacy class is a powerful teaching aid. Ordinary objects of life, like spades, are 'decoded' and their political significance made clear.

Midwinter seems to be saying that teachers in 'disadvantaged' areas of Britain can be effective only if they teach revolution or at least very fundamentally call into question the status quo;[125] Zimmer explicitly advocates revolution as the curriculum for Germany's industrial working class. He is quite explicit: children of the workers must be able to 'present a united front against oppressive aspects of the reality of late capitalist society'.[126] There is no doubt that a Marxist sociology of education will reveal social-class conflicts in our schools which nobody imagined were there.

UNIVERSITY EDUCATION AND AFTER: THE LAGGED EFFECT

There is no connexion between social class and attainment in British universities. There are some indications of an inverse relationship, especially in more socially exclusive institutions.[127] At Oxford and Cambridge ex-public schoolboys are unduly prominent among those who get poor degrees.[128] The Robbins Report summarized the position:

> ... once in higher education, working class children do at least as well as children from middle-class homes. Both in terms of degrees obtained and in terms of wastage, the performance of university students with fathers in manual occupations has been as good as that of students from other homes, where there is likely to have been a longer tradition of education.[129]

'Class bias' in English universities is at the point of entry. In the post-war period approximately 40 per cent. of English university students have been working class (if we define this as the Registrar General's 'social classes' three to five) and 60 per cent. middle class (the Registrar General's classes one and two).[130] A higher proportion of students taking science and technology come from working-class homes—in the region of 50 per cent. This is, of course, an 'underrepresentation' of the working class, but it is the unskilled and semi-skilled end that accounts for a large measure of working-class underrepresentation. Whereas adult male workers at these lowest occupational levels account for more than 20 per cent. of all male workers, their sons are only 6 or 7 per cent. of university students.

By the nineteen-seventies, if all institutions of higher education which provide degree courses are taken into account, students were as much working class as middle class. Probably some 10 per cent. of working-class children nowadays proceed to institutions of higher education (universities, polytechnics, technological universities, and colleges of higher education) and so constitute some 50 per cent. of all students.[131] What is of much greater significance for social justice than this crude breakdown is 'class-bias' in recruitment to particular fields of study. In France working-class students go disproportionately into general degree courses in Arts and Sciences and are destined for unemployment, underemployment, or work in proletarianized 'administrative' jobs; the professional schools—notably Law and Medicine—recruit disproportionately from the middle class.[132] There are similar trends in America, and the same is probably happening in Britain.

When I made an extensive study of social class in a new technological university fifteen years ago, I found that more than half of a year's student intake (54 per cent.) were from working-class homes as defined above. The proportion was substantially higher in scientific and engineering departments: no less than 70 per cent. of students of mechanical engineering and 65 per cent. of electrical engineering were from working-class homes. By contrast only 26 per cent. in ophthalmic optics were working class. Again it was the semi-skilled and unskilled levels of the working class that were markedly underrepresented: they contributed 9 per cent. of all the students (14 per cent. of students of mechanical engineering, but none at all to ophthalmic optics—and, indeed, none to the socially prestigious field of civil, as distinct from mechanical, engineering).[133]

It has been alleged nevertheless that social class enters English universities in two respects: it influences who your friends are and what kind of job you want. On both counts, it is said, English universities are not social-class melting pots after all. And on both counts the argument is false.

Abbott's is the major study of friendship and class. The research was carried out at the universities of Edinburgh, Newcastle, and Durham. It is not based on studies of who was friendly with whom, but on whether students thought—when the ideas was put to them in a questionnaire—that they were influenced by class when making friends. The preliminary, published report (1965) said that approximately 55 per cent. of male students at Edinburgh and about 35 per cent. at Newcastle and Durham 'expressed themselves influenced in some way by consideration of class when making friends of the same sex'.[134]

These percentages look impressively large. The book that followed made it clear that they were a summation of two response categories: in fact only 18 per cent. at Edinburgh, 10 per cent. at Newcastle, and a mere 5 per cent. at Durham thought they were influenced by such considerations; but 37 per cent. at Edinburgh, 31 per cent. at Newcastle, and 29 per cent. at Durham thought they were 'possibly unconsciously influenced'. On the basis of these percentages Abbott felt able to say: 'Social class may "not matter" in certain situations but it nevertheless exists as meaningful social category with which students identify.'[135]

When I reviewed Abbott's book, I referred to the quite contrary findings of the research I was directing, which was based not on whether students thought they might possibly be unconsciously influenced by class, but on who their friends actually were.[136] What determined friendships was not social class but subject department:

There was no statistically significant social-class bias in friendship groups:

C

the over-riding influence was membership of academic departments. This influence was especially strong among students living at home and in digs. Large halls of residence did little to moderate departmental influence, but small halls of residence forced students into relationships with others from different academic areas. Propinquity promoted by academic departments and small halls was decisive.[137]

Abbott's book does not 'prove' or even make a plausible case that social class is a major influence on students' friendships. As I went on to point out:

There is no demonstration anywhere in the book that friendships among students of the same social class occur more frequently than could be expected by chance. A very few students think they were influenced by 'class'; rather more think they may have been influenced 'unconsciously'; none of them may have been able to recognize social class when they saw it. The danger is that this substantial volume will be widely cited as evidence that our universities not only reflect but exacerbate the social divisions and distinctions that exist outside them.

Kelsall's is the most influential English study of the relationship between social class and students' career ambitions and the jobs they actually get. A postal survey was carried out in 1966 of graduates who entered their universities nine years before and took their degrees in 1960. Subjects were asked to recollect what their career intentions were nine years and six years earlier. Of those who replied, 50 per cent. of the women thought they had no particular career in mind nine years earlier and 20 per cent. thought they still had none after graduating; 40 per cent. of the men thought they had no particular career in mind nine years earlier and 13 per cent. still had none after graduating.[138] But on the basis of these recollections nine years and six years after the event, Kelsall feels able to offer a highly confident non-melting-pot version of English universities.

One of Kelsall's key points is that graduates from working-class homes went disproportionately into school teaching and to a relatively minor extent into more prestigious professions like law, or management and the administrative Civil Service. This is true, although the picture is not quite as stark as Kelsall paints it. The problem is not so much what they did as what they intended. Kelsall has no warrant for erecting an emphatic class-culture view of students' motivations, values, and aspirations on the basis of these long-term recollections.

Forty per cent. of the male graduates from the homes of manual and routine non-manual workers (Kelsall's working class) went into education; 30 per cent. of the graduates from the homes of professional, managerial, and 'intermediate' workers did so. This is a large, but hardly a dramatic difference.[139] Kelsall's own data show that these eventualities do not reflect intentions: only 28 per cent. of the working-class students had thought of entering teaching, although 40 per cent. did so; 10 per cent. of the middle-class students had thought of entering teaching but 30 per cent. did so.[140] (These figures mean that 66 per cent. of those male graduates who entered teaching were from working-class homes.[141] This is still a marked 'under representation' of the working class—83 per cent. of the population on Kelsall's definition—in the graduate entry into teaching.)

On the basis of this retrospective study of intentions Kelsall presents a report which, like Abbott's, is shrill in its strident insistence on the influence of 'class' in English universities. Working-class students had depressed aspirations which the university experience did nothing to raise: '... the universities failed generally to provide a "melting pot" environment in which students' career horizons could be significantly widened.'[142] Kelsall proceeds boldly to an explanation of students' actions and intentions in terms of class culture: 'They were (aside from their qualifications) not part of a common culture, but had come up to university with attitudes profoundly influenced by their family backgrounds and these were in many cases reinforced and certainly not attenuated by the process of higher education itself.'[143] There is no warrant in Kelsall's data for this statement.

My own research in the nineteen-sixties into the aspirations not only of university students but of grammar school pupils showed no social-class influence after the age of fifteen. Educational selection eliminated social class (at least for those who had been selected). By contrast with America, where a great deal of research had shown the powerful impact of class on the levels of aspirations of high school pupils,[144] I found none and concluded as follows:

> At least for children who enter English grammar schools and remain until the fifth or sixth forms, the influence of social origins appears to be eliminated in shaping occupational and social aspirations. The school is the decisive frame of reference rather than the family or peer group. In this sense at least the English grammar school can claim to be 'democratic'; the American high school, by contrast, fails to reduce the force of the social-class system in determining the life chances of the young.[145]

At the university level I found little influence of class when I investigated students actually on-course. What mattered was the field of study. Thus students of mechanical engineering with very weak academic careers behind them and lower working-class homes had very positive self-concepts and very high ambitions; middle-class students of modern languages with outstanding academic records had serious doubts about themselves and their future careers.[146] Working-class students of science and engineering seemed to have been progressively raising rather than lowering their sights; class origins had not prevented a very considerable escalation of ambition.[147] Indeed, 'class' was irrelevant.

But it is not irrelevant to the jobs graduates actually get, and still less to career jumps in later life. In this respect Kelsall is quite correct: graduates do not 'have equal opportunities in the world of work, even if they experienced an identical form of education and had performed equally well or badly'. It is Kelsall's 'soft' explanation, in terms of values and class 'culture', that is false; the true explanation is 'hard', in terms of actual opportunities and the resources to take advantage of them. Education in England is a relatively insulated, class-free zone—a no-go area with regard to social class. It is afterwards that class bites. The bite is known technically as 'counter-mobility' or 'the lagged effect'.

Quite often upper-class people inherit wealth, property, or perhaps a business or professional practice some years after they have begun their careers, perhaps in middle life, and so gain a substantial lift; but this is not the only, or even the principal, explanation of the 'lagged effects' of social class. Counter-mobility occurs quite often at more modest levels, when sons of non-manual workers begin in manual jobs but later climb back to the status of their fathers.[148] Educational qualifications have a stronger effect on the first job than on subsequent jobs, and the class of origin grows in importance throughout life. Carlsson has illustrated this delayed effect of class in Sweden,[149] and we now have quite good international, comparative data. But precisely how it works is still not very well understood. There are indications that, somewhat paradoxically, lagged effects are most pronounced in societies where qualifications rather than experience matters in career advancement—perhaps because unprofitable experiences can be more easily jettisoned and fresh starts made (with a little help from one's friends).[150]

Even among the quite socially (and intellectually) homogeneous boys at Winchester College the 'lagged effects' of social class on careers in later life are not only pronounced but increasing. It has become more rather than less important to have titled or propertied parents. In the nineteenth century this did not seem to influence whether or not a Wykehamist moved to the foremost rank in his career; it has mattered increasingly since. In the light of his exhaustive and painstaking analysis, Bishop says of this change:

> It shows that, for all Britain's march towards political democracy, the career success achieved by the Wykehamist status group has become increasingly hereditary and increasingly won by Wykehamists of the most upper class families. One might have expected social class to have become chiefly a matter of occupation; it is striking, therefore, to find titles and property playing an increasing part in career success.[151]

If we are to achieve a richer measure of social justice in Britain, we must (apart from abolishing the Public Schools) turn our attention to where class actually bites, rather than remaining obsessed with areas where it does not. This means guiding working-class children more firmly away from non-professional degree courses (general arts degrees in colleges of higher education should be reserved for the upper class). They should be especially deterred from going to colleges of art. But above all we must build massive support systems and subsidies into career making in the seven or eight years after they have taken their degrees. They, too, must be able to take chances, make fresh starts, and survive the early 'starving period' that worthwhile careers still commonly entail.

NOTES

1. Herbert Marcuse, *One-Dimensional Man*, Sphere Books, London, 1968, p. 12.

Categories like 'class' and 'private' had lost their oppositional and critical connotation.

2. Ralf Dahrendorf, *Class and Class Conflict in Industrial Society*, Routledge and Kegan Paul, London, 1959:

> One might question whether this new conflict (between propertyless managers and workers), in which labor is no longer opposed to a homogenous capitalist class, can still be described as a class conflict at all. In any case it is different from the division of the whole society into two great and homogeneous hostile camps with which Marx was concerned (pp. 47–48).

3. Herbert Gintis, 'Toward a political economy of education: a radical critique of Ivan Illich's *Deschooling Society*', *Harvard Educational Review*, **42** (1972).
4. S. Hall and T. Jefferson (Eds.), *Resistance Through Rituals*, Hutchinson, London, 1976: 'The various interpretations of post-war change, enshrined in the holy trinity of affluence, consensus and embourgeoisement, rested on a singular social myth—that the working class was disappearing' (p. 25).
5. J. H. Goldthorpe *et al.*, *The Affluent Worker: Industrial Attitudes and Behaviour*, Cambridge University Press, 1968.
6. M. Brake, 'The skinheads: an English working-class subculture', *Youth and Society*, **6** (1974). The Skinheads were notable for supporting the 'work ethic', for queer-bashing, Paki-bashing, and bashing 'layabouts'.
7. S. Hall and T. Jefferson (Eds.), *Resistance Through Rituals*, Hutchinson, 1976, pp. 9–79.
8. These calculations are based on data in D. V. Glass (Ed.). *Social Mobility in Britain*, Routledge and Kegan Paul, London, 1954, Table 1, pp. 294–295. Out of 274 sons of fathers in the first two status categories (Professional and High Administrative, Managerial and Executive), 124 (46 per cent.) had remained at the same status level and 150 (54 per cent.) had gone down. Out of the 160 sons who went to grammar schools, 64 (40 per cent.) went down. Out of 2,306 who had fathers who were unskilled, semi-skilled, or skilled manual workers or routine non-manual workers, 768 (33 per cent.) went up.

   The school system in America similarly failed in the first half of this century to maintain a majority of sons from the higher social classes at their fathers' social level. Referring to 1952 survey data, Lipset and Bendix observe that '... the majority of the sons of professionals, semiprofessionals, proprietors, managers, and officials—the most privileged occupations—are not able to maintain the rank of their fathers, and about one-third of them are actually in manual employment.' See Seymour Martin Lipset and Reinhard Bendix, *Social Mobility in Industrial Society*, University of California Press, Berkeley and Los Angeles, 1964, p. 90.
9. A. H. Halsey, 'Towards meritocracy? The case of Britain', in Jerome Karabel and A. H. Halsey (Eds.), *Power and Ideology in Education*, Oxford University Press, New York, 1977. Halsey is properly very cautious in comparing the LSE mobility study of 1949 and the Nuffield study of 1972, and points out that a good deal of family influence is via education; nevertheless, he concludes that: 'The direct effect of paternal status on respondent's first job is low and decreasing ...' (p. 182).
10. A. Little and J. Westergaard, 'The trend of class differentials in educational opportunity in England and Wales', *British Journal of Sociology*, **15** (1964): 'As between the generations born in the 1920's and the late 1930's, the chances of entering a grammar school or the equivalent rose by about two-fifths for children of the lowest social group, by about a fourth for the middle group, and by only about one fifth for those of the upper group', i.e. a 40 per cent. improvement for the lower working class, a 25 per cent. improvement for the upper working class and lower middle class, and a 20 per cent. improvement for the upper middle class.
11. J. C. Goyder, 'A note on the declining relationship between subjective and objective

64

class measures', *British Journal of Sociology*, **26** (1975).

12. Audrey Weinberg and Frank Lyons, 'Class theory and practice', *British Journal of Sociology*, **23** (1972).

13. Joseph Schumpeter, 'The problem of classes', in Richard Bendix and S. M. Lipset (Eds.), *Class, Status and Power*, Routledge and Kegan Paul, London, 1967.

14. W. G. Runciman, *Relative Deprivation and Social Justice*, Routledge and Kegan Paul, London, 1966, p. 45.

15. *Ibid.*, p. 44.

16. K. I. Macdonald, 'The Hall-Jones scale: a note on the interpretation of the main prestige coding', in J. M. Ridge (Ed.), *Mobility in Britain Reconsidered*, Clarendon Press, Oxford, 1974.

17. D. Swift, 'Social class and educational adaptation', in H. Silver (Ed.), *Equal Educational Opportunity*, Methuen, London, 1973.

18. D. Silverman, 'Clerical ideologies: a research note', *British Journal of Sociology*, **19** (1968).

19. David Lockwood, *The Blackcoated Worker*, Allen and Unwin, London, 1958: 'The twentieth century has witnessed the progressive social devaluation of clerical work. Yet it would be a mistake to assume that because the clerk is no longer clearly part of the middle classes he is now indistinguishable from the working class' (p. 125).

20. Anthony Giddens, *The Class Structure of Advanced Societies*, Hutchinson, London, 1973, pp. 180, 192–193.

21. Ralf Dahrendorf, *Class and Class Conflict in Industrial Society*, Routledge and Kegan Paul, 195, pp. 55–56.

22. Nicos Poulantzas, *Classes in Contemporary Capitalism*, New Left Books, 1975. Whereas Dahrendorf talks of 'sectors' of the middle class moving different ways, Poulantzas talks of 'fractions'. Some 'fractions' of the middle class have 'an objectively proletarian polarization' (p. 316), but even Poulantzas hesitates to put them unequivocally in the working class.

23. Gavin Mackenzie, 'The "affluent worker" study: an evaluation and critique', in Frank Parkin (Ed.), *The Social Analysis of Class Structure*, Tavistock, 1974. Mackenzie also stops short of assigning clerks to the working class (pp. 250–251).

24. E. P. Thompson, *The Making of the English Working Class*, Penguin Books, Harmondsworth, 1968, p. 22. Thompson does not seem to find these superior economic conditions of the founder members problematical, but see Perkin's observations on the London Corresponding Society in which Thompson locates the source of the working class movement (H. Perkin, *The Origins of Modern English Society 1780–1880*, Routledge and Kegan Paul, London, 1969):

> The London Corresponding Society of 1792—proletarian according to the theory but in fact composed of 'tradesmen, mechanics, and shopkeepers' who in old society terms belonged to the middle ranks rather than the lower orders, or at least cut across both—was connected with Major Cartwright and the Society for Constitutional Reform (p. 194).

25. E. J. Hobsbawm, *Labouring Men*, Weidenfeld and Nicolson, London, 1964, Chap. 15: 'The labour aristocracy in nineteenth-century Britain'.

26. H. Perkin, *The Origins of Modern English Society 1780–1880*, Routledge and Kegan Paul, 1969, p. 256.

27. Gosta Carlsson, *Social Mobility and Class Structure*, C. W. K. Gleerup, Lund, Sweden, 1958, p. 188. The problem is the familiar one of the relative positions of skilled manual and routine non-manual workers.

28. C. Wright Mills, *White Collar*, Oxford University Press, New York, 1951. Mills saw the new middle class as a pyramid rather than a horizontal layer, but: 'The great bulk of the new middle class are of the lower middle-income brackets ...' (p. 64).

29. Alain Touraine, *The Post-Industrial Society*, Wildwood House, 1974. 'We are not thinking of the new "proletariat", the employees whose tasks are as repetitive, monotonous, and restrictive as those of assembly-line workers. Rather, we are thinking of relatively advanced groups: technical workers, designers, high ranking office workers, and technical assistants ...' (p. 58).

30. Herbert Gintis, 'The new working class and revolutionary youth', *Continuum*, Spring/Summer **1970**. See also Samuel Bowles and Herbert Gintis, *Schooling in Capitalist America*, Routledge and Kegan Paul, London, 1976, p. 204. White-collar labour has been integrated into the dominant wage–labour system through the fragmentation and compartmentalization of white-collar work.

31. Frank Parkin, *Middle-Class Radicalism*, Manchester University Press, 1968. 'The educated middle class is that stratum whose social position and life chances rest primarily upon its intellectual attainments and professional qualifications, and not upon the ownership of property or inherited wealth' (p. 179).

32. John Westergaard and Henrietta Resler, *Class in Capitalist Society*, Penguin Books, Harmondsworth 1976, p. 292.

33. Stanislav Andreski, *Prospects of a Revolution in the USA*, Tom Stacey, 1973, p. 46.

34. John Porter, *The Vertical Mosaic*, University of Toronto Press, 1965, p. 52.

35. Richard Bland, 'The operational definition of downward mobility', *British Journal of Sociology*, **29** (1978).

36. There are some important chapters on education in D. V. Glass (Ed.), *Social Mobility in Britain*, Routledge and Kegan Paul, 1954. The best-known study is probably J. E. Floud, A. H. Halsey, and F. M. Martin, *Social Class and Educational Opportunity*, Heinemann, London, 1956.

37. See H. T. Himmelweit, 'Social status and secondary education since the 1944 Act: some data for London', in D. V. Glass (Ed.), *Social Mobility in Britain*, Routledge and Kegan Paul, 1954.

38. A recent study of 7,000 men in England by George Psacharopoulos of the London School of Economics gives a correlation between a father's occupational status and his son's schooling (years of schooling) as 0.293. The correlation of the father's occupational status and O-level examination success is somewhat lower (0.223). See George Psacharopoulos, 'Family background, education and achievement', *British Journal of Sociology*, **28** (1977). The Oxford Nuffield College Study of 1972 yields a higher correlation between a father's occupation and the son's education: 0.358. See A. H. Halsey, 'Towards a meritocracy? The case of Britain', in J. Karabel and A. H. Halsey (Ed.), *Power and Ideology in Education*, Oxford University Press, New York, 1977. In America the correlation for non-farm White Americans is of roughly the same order: Jencks calculates 0.382. See Christopher Jencks, *Inequality*, Penguin Books, Harmondsworth, 1975, p. 322. In this case educational attainment means: 'The highest grade of school or college completed by the respondent. No correction is made for the quality of schooling or for how much the respondent learned in school' (p. 320).

39. *Early Leaving: A Report of the Central Advisory Council for Education (England)*, HMSO, London,9 1954, p. 4, para 13 and App. IV, 'Occupational Grouping'.

40. These calculations are based on data in *Early Leaving, ibid.*, Table K, p. 18.

41. C. Lacey, *Hightown Grammar*, Manchester University Press, 1970, pp. 56–57.

42. J. W. B. Douglas, *The Home and the School*, MacGibbon and Kee, 1964, pp. 42–45.

43. The average test scores were: upper middle class 56.99; lower middle class 53.88; upper working class 50.05; lower working class 47.55. See *ibid.*, p. 46.

44. Ronald King, *Values and Involvement in a Grammar School*, Routledge and Kegan Paul, London 1969, Tables 1 and 2, pp. 20–21.

45. *Ibid.*, p. 54.

46. *Ibid.*, pp. 155–156. The hypothesis that King had set out to test was: 'The holding of school-approved values will be associated more with pupils from middle-class families than pupils from working-class families' (p. 27).

47. Allison Davis, *Social Class Influences Upon Learning*, Harvard University Press, 1949, p. 90. 'Class' is seen as an environment which provides an 'adaptive training' (p. 88).
48. Marjorie E. Ainsworth and Eric J. Batten, *The Effects of Environmental Factors on Secondary Educational Attainment in Manchester: A Plowden Follow-up*, Macmillan, London, 1974, p. 81.
49. *Children and Their Primary Schools · A Report of the Central Advisory Council for Education (England)*, Vol. I, HMSO, London, 1967, p. 35.
50. Stephen Wiseman, *Education and Environment*, Manchester University Press, 1964, p. 48. Wiseman's curiously old-fashioned study—it is a repeat of Burt's ecological studies of 'backwardness' in the nineteen-thirties—not only plays down social class but rejects it as having any serious meaning or explanatory value. His study of the social environment has no data on the father's occupation. But Warburton's Salford survey is included (Chapter 6) and does include measures of socioeconomic status (like having a front garden) which do correlate with scholastic attainment.
51. D. M. Toomey, 'Home-centred working class parents' attitudes towards their sons' education and careers', *Sociology*, 3 (1969).
52. This picture owes much to an important book published in the late nineteen-sixties, David H. Hargreaves, *Social Relations in a Secondary School*, Routledge and Kegan Paul, London, 1967. Hargreaves is aware of the limitations of his data and interpretation:

> Our distinction between the academic and the delinquescent subcultures is a considerable over-simplification of the facts. Although the extremes can be clearly distinguished, there remains a large proportion of boys who, whilst tending towards one of the poles, cannot easily be contained in either. ... It may be that our analysis of the subcultural differentiation raises more problems than it solves (pp. 180–181).

53. See David Reynolds, 'When pupils and teachers refuse a truce: the secondary school and the creation of delinquency', in G. Mungham and G. Pearson (Eds.), *Working Class Youth Culture*, Routledge and Kegan Paul, London, 1976; 'The delinquent school', in M. Hammersley and P. Woods (Eds.), *The Process of Schooling*, Routledge and Kegan Paul, London, 1976; and 'Schools do make a difference', *New Society*, 29 July 1976.
54. W. G. Quine, 'Polarized cultures in comprehensive schools', *Research in Education*, **1974,** No. 12.
55. Christopher Jencks, *Inequality*, Penguin Books, Harmondsworth, 1975, p. 140.
56. Eva Bene, 'Some differences between middle-class and working-class grammar school boys in their attitudes towards education', *British Journal of Sociology*, **10** (1959).
57. Ralph H. Turner, *The Social Context of Ambition*, Chandler, San Francisco, 1964, pp. 9, 107.
58. *Ibid.*, p. 208.
59. F. Musgrove, 'Role-conflict in adolescence', *British Journal of Educational Psychology*,, **34** (1964).
60. J. Floud, 'The educational experience of the adult population of England and Wales as at July 1949', in D. V. Glass (Ed.), *Social Mobility in Britain*, Routledge and Kegan Paul, 1954, p. 108.
61. Stephen Wiseman, *Education and Environment*, Manchester University Press, 1964. Wiseman's strictures relate not only to unsatisfactory samples and inadequate control groups (p. 48) but to the book's failure to carry conviction with people who knew schools and teachers well in their professional capacity (p. 169).
62. Brian Jackson and Dennis Marsden, *Education and the Working Class*, Routledge and Kegan Paul, London, 1962, p. 114.
63. *Ibid.*, p. 215.
64. *Ibid.*, p. 224.

65. *Ibid.*, p. 241. The real trouble was keeping up with the work or catching up after a setback such as illness.
66. C. Lacey, *Hightown Grammar*, Manchester University Press, 1970, p. 130.
67. Barry Sugarman, 'Involvement in youth culture, academic achievement and conformity in school', *British Journal of Sociology*,**18** (1967).
68. James S. Coleman, *The Adolescent Society*, Free Press, New York, 1961.
69. Bennett M. Berger, 'Adolescence and beyond', *Social Problems*, **10** (1963).
70. C. Lacey, *Hightown Grammar*, Manchester University Press, 1970, pp. 137–142.
71. Ian K. Birkstead, 'School versus pop culture? A case study of adolescent adaptation', *Research in Education*, **1976s** No. 16.
72. C. Lacey, *Hightown Grammar*, Manchester University Press, 1970, pp. 71, 119–122.
73. See Graham Murdock and Robin McCron, 'Youth and class', in G. Mungham and G. Pearson (Eds.), *Working Class Youth Culture*, Routledge and Kegan Paul, London, 1976. Murdock and McCron argue that class must be restored 'to the centre of the sociology of youth' (p. 24).
74. David Reynolds, 'When pupils and teachers refuse a truce', in G. Mungham and G. Pearson (Eds.), *Working Class Youth Culture*, Routledge and Kegan Paul, London, 1976.
75. Ian Birksted, 'School performance viewed from the boys', *Sociological Review*, **24** (1976).
76. P. Bourdieu, *Outline of a Theory of Practice*, Cambridge University Press, 1977, p. 87.
77. P. Bourdieu, 'The school as a conservative force: scholastic and cultural inequalities', in J. Eggleston (Ed.), *Contemporary Research in the Sociology of Education*, Methuen, London, 1974.
78. C. Lacey, *Hightown Grammar*, Manchester University Press, 1970, pp. 148–152, 192–193.
79. B. Bernstein, 'Some sociological determinants of perception: an enquiry into sub-cultural differences', *British Journal of Sociology*, **9** (1958).
80. E. L. Eisenstein, 'The impact of printing on European education', in P. W. Musgrave (Ed.), *Sociology, History and Education*, Methuen, London, 1970.
81. Jack Goody, 'Literacy and the non-literate', *Times Literary Supplement*, 12 May 1972.
82. Tony Ellis, Jackie McWhirter, Dorothy McColgan, and Brian Haddow, *The Teachers' Story*, Writers and Readers Publishing Co-operative, 1976, pp. 46–47.
83. Rachel Sharp and Anthony Green, *Education and Social Control*, Routledge and Kegan Paul, London, 1975, p. 58.
84. Basil Bernstein, 'Education cannot compensate for society', in B. R. Cosin (Ed.), *School and Society*, Routledge and Kegan Paul, London, 1971.
85. Eleanor Leacock, 'Abstract versus concrete speech: a false dichotomy', in J. Beck, C. Jenks, N. Keddie, and M. F. D. Young (Eds.), *Worlds Apart*, Collier-Macmillan, 1976.
86. William Labov, 'The logic of nonstandard English', in Nell Keddie (Ed.), *Tinker, Tailor ... The Myth of Cultural Deprivation*, Penguin Books, Harmondsworth, 1973.
87. Thomas Gladwin, *East is a Big Bird*, Harvard University Press, Cambridge, Mass., 1971, p. 225.
88. Basil Bernstein, 'Some sociological determinants of perception', *British Journal of Sociology*, **9** (1958).
89. Robert W. Witkin, 'Social class influence on the amount and type of positive evaluation of English lessons', *Sociology*, **5** (1971).
90. Allison Davis, *Social Class Influences upon Learning*, Harvard University Press, 1949, p. 91.
91. William Coleman and Annie W. Ward, 'A comparison of Davis–Eells and Kuhlmann–Finch scores of children from high and low socio-economic status', *Journal of Educational Psychology*, **46** (1955).
92. See J. W. B. Douglas, *The Home and the School*, MacGibbon and Kee, 1964, p. 46.
93. See Dorothy Henderson, 'Contextual specificity, discretion and cognitive socialization:

68

with special reference to language', in B. R. Cosin (Ed.), *School and Society*, 2nd ed., Routledge and Kegan Paul, London, 1977.

94. Douglas Barnes, *Language, Learner and the School*, Penguin Books, Harmondsworth, 1969, pp. 48–49.

95. L. A. Jackson, 'The myth of elaborated and restricted code' in B. R. Cosin (Ed.), *School and Society*, 2nd ed., Routledge and Kegan Paul, 1977. This is a powerful and forthright attack which ably exposes the sham of Bernstein's sociolinguistics (and the fraudulent nature of a sociology which can so readily accept it).

96. George C. F. Payne, 'Making a lesson happen: an ethnomethodological analysis', in Peter Woods (Ed.), *The Process of Schooling*, Routledge and Kegan Paul, London, 1976.

97. David H. Hargreaves *et al.*, *Deviance in Classrooms*, Routledge and Kegan Paul, London, 1975, p. 64.

98. A. J. M. Sykes, 'Economic interest and the Hawthorne researches', *Human Relations*, **18** (1965), and Alex Carey, 'The Hawthorne studies: a radical criticism', *American Sociological Review*, **32** (1967).

99. Christopher Jencks, *Inequality*, Penguin Books, Harmondsworth, 1975, p. 139.

100. C. Lacey, *Hightown Grammar*, Manchester University Press, 1970, p. 180.

101. Ray, C. Rist, 'Student social class and teacher expectations: the self-fulfilling prophecy in ghetto education', *Harvard Educational Review*, **40** (1970).

102. R. Rosenthal and L. Jacobson, *Pygmalion in the Classroom*, Holt, Rinehart and Winston, New York, 1968.

103. D. H. Hargreaves, *Social Relations in a Secondary School*, Routledge and Kegan Paul, London, 1967, pp. 104–107.

104. D. H. Hargreaves, *Interpersonal Relations in Education*, Routledge and Kegan Paul, London, 1972, p. 58.

105. *Ibid.*, pp. 63–66.

106. Rachel Sharp and Anthony Green, *Education and Social Control*, Routledge and Kegan Paul, London, 1975, pp. 125–127.

107. F. Musgrove, 'A home for the disabled: marginality and reality', *British Journal of Sociology*, **27** (1976).

108. F. Musgrove, *Margins of the Mind*, Methuen, London, 1977, Chap. 6: 'The world of the blind: a supernormality'.

109. See S. Cohen and L. Taylor, *Psychological Survival*, Penguin Books, Harmondsworth, 1972, p. 148.

110. Ray C. Rist, 'On understanding the process of schooling: the contribution of labeling theory', in J. Karabel and A. H. Halsey (Ed.), *Power and Ideology in Education*, Oxford University Press, New York, 1977.

111. See James Murphy, 'Teacher expectations and working-class under-achievement', *British Journal of Sociology*, **25** (1974).

112. Basil Bernstein, *Class, Codes and Control. (Vol. 3) Towards a Theory of Educational Transmissions*, Routledge and Kegan Paul, London 1977, p. 138.

113. *Ibid.*, p. 140.

114. Rachel Sharp and Anthony Green, *Education and Social Control*, Routledge and Kegan Paul, 1975, pp. 208–209.

115. P. E. Woods, *Secondary School Realities*, Ph.D. thesis, Open University, 1978, p. 132. See also Peter Woods, *The Divided School*, Routledge and Kegan Paul, London, 1979.

116. See J. M. and R. E. Pahl, *Managers and Their Wives*, Penguin Books, Harmondsworth, 1972.

117. F. Musgrove, 'Late-entrants to the Anglican ministry: a move into marginality', *Sociological Review*, **23** (1975).

118. See S. R. Parker, 'Work and non-work in three occupations', *Sociological Review*, **13** (1965).

119. A. Giddens, 'Notes on the concepts of play and leisure', *Sociological Review*, **12** (1964).

120. Tony Ellis, Jackie McWhirter, Dorothy McColgan, and Brian Haddow, *William*

Tyndale: The Teachers' Story, Writers and Readers Publishing Co-operative, 1976, p. 11.

121. *Ibid.*, p. 70.
122. John Gretton and Mark Jackson, *William Tyndale: Collapse of a School—or a System?*, George Allen and Unwin, London, 1976, p. 68.
123. See especially Tony Ellis, Jackie McWhirter, Dorothy McColgan, and Brian Haddow, *William Tyndale: The Teachers' Story*, Writers and Readers Publishing Co-operative, 1976, pp. 2–3.
124. *William Tyndale Junior and Infants Schools Public Inquiry (1976)*, A Report to the Inner London Education Authority by Robin Auld, Q.C.
125. Eric Midwinter, *Priority Education*, Penguin Books, Harmondsworth, 1972, pp. 145–146.
126. Jurgen Zimmer, 'Aspects of a curriculum for working-class children: from the example of a planned model school in the German Federal Republic', *Paedagogica Europaea*, **9** (1974).
127. R. R. Dale, 'Reflections on the influence of social class on student performance at the university', in Paul Halmos (Ed.), *The Sociological Review Monograph No. 7: Sociological Studies in British University Education*, Keele, 1963, p. 136.
128. D. G. Worswick, 'The anatomy of Oxbridge', *Times Educational Supplement*, 3 May 1957; and T. R. W. Evans, 'The physiognomy of Cambridge', *Times Educational Supplement*, 16 October 1959.
129. *Report of the Committee on Higher Education*, HMSO, London 1963, App. I, pp. 80–81.
130. *Ibid.*, App. II (B). Calculations based on A. Little and J. Westergaard, 'The trend in class differentials in educational opportunity' *British Journal of Sociology*, **15** (1964), give (male) university entrants in the late nineteen-fifties as follows: 56 per cent. from Registrar General classes I and II, 38 per cent. from class III and 6 per cent. from IV and V (based on data in Table 5).
131. Calculations are based on John Westergaard and Henrietta Resler, *Class in Capitalist Society*, Penguin Books, Harmondsworth 1976, p. 323. A Report of a study (late nineteen-sixties) in the North and Midlands gives 30 per cent. of students from non-manual homes and 8.5 per cent. from manual workers' homes: this gives approximate social-class parity in actual numbers.
132. Pierre Bourdieu and Jean-Claude Passeron, *Reproduction in Education, Society and Culture*, Sage Publications, London 1977, pp. 221–233.
133. F. Musgrove (Ed.), *Preliminary Studies of a Technological University*, Bradford University 1967, App. I, pp. 196–199.
134. Joan Abbott, 'Students' social class in three northern universities', *British Journal of Sociology*, **16** (1965).
135. Joan Abbott, *Student Life in a Class Society*, Pergamon, Oxford, 1971, p. 269.
136. C. J. Willig, 'Student social relationships: social class and patterns of friendship', in F. Musgrove (Ed.), *Preliminary Studies of a Technological University*, University of Bradford, 1967.
137. F. Musgrove, 'Student Life in a Class Society' (review), *British Journal of Sociology*, **23** (1972).
138. R. K. Kelsall, Anne Poole, and Annette Kuhn, *Six Years After*, Sheffield University, 1970, p. 62.
139. R. K. Kelsall, Anne Poole, and Annette Kuhn, *Graduates: The Sociology of an Elite*, Methuen, London 1972, Table 42, p. 212.
140. *Ibid.*, p. 73.
141. *Ibid.*, Table 46, p. 216.
142. *Ibid.*, p. 111.
143. *Ibid.*, p. 99.
144. For example, E. Youmans, 'Occupational expectations of Twelfth Grade Michigan boys', *Journal of Experimental Education*, **24** (1956).

145. F. Musgrove, *Youth and the Social Order*, Indiana University Press, Bloomington, 1965, pp. 31–32.
146. F. Musgrove, 'Social class and levels of aspiration in a technological university', *Sociological Review*, **15** (1967).
147. F. Musgrove, 'Some aspects of the swing from science', *British Journal of Educational Psychology*, **39** (1969).
148. John H. Goldthorpe and Catriona Llewellyn, 'Class mobility in modern Britain: three theses examined', *Sociology*, **11** (1977).
149. Gosta Carlsson, *Social Mobility and Class Structure*, C. W. K. Gleerup, Lund, Sweden, 1958, p. 137.
150. Jonathan Kelley, 'Wealth and family background in the occupational career: theory and cross-cultural data', *British Journal of Sociology*, **29** (1978).
151. T. J. G. Bishop, *Winchester and the Public School Elite*, Faber, London, 1967, p. 196.

CHAPTER 4

Education and Social Control

'Liberal education' is now widely seen as a contradiction in terms. Schools do not liberate; at best they domesticate.[1] An extensive neo-Marxist literature on schooling and social control advances two simple and contradictory propositions: the first is that schooling teaches subordinate classes servility; the second is that it does not. Defiance brings retribution and thus the subordinate classes 'ensure the continuity of their own underprivilege'.[2] Both propositions find apparent support in 'correspondences' between conditions in schools and servility or defiance at the site of capitalist production. In the first case social control is achieved because the school succeeds; the second because it fails.

All societies need their members to behave reasonably consistently, predictably, and honestly. This is what the social order is. In relatively small-scale, homogeneous societies families ensure that the young will have these characteristics by the time they assume adult rights and responsibilities, but in less close-knit communities like modern industrial countries families themselves may vary considerably. In these circumstances schools come to the fore: they help to cut down variations in behaviour that is important to the society and the economy. Young people learn in schools to have some respect for adults who are not kinsmen, to carry out work not of their own choosing, to be punctual and truthful, and to work for longer-term rewards. This is not a recipe for tyranny; it is a simple blueprint for an orderly society and the satisfaction of its members.

Everett Reimer says that: 'The main thing children learn in schools is how to lie.' He equates domestication with castration: 'School domesticates—socially emasculates—both boys and girls by a process much more pervasive than mere selection by sex.' Actual physical castration is unnecessary: the job is done much more effectively 'at the libidinal level'.[3] It is in such highly theatrical terms that the school was often portrayed in the nineteen-seventies not as a place of personal opportunity and growth but of enslavement.

It seems that it was middle-class children in particular who, in mid-twentieth-century America, were taught by their schools to lie, to be self-effacing, and to conform. They were apparently being taught these essential organizational skills even in nursery schools. But this was not for capitalism; it was for bureaucracy. In her study of 'the organization child' in the mid-nineteen-sixties Kanter portrayed nursery school children from professional families in a Mid-western American town. Competition was discouraged; 'play was highly routinized'; 'only pleasant beliefs about the world and about themselves were encouraged ... the child was never asked to face unpleasant facts'; the organization, its 'needs' and procedures, had more reality than any individual. Kanter advances a very simple correspondence theory: 'There is relationship between the structure of education and the major institutional forms of society.'[4] But the upper-class education that she describes seems to be a singularly inauspicious start for any would-be capitalist.

This illustrates the difficulty with the now widely accepted view that 'mass schooling' in modern industrial societies arose as an apparatus to control the working class; comparative data on the middle and upper classes are rarely or never used. When attention is focused on the education of the labouring poor, 'social control' aspects appear prominent; but when attention is turned to the upper classes at the same time, the repression which they experienced seems outrageous. In the new mass elementary schools very few pupils were actually killed. What needs explanation is not the control of an uprooted peasant population in raw industrial towns; it is the quite savage repression that the upper classes imposed upon themselves. It was not only the systems and procedures to which they subjected themselves; even more remarkable are the self-inflicted ideological wounds. England's ruling class was the principal victim of its own ideology.

It was the upper classes of early Victorian England that were in particular need of constraint: to curb their idleness, brutality, drunkenness, gambling, and vice. Upper-class codes of honour—tied to families and upheld to defend the family name—had been an important form of social control; they were diluted (and duelling declined) as families increasingly 'married out' into new wealth. But only when upper-class proconsuls were reasonably trustworthy and preferably sober could the New Empire survive. The cleaning up of England's upper class in the reformed Public Schools was one of the most ruthless sanitary operations of Victorian England.

This chapter will examine (with special reference to England) the role of mass schooling as a form of 'social control' during the rise of modern industrial-urban societies. But schooling must be kept in its proper perspective; it was only one among many 'agencies of social control'. The Royal Society for the Prevention of Cruelty to Animals, no less than the Royal Society for the Prevention of Cruelty to Children, has significance in this context; factories; the temperance movement; the Lord's Day Observance Society; the shift from individualistic sports to competitive games; boys' clubs; the Boy Scouts and fox-hunting: all played their part. None is a straightforward imposition by the upper classes on the lower classes (workers wanted the Lord's Day observed—it removed at least one day in seven from the sphere of employers; many workers wanted a teetotal working class—radicals knew they could be more effectively subversive when cold sober). But perhaps one of the most potent means of social control was the rise of the child-centred ideology which required fathers to 'sacrifice' themselves for their children and give them their 'chance in life'. Today a father with two children is effectively disciplined for thirty years. The direct consequences of mass schooling are, in comparison, probably quite trivial.

CORRESPONDENCES BETWEEN SCHOOLING AND INDUSTRY

Inter-war Marxist historians attacked capitalists for withholding education from the workers; today's neo-Marxists attack them for providing it. It is through the provision of mass schooling that great inequalities have been perpetuated, capitalist power sustained, and individuals enabled 'to move smoothly into an alienated and class-stratified society'.[5] Popular or mass schooling has operated on a principle of 'correspondence': the authority relations of capitalist production have been replicated and reinforced in the schools. This may not always be apparent: the correspondences are embedded in 'the hidden curriculum'.

These ideas were most vigorously propagated in the nineteen-seventies by two American economists, Herbert Gintis and Samuel Bowles. They published a large number of specialized papers on this theme in economic and educational research journals. Their work was an important contribution to the resurgence of Marxist interpretations of 'schooling'. The new wave of Marxist thinking on education broke in the mid-nineteen-seventies. In 1976 Bowles and Gintis published the book which saw the culmination of their work: *Schooling in Capitalist America*. This book was also published in England in 1976 and reprinted within the year.[6] This was the year in which educational theory was stripped of its liberal illusions and finally lost its innocence.

Bowles and Gintis dethroned the consumer and reinstated the producer (they were wise to dethrone the very self-conscious parent-consumers involved in highly rational 'micro-decision making' who had recently been invented by economists). It was not demand (by parents) but supply (by providing agencies) that explained the nature of mass schooling. In other words, schooling was imposed. It could not be understood, except at a very superficial level, in currently fashionable terms of personal investment in human capital.[7] That is to say, it did not develop because individuals thought that by going to school they would get some economic benefit out of it.

The basic point that Bowles and Gintis are making is quite simply this: mass schooling has arisen since the mid-nineteenth century not to provide skills and trained intelligence for industrial employment but to ensure a suitably docile labour force. It can do this more effectively because it also 'legitimates' this process and the system: 'Education reproduces inequality by justifying privilege and attributing poverty to personal failure.'[8] The argument necessarily involves an historical interpretation of the role of popular or mass schooling over the past century. The argument also rests on a simple theory of correspondences ('a straightforward correspondence principle'). If factories have 'mass' characteristics and if schools developed 'mass' characteristics, then the latter arose to fit the former. Evidence of 'congruence' is usually enough to claim a real connexion. All explanation in the natural and social sciences is a matter of establishing connexions. Usually they are established by showing 'concomitant variation'. This means making comparisons. Bowles and Gintis make no attempt to show concomitant variation; and they make no comparisons.

What they say about correspondences is this: the educational system is essentially about shaping the consciousness of future workers to fit the system, and 'the educational system's ability to reproduce the consciousness of workers lies in a straight forward correspondence principle. For the past century at least, schooling has contributed to the reproduction of the social relations of production largely through the correspondence between school and class structure.' School and industrial employment, as well as school and class, have the same basic 'structure' and so young workers leave their schools with the correct posture:

> The educational system helps integrate youth into the economic system, we believe, through a structural correspondence between its social relations and those of production. The structure of social relations in education not only inures the student to the discipline of the workplace, but develops the type of demeanor, modes of self-presentation, self-image, and social class identifications which are crucial ingredients of job adequacy.[9]

The school and the workplace are alike, say Bowles and Gintis, in three crucial respects: they are hierarchical in their organization (although schools do not need to be to promote effective learning); they exact 'alienated' labour for extrinsic rewards; and the work in which pupils and workmen alike are engaged is 'fragmented'. These attributes of schools and their activities constitute the hidden curriculum, and 'the hidden curriculum in mass education reproduces the social relations of production'.[10]

There are mechanisms which ensure congruence and correspondence and correct possibly inherent tendencies towards non-alignment and mismatch: these mechanisms are subsumed under the heading of 'pluralistic accommodation'. Bowles and Gintis point to the way in which educational reforms in America have followed periods of labour unrest and in essence appear to be arguing that mass education was a means of avoiding class war under the conditions of nineteenth-century entrepreneurial capitalism. They are almost in danger of reinstating the consumer in a free-market process of accommodation, but they claim that these processes have always been led by the changing structure of economic production.[11]

This thesis is basically wrong. It greatly overstates the role of economic influences in the development of education. The argument is riddled with difficulties of logic and evidence. It is falsified cartographically. If we map types of educational provision and industrial development at different times over the past two centuries, we find, when we superimpose one map on the other, a quite astonishing lack of correspondence. Mass education developed as a rural phenomenon. Tyack has underlined the fact that in late nineteenth-century America there was '... widespread provision of schooling and numerous compulsory-schooling laws in communities and states in which the farm family was the predominant mode of production'.[12] In England in the middle of the nineteenth century the least schooled places were Oldham and Rochdale; the most schooled regions were the vast rural expanses of Northumberland, Cumberland, Westmorland, and the East and North Ridings of Yorkshire.

Even Lawrence Stone was perplexed. His impressive study of literacy and education between the seventeenth and twentieth centuries does not suggest the total irrelevance of education to economic growth; there were rising educational levels in eighteenth century England as a prelude to the Industrial Revolution (but evidence of deterioration under its initial impact). What puzzled Stone was the geographical distribution of literacy by the eighteen-forties. An inversion had occurred since the seventeenth century: formerly high literacy rates were found in the south of England; by 1840 they were in the far rural north. Stone referred to this distribution as 'the oddest feature of the educational scene in the early Victorian period'. He had no tidy explanation: 'This strange distribution of literacy does not appear to correlate with any of the obvious factors.'[13]

In fact he was wrong. There is a high correlation between the Education Census of 1851 and the Religious Census of the same year: where church attendance was high, so was school attendance. No understanding of mass education (or any other) in Victorian England is possible without a firm grasp of religious influences. And they lie behind the phenomenon to which Stone drew attention: the superior literacy rates of 'the countryside and small towns'.

The capitalists who owned the new textile factories of early Victorian Lancashire prospered without benefit of a mass-schooled population. Michael Sanderson's close study of education and the economy at the site of the Industrial Revolution shows how in 1830 literacy rates in such traditional, pre-industrial occupations as joiner, carpenter, and wright were very high (82 per cent.); in the new factory occupations such as weaver, carder, and rover they were very low (35 per cent.). In the new factories children could start work at the age of eight or nine; in the old crafts eleven or twelve was usual. Schooling suffered, in spite of factory schools and part-time instruction. An essentially mercantile economy, which still survived in the town of Lancaster, called for a more educated population, but '... the whole of that great manufacturing quadrilateral area, Manchester–Bolton–Rochdale–Oldham, enjoyed its booming growth with a labour force forty per cent. of which was literate'. Sanderson shows how weak were the links between early industrial capitalism and mass elementary education, and characterizes industrial England before 1840 as '... a sub-literate society ... where the motive behind education was religion and not the economy'.[14]

Thomas W. Laqueur has taken him seriously to task. He maintains that the decline in literacy was not caused but reversed by the Industrial Revolution. His argument is based on the chronology of factory development. Sanderson has made a spirited and cogent rejoinder.[15] But whether caused or reversed by industrialization, Laqueur does not dispute the very low literacy rates in the new industrial areas at the mid-century: 'In 1851 the percentage of children in day school in industrial Lancashire was well below the national average.' Oldham, with male literacy 21 per cent. below the national average in 1841, was notorious for its educational backwardness.

To point to the rural–urban distinction in literacy rates in itself explains nothing, although it automatically questions the very close connexion that Marxists (and others) have alleged between urban-industrial capitalism and mass elementary schooling. The link between high levels of schooling and rural life is in any event far from perfect: Stone pointed to the puzzlingly low literacy rates in the rural regions to the north and east of London in Bedfordshire, Essex, and Suffolk. It was (some) rural areas and relatively small, ancient, unchanged (especially cathedral) towns which showed high literacy rates. Rural areas were perhaps outstanding for an educated populace if the ecclesiastical organization was ancient and strong. At Census Day in 1851, 52 per cent. of the nation's children between the ages of five and fourteen were at school: among the towns with between 65 and 75 per cent. were Chichester, Dorchester, Exeter, Lincoln, Salisbury, Truro, Winchester, and York (Gloucester, Bath, and Canterbury were not far behind, with more than 60 per cent.); among the towns with 36 per cent. or less were Birmingham, Blackburn, Bolton, Bradford, Coventry, Manchester, Stockport, and Oldham.[16] Ancient market towns and cathedral cities relatively untouched by industrial capitalism did far more than the new factory towns to subject their children to the rigours of mass elementary schooling.

For some American economists industrialization had such a potent influence on the development of elementary education that legislation to make schooling compulsory was almost superfluous; it merely signalled, ratified, and applauded what was in any event taking place. The states which passed laws for compulsion in the eighteen-seventies were those which had already achieved high levels of investment in the public education.[17]

This picture does not fit England. There the background to compulsion was the persistent and indeed deepening failure of the schools to bring in lower-working-class children (the 'sunken classes') and an actual decline in juvenile employment in the great industrial cities. The Manchester Statistical Society monitored these changes, providing survey evidence that between 1834 and 1861 the number of day scholars in the city (per 10,000 inhabitants) fell significantly.[18] Another survey of the eighteen-sixties showed that 40 per cent. of children between the ages of three and twelve were at school: only a very small percentage (5 or 6 per cent.) were at work; the majority were simply 'idling in the streets and wynds; tumbling about in the gutters ... cared for by no man'.[19] The problem was not that industry wanted them but that it did not. Public policy as expressed by the first permanent Secretary of Education, Sir James Kay-Shuttleworth, had always kept the essentially nurturant aspects of schooling to the fore; schools were increasingly necessary to provide the moral and physical care that parents should provide but did not.[20] Compulsory mass schooling, when it came, was not to provide a disciplined work force; it was a gigantic device for cleaning the streets.

MASS SCHOOLING AS IDEOLOGICAL ASSAULT

Marxist historians and sociologists today interpret mass schooling (including the early Sunday schools) as an ideological assault on the working class: a massive act of cultural aggression by the capitalist bourgeoisie. Popular education in the nineteenth century was an instrument to prevent the reproduction of traditional working-class culture which was at best inconvenient and at worst hostile and threatening to the new industrial order. For the ideologically vulnerable working class, school was defeat.[21] It was not simply an agency of social control but of 'class-cultural control'.[22] 'Cultural aggression of this kind was organic to this phase (1780–1850) of capitalist development.'[23]

There are two simple but quite crucial problems about this view: the first is why the working classes should have gone along to the schools, before education was made compulsory at the end of the nineteenth century, to submit themselves to this assault; the second is who was actually dominated by the dominant ideology. The working classes seem to have been remarkably resistant (that is why the upper classes were so loud in their complaints, so obsessed with lower-class morals). It was the dominant and not the subordinate classes who were the principal victims of the dominant ideology.

There is a third problem, scarcely less difficult: what was the dominant ideology anyway? There are numerous contenders: individualism, utilitarianism, and Methodism have all been canvassed. Beliefs about the sanctitity of property and the family might also be seen as key elements in the ideology of early industrial capitalism. The 'dominant ideology', like the number of social classes, often seems to be a principal product of the sociological imagination.

Marx and Engels are of little help. Their writing on this theme obscures rather than clarifies. In a famous aphorism (in *The German Ideology*) they state that the ideas of the ruling class are in every epoch the ruling ideas: the ruling material force is the ruling intellectual force. But elsewhere they regard each class as having its own distinctive ideology because of its peculiar economic circumstances.[24]

Recent studies of the pervasiveness of ruling ideologies in the past show only their failure to pervade. The 'Ages of Faith', it seems, were singularly faithless, largely because the lower classes would not go to church. The church was unable to get over its views on monogamy to a mainly polygamous Carolingian Germany. Only members of the elite were efficiently exposed to the Church's teaching, actually believed in monogamy, and sometimes practised it.[25]

Even the 'aristocracy of labour' of Victorian England were not, apparently, class traitors after all. They did not take their beliefs in respectability and self-help from their betters: they had worked them out for themselves in relation to the facts of economic and social life in the communities in which they lived.[26] Their apparent (partial) embourgeoisement was not an imposition of the bourgeoisie.

Other recent studies have shown how subordinate classes in the past have rarely shared the ideology of the dominant class. The apparatus for transmitting and imposing an ideology (books, churches, parsons, teachers, schools) have usually been more effective for the upper classes than for their inferiors. One important recent examination of this subject argues that '... the education available to the elite, particularly in the nineteenth and first half of the twentieth century, is a great deal more intensive and more likely to be formative of a coherent set of beliefs than that provided for the subordinate classes'. Elites have the most efficient means to indoctrinate themselves: 'We conclude that, until fairly recently, the dominant classes were greatly more exposed to the apparatus of ideological distribution than were the subordinate classes and that they still are exposed to at least the same degree.'[27]

E. P. Thompson's famous book, *The Making of the English Working Class*, has been interpreted as a story of middle-class ideological assault; Laqueur engaged in an important programme of research on Sunday schools to test the truth of Thompson's view.[28] The trouble with Thompson is that his account of the working class between

1780 and 1830 can be variously interpreted (and has been by numerous excited reviewers). His images are as vivid as his explanations are confused. It is true that he writes of 'psychological atrocities' and 'religious terrorism' in the early Methodist Sunday schools; but it is not always clear who the terrorists were. In other writing (for instance on time and work discipline in the early factories)[29] he presents a view (rather like Sidney Pollard's[30]) of the factory and Sunday school destroying an ancient working-class culture and imposing an essentially middle-class morality. But in his book he speaks at times as if the poor themselves evolved this alien discipline and imposed it on themselves.[31]

Methodism was the desolate inner landscape of utilitarianism and together they constituted the dominant ideology of the Industrial Revolution; the blackened box-like chapels in the new industrial districts were great traps for the human psyche; work was the cross from which the refashioned worker hung; and God was the most vigilant overlooker of all. This is Thompson's thesis. It is not altogether surprising that he concedes there is some difficulty in understanding '... why so many working people were willing to submit themselves to this form of psychic exploitation'.[32] Why did they troop into these black, forbidding psychic traps that (capitalists?) had set for them.

Thompson's explanation gives pride of place to direct indoctrination ('it cannot be overstated'): 'Long before the age of puberty the child was subject at Sunday school and at home (if his parents were pious) to the worst kind of emotional bullying to confess his sins and come to a sense of salvation.' This does not solve the problem of why people submitted to bullying; it merely adds to it.

It is never altogether clear in Thompson's account whether by these means the poor were tamed for employment in industrial capitalism or turned into radicals and subversives. It is true that he rejects Halevy's argument that Methodism saved England from revolution; however, the 'psychic masturbation' and 'Sabbath orgasms' which the poor experienced in their chapels every week apparently diverted their attention from their grievances and material sufferings. Nevertheless, Thompson agrees that a few Methodists were Jacobins, more were Luddites, and still more were Chartists and trade unionists. But his key contention seems to be that this ideology was essentially diversionary: it was the 'chiliasm of despair'.[33]

He would like to have it both ways and so posits an 'oscillation' between positive and negative poles (which reviewers have found puzzling, unconvincing, and inconsistent).[34] But Thompson himself points to the biggest puzzle of all: the dual role of the Methodist ideology in serving both capitalist employers as 'exploiters' and their workers as the 'exploited'. 'How was it possible for Methodism to perform, with such remarkable vigour this double service?' asks Thompson. And he has no answer—principally because it is a nonsensical question. The ideology of the dominant class has this unfortunate characteristic: while it effectively controls the dominant classes, when the subordinate classes get hold of it it is not an instrument of social control but of subversion. The 'correspondence' between Methodist Sunday schools and industrial employment has been overstated—distorted, perhaps, by Andrew Ure's celebrated picture of closely matched regimentation (in his *Philosophy of Manufactures*) in Stockport in the eighteen-thirties. The Sunday school movement was in any event a rural movement in origin, as Laqueur has emphasized; the highest enrolments in the early nineteenth century were in Wiltshire, Dorsetshire, Buckinghamshire, and Bedfordshire:

> Sunday schools began at a time when the factory system had scarcely gained a foothold and grew to contain millions of children before the factory became the dominant organization of production. They were as much a rural as an urban phenomenon, as much part of an agrarian as of an industrial economy.[35]

They were not 'middle-class institutions'. The 'overwhelming verdict of scholars' that Sunday schools 'existed as more or less overt agencies of social control and class manipulation' is wrong.[36] Laqueur has effectively reinstated the Sunday school as a working-class institution.

Laqueur relates the origin and growth of Sunday schools as much to leisure as to work: the working class re-made itself along less picaresque, more restrained, and 'respectable' lines which involved substituting the Sunday school anniversary outing for the traditional, less decorous feast, and 'excursions' and the Sunday school 'treat' for the drunken Whitsuntide celebrations of the friendly societies. The railway day-trip took the place of pagan festivals. This was not because workers were bullied by capitalists intent on assaulting and remodelling the pre-industrial personality; it was part of the essentially working-class culture of self-improvement.

The Methodist Sunday schools were in the main working-class in their origin, organization, administration, and finance: 'the teachers were almost all from the same social strata as those they taught'; the schools, by the early nineteenth century, were embedded in and supported by local working-class communities; and fund-raising sermons were an important and popular feature of working-class community life. The upper classes had often founded and financed (and even taught in) Sunday schools in the late eighteenth century, but in the early nineteenth century the annual sermons rather than subscription was the principal source of funds. Employers sometimes bullied and cajoled workers and their families into attending,[37] but an ideology of hard work, self-discipline, and self-help was just as 'serviceable' to working-class leaders as to industrial entrepreneurs. (It may not have fuelled revolution, but it helps to explain why the grammar school was such a triumphant working-class institution by the mid-twentieth century.) The general picture is not one of upper-class imposition: 'A model which regards Sunday schools primarily as a weapon in an alleged bourgeois assault on working-class culture simply will not do.'[38]

MONITORS AND THE SELF-CONFIDENCE OF THE NEW WORKING CLASS

Work in a factory was a useful training for any boy or girl who wished to become a pupil in a nineteenth-century elementary school. Anyone who had become used to factory routines would find the rigours of school life relatively undemanding. The typical elementary school pupil in the first half of the nineteenth century was a highly intermittent pupil: he constantly withdrew, went to work, and returned after six months or a year. School and work were not necessarily or even normally 'end-on'; they were simply alternative. If work was not available for children, school was a place where they could be safely and perhaps profitably occupied.[39]

Of course there were 'correspondences' between the massed hierarchical arrangements of many nineteenth-century factories and many nineteenth-century schools of the kind that Bowles and Gintis have emphasized; but there were important differences. The classroom in the monitorial school was intensely individualistic and competitive; work for children in textile mills was usually a closely collaborative effort; Andrew Ure applauded this as a highly moral feature of factory employment, quoting with approval reports that in the factory 'not half an hour passes but what children are laying each other under obligations important to them'.[40] In the monitorial schools prizes, badges, and similar marks of personal achievement and distinction were freely employed to encourage children in their studies. This was not an appropriate training for less individualistic work in mass production. Of course it is still possible to argue—and in America it has been argued—that this kind of competitive training in school weakened the working class by setting every man against every man, so undermining the working class as a cohesive and threatening force.[41]

The monitorial organization of schools provided a training not in subservience but in command. The Professor of Education at Edinburgh University, Professor Pillans, saw the system as a training in 'cool judgement and prompt decision'; by the age of eleven or thereabouts, these working-class boys who were Monitors—a high proportion of all pupils—were, as one headmaster said, 'a kind of aristocracy in the school'. These eleven-year-old working-class aristocrats carried heavy responsibilities and exercised wide powers—'a sort of magisterial authority in settling petty disputes among the boys'. They received an excellent training not only in exercising control but in the bureaucratic procedures of record-keeping: it was their responsibility to keep attendance records, the lesson progress book, and the proficiency register.[42] It is little wonder that their authority often clung to them after school hours and gave them remarkable powers of command in the neighbourhood.[43]

The problem with pupils in monitorial schools was not that they were abject and downtrodden: the problem was their finery—they flaunted themselves. It was difficult (in one monitorial school in South Wales in the eighteen-forties) to prevent girls appearing decked out in all the finery of many-flounced dresses and long sashes. On school outings it was wholly impossible: fine gauze veils appeared to protect tender complexions and numerous parasols were spread for the same purpose.[44] A close examination of what actually happened in nineteenth-century monitorial schools does not support an interpretation of the working classes as victims; all the indications are that they were the victors.

Indeed, they called the tune. Laqueur has reinstated the consumer in the interpretation of the rise and development of mass schooling. Marxist explanations from the supply side—in effect that schools were imposed—is unconvincing in relation to both England and America. Only the handful of new, small, self-contained industrial villages remote from the great industrial cities, often run on highly paternalistic lines, gave the capitalist sufficient opportunity for surveillance and blackmail. Cromford under Arkwright, Styal under Greg, Marple under Oldknow, Saltaire under Titus Salt, and Copley under Akroyd were such enclosed communities.[45] But the picture generally in urban-industrial England is not of a work force whose children could be schooled under duress.

England's new working class did not in fact troop into the Sunday schools for psychic masturbation or a Sabbath orgasm: they went to acquire the secular skills of reading and writing which were the core curriculum. Hartwell asks whether the poor really needed taming for factory (as compared with agricultural or workshop) employment and points to the free-market aspects of educational provision: 'Most education for the poor in the eighteenth century was demanded, and paid for, by the poor.'[46] Laqueur has given close and detailed attention to this free market in the nineteenth century in relation to both Sunday schools and day schools. He emphasizes the wide range of secular instruction offered in the Sunday schools (and with regard to religious indoctrination through tracts observes that: 'Like the mass literature directed against the working-class reader, there is good reason to think that it missed its mark'). Sunday schools which offered an extensive curriculum prospered; those that provided more restricted fare failed.[47] Private day schools for working-class clients held their share of the market until the late eighteen-thirties. It was only the advent of compulsory education at the end of the century that eventually curtailed the working-class parent's '... ability to determine the content or structure of his children's education'.[48]

The recent emphasis by Marxists on the social control aspects of 'schooling' relegates the working-class consumer to at best a passive role in the origins and growth of elementary education. Often he is not simply passive: he is subjected to an intense and effective ideological bombardment to which he abjectly succumbs (reduced, in E. P. Thompson's phrase, 'to one of the most abject of beings'), and the school is represented as a means of repression and class domination. Laqueur rescues the Sunday school (and in many respects the day school) as a working-class institution, the product of the 'infinite inventiveness and ingenuity' of working-class men and women, strands in 'a uniquely working-class cultural constellation', and a base from which to wage the battle for a fair share in the new industrial society.

And yet there is an incompleteness in Laqueur's picture and analysis. Like E. P. Thompson he fails to distinguish sharply between the respectable, skilled working class (who wanted schooling for their children and were prepared to pay for it) and the unskilled, casual working class (which David Stow called the 'Sinking and Sunken Classes' and put at more than a third of a large industrial city like Glasgow).[49] Mary Carpenter called them the 'Perishing and Dangerous Classes' and was acutely aware of them as a special problem. Laqueur's free-market picture of bouyant working-class demand does not, as it stands, square with the need to introduce compulsory education in the eighteen-seventies. Stone draws the correct inference from the literacy rate (two-thirds) at the mid-century:

In early Victorian England the bottom third of the population was cut off from the rest, not only by its abject poverty, but also by its illiteracy. There must have been a significant cultural barrier between the respectable, newspaper-and-Bible-reading working class and the illiterate proletariat at the bottom of the heap.[50]

A strong demand for schooling by the respectable, skilled working class was well attested in the eighteen-sixties. As far as they were concerned, there was no need to make schooling either compulsory or free. But instead of 'working downwards', as administrators and policy-makers hoped, there was a tendency (as one report on Liverpool in the eighteen-fifties said) for the system to work upwards.[51] 'The present Government system of aid,' wrote Brotherton in *The Manchester Guardian* (21st November 1865), 'does not send any more children to school. ... It is now perfectly well known that the poorest people entirely escape its operations, and that those who benefit would have been at school if no Government aid had existed.' Hole similarly maintained in the eighteen-sixties that the educational system reached '... the better and more accessible portions of the working class' but was still leaving 'a broad and deep stratum untouched'.[52] The respectable working class were getting what they wanted and were willing to pay for it, but only a compulsory system could reach the neglected and destitute at the bottom of the heap.[53]

THE PUBLIC SCHOOLS: VICTIMS OF THE DOMINANT IDEOLOGY

The effective religious terrorism (because there was no way of escaping it) and the real 'chiliasm of despair' were in the middle-class, denominational boarding schools. In the eighteen-thirties the most powerful trap for the human psyche was probably Mill Hill School (closely followed by Woodhouse Grove).

The victims of the dominant ideology in Victorian England were the dominant classes. The educational apparatus which they created and to which they unflinchingly subjected themselves functioned with ruthless efficiency. It was the upper classes who, in the Public Schools, installed God as the Senior Prefect, eliminated all privacy, promoted total exposure, and pruned the traditional rather leisurely school life of any unprogrammed margins in which to hide. It was the great Public Schools, and not the Sunday schools, which were periodically under siege by the Brigade of Guards to enforce the new utilitarian work ethic (and curtailment of 'bounds'). The Prefect system could not effectively rehabilitate victims of sustained abasement and humiliation. (Becoming, eventually, a Monitor at Harrow did nothing whatsoever to restore Anthony Trollope's depleted self-confidence and self-esteem.) A brief respite as a Prefect could not rectify the damage done by years of terror and degradation. The alleged self-confidence of Public Schoolboys must find an explanation not in their experiences at school but in the network of support (often in the past including a private income) that awaits them afterwards.

One of the few educational studies to make explicit social-class comparisons is Goldstrom's recent work on the religious and social context of the nineteenth-century school curriculum. This is a study principally of elementary schools, but class comparisons are made and the point underscored that middle-class people who involved themselves in public education '... were not, after all, asking anything of the lower orders that they were not asking of themselves and their own children. A high standard of virtue was expected of middle class children, and this standard included everything expected of poor children, not excepting respect for one's betters.' Goldstrom finds no reason to support the currently fashionable view that elementary education was 'a conspiracy by the upper classes to hold on to their privileges', and concludes that: 'In at least some respects education seemed to run counter to middle-class interests.'[54] They imposed extra and often formidable restraints and moral burdens on themselves precisely because of their social standing.

The intense religiosity found in some boarding schools long pre-dates Arnold's reinstatement of Christianity at Rugby. Religious hysteria was constantly induced by the staff of Kingswood School in the late eighteenth century: the writing master, Hindmarsh, produced orgies of religious emotion in March 1768 and again in September 1770 when he took the boys to see the body of a dead neighbour and urged on them the need for repentance.[55] In the eighteen-twenties and -thirties any convenient corpse was used with similar effect at Mill Hill School.[56] But at Woodhouse Grove mass hysteria was perhaps still more common (high peaks were reached in 1817, 1827, 1833, 1843, and 1862). In 1818 a sermon on death left 'a large number of boys on their knees bewailing their sins, and crying to God for mercy and forgiveness'. The headmaster, Mr. Martindale, and his wife joined the boys in their prayers until the early hours of the following morning.

Religious hysteria and 'chiliasm' at this time was not the monopoly of any social class (although it was probably more prevalent in the non-conformist churches). The millennial Presbyterian 'Irvingites' of the eighteen-thirties were not simply middle class: they were distinctly upper class and even aristocratic (the duke of Northumberland was among the adherents).[58] The great Public Schools at the mid-century were not invariably scenes of unbridled religious terrorism; indeed, neither Butler nor Kennedy inspired the boys at Shrewsbury with religious fervour (and this is probably a major reason why numbers declined). Hawtrey at Eton exerted no strong religious influence. But the story is quite otherwise at Winchester and Harrow. Vaughan, who had been one of Arnold's pupils, was notable for his religious views and teaching (and numbers during his fifteen years at Harrow rose from 69 to 466); Moberly at Winchester saw religious instruction and inspiration as his central concern: 'Make the boys religious ... catechize them faithfully and painfully. ... Hear them express, as they readily will, their penitence for the past.'[59] In pre-Confirmation spiritual exercises boys were embarked on a process of self-examination and recollection of sins from earliest childhood.

But the real substitute for the Life Guards was organized games. Mutinies at Eton and Winchester persisted into the nineteenth century (and as late as the eighteen-seventies an Eton housemaster went, with good cause, in fear of his life; in 1900 there was a serious demonstration at Haileybury because Lyttleton refused a half-holiday to mark the relief of Ladysmith). But the last of the great rebellions was at Marlborough in 1851. It led to the resignation of Wilkinson, the first headmaster.

Cotton succeeded him. It was Cotton who invented organized games.[60]

Formerly boys at Public Schools had enjoyed large stretches of unsupervized time, jealously protected by tradition, in which to engage in individualistic sports like falconry, coursing, fishing (and cock-fighting and poaching). The playing fields of Eton at the time of Waterloo were not the scene of tidily organized compulsory games; they were the site of semi-organized brawls and fisticuffs in which from time to time a boy would be killed. Cotton stumbled on a remarkably effective means of curbing the independent spirit of England's upper class.

The Vice-Principal of St. John's Training College at Battersea (who had been educated at Marlborough) put it rather differently in 1900: he said that organized games had radically changed '... the bestial habits of the well-born and the well-to-do'. The change in the morals of Public Schoolboys since the eighteen-thirties, he said, was enormous. But the lower classes had not yet been similarly tamed. His hope was that the means that had proved so effective in civilizing the upper classes '... may gradually improve the habits of the very poorest'.[61]

There was widespread dismay that such means had worked only too well. That is why more independent spirits (like Edward Carpenter, Cecil Reddie, and J. H. Badley) invented the 'New' (Progressive) Schools in the eighteen-eighties. (They did so quite explicitly to rescue the upper classes from the stupefied overconformity of the Public Schools.) When Arthur Ponsonby wrote his book *The Decline of the Aristocracy*, in 1912 he was able to point to the evidence of photography that upper-class schoolboys had been cleaned up and standardized. Photographs of mid-nineteenth-century football teams showed boys 'lounging about in different attitudes with a curious variety of costumes'. But by 1912:

> The group of today consists of three rows of boys beautifully turned out with immaculate, perfectly fitting clothing. They stand and sit so that the line of the peaks of their caps, of their folded arms, and their bare knees, is mathematically level. And even their faces! You can hardly tell one from another.

Ponsonby saw public examinations (originated in the eighteen-sixties) as an important standardizing influence; but whatever the causes, he maintained that: 'This stereotyping constitutes perhaps the strongest indictment that has been brought aginst our Public Schools.'[62] He spoke of the 'iron mould' which produced 'fixed patterns' and concluded: 'We sacrifice individuality and suppress originality so as to produce a conventional average type.'[63]

The terrorism was real and for many self-confidence was undermined for life. Even Marjoribanks, Captain of the school for a time when Cyril Connolly was at Eton, a passionate beater who one evening flogged all the lower half of the college, later committed suicide.[64] The Prefect system varied considerably in Victorian Public Schools and it is not a convincing explanation of leadership in later life. It is difficult to see how young Powys Lybbe at Eton and young Meyrick at Westminster, who were bullied systematically and continuously for years, almost to death, could be saved for leadership by a final year as a Prefect or Monitor. The remarkable fact is that the fathers of these boys were men of wealth and power and position (Lybbe's father was a Member of Parliament). Both fathers gave evidence to the Clarendon Commission and produced medical evidence to support their allegations.[65]

Trollope, after nine years at Winchester and Harrow, left school as a Monitor at the age of nineteen with an abiding sense of humiliation and failure. His long years of degradation at these two great schools had totally destroyed his self-confidence. This was partly because of his poverty (and at Harrow being a day boy), but he always had an insuperable sense of rejection. (His father was a barrister, a Wykehamist, and a former fellow of New College, Oxford.) But his background secured him a job in the Post Office, although he was virtually illiterate; later, as a successful novelist in his forties, membership of the hunt and of the Garrick Club gave him what Winchester and Harrow and his monitorship wholly failed to provide: a sense of social acceptance and personal worth.[66]

Lugard, the future Governor General of Nigeria, often contemplated suicide during his degrading six years at Rossall. Like Trollope, one of his difficulties was poverty, but it was also the harshness and humiliation of the system (his friend Greenway died at the school of cold and exposure). As a young man he faced physical punishment for poor school work: 'Fancy the disgrace of being thrashed like a dog.' On his first night senior boys beat him and poured cold water over him in bed and the next day he was in hospital. Over the next six years the future empire-builder's self-confidence was not restored but systematically eroded. For an 'explanation' of Lugard we must look beyond his school and his impoverished ex-missionary father to his background of gentry connexions, of which he was intensely aware: he refused to be saved from the agony of Rossall by a managerial post in a sugar factory: '... the Lugards have been in the Army and in the Church, good servants of God and the Queen, but few if any have been tradesmen.'[67]

Lack of privacy and pressure to conformity seem to be central characteristics of the post-Arnold Public School. Bishop characterizes life at Winchester as 'a collectivism supported by lack of individual privacy and a host of unquestioned, unwritten rules'.[68] This was certainly the experience of Cecil King, the future chairman of the *Mirror* group of newspapers: 'When I say you were never alone, even the lavatories were without doors.'[69] King also became a Prefect, but claims: 'I hated almost every day of my time at Winchester. ...' He never learned to stand to the fore as a leader; his sole aim was to make himself invisible, and in this he claims to have had considerable success. He, too, thought often of suicide. In his late sixties he wrote: '... at least until recently I have always hated myself and always wanted to commit suicide.' Although he always found life 'like walking in thick treacle up to your neck', it was some assistance to have Lords Northcliffe and Rothermere as uncles.

Six centuries of gentry background—a great web of gentry connexions in Devonshire, including six baronetcies—may help to account for Francis Chichester's unexpected recovery from the damage he suffered at Marlborough. He left before he could become a Prefect; but the man who flew solo across the Tasman Sea in 1931 and later sailed single-handed round the world recalled the almost total destruction of his self-confidence at school: '... I would shake with fear if I had to get up and speak to more than half a dozen people, because the terror of doing or saying anything which would not be approved of by a mob code was so rooted in me.'[70]

Perhaps Trollope should be allowed the last word on self-confidence. He was an authority. When he introduced Bernard Dale, one of his characters in *The Small House at Allington*, he said this: 'Moneys in possession or expectation do give a set to the head, and a confidence to the voice, and an assurance to the man, which will help him much in his walk in life.' Neither years at Harrow, nor even being Captain of the school, had quite the same effect.

CONCLUSION: DEFIANCE, DOCILITY, AND SOCIAL CLASS

The very latest version of control theory places far less emphasis on the way schools can change people; it claims instead that schools reward (or punish) the different social classes for what they in any case are. This simple proposition is nowadays usually advanced in Bourdieu-type terminology which obscures its undoubted simplicity and probable falsity. The basic idea is that middle-class children are docile conformists and do not cause trouble because of their upbringing (socialization); working-class children are more of a nuisance, often stand up for themselves, and do not do as they are told (they 'reject the teacher's definition of the situation'). This is because of the differert child-rearing methods of the working class. Middle-class children are rewarded for being good boys and girls; working-class children are punished for being bad boys and girls. This is called 'refereeing the strategies of child rearing through the schools' certifying arrangements'.[71] In this way it is said in Bourdieu-type language, schools promote 'social reproduction' and ensure that the upper classes remain in control. The working class remain underprivileged not because they are controlled and made servile but because they are not.

The very man—Samuel Bowles—who placed so much reliance on the authority relationships of the school now says, in effect, that this does not work: '... given the existing institutional arrangements, the ability of a school to change a child's personality, values and expectations is severely limited.' The control system works more deviously by accepting what it is in any case powerless to change: 'The educational system serves less to change the results of the primary socialization of the home than to ratify them and render them in adult form.' The superior power of the upper class shows itself not in the ability to constrain and change pupils' behaviour but to impose its own special 'rules of the game' which make it unlikely that lower-class children will win.[72]

The docility of middle-class children—probably far more apparent than real—has become a cliché in educational literature since Allison Davis popularized it in the years immediately after the Second World War. The middle-class child, we were told, has a socially adaptive fear of poor grades and early sex; but the lower-class child is taught by the gang to fear being taken in by the teacher and to conceal good grades if he actually gets any.[73] American anthropologist Jules Henry has also described how middle-class children in their classrooms 'give the teacher what she wants' because, apparently, they fear to lose her love.[74]

The school, it seems, does not curb the (often celebratory) defiance of working-class pupils, but social control operates indirectly because their behaviour is a form of self-damnation. They are their own worst enemies. This is Paul Willis's argument which he presents as a 'bleak reversal' of Bourdieu's reproduction thesis. Throughout the entire working-class subculture, he says, 'there is an element of self-damnation in the acceptance of subordinate roles.'[75] But Willis knows that 'the lads' who stand up for themselves at work or at school are not a really serious threat to the established order. It is the clever silent conforming (perhaps middle-class) youth on the back row who is the real malcontent and subversive.

The power of the dominant class not to change people but to lay down the rules of the game and define (in upper-class interests) what 'counts as knowledge' is the burden of a well-known study by Nell Keddie.[76] She also finds unquestioning docility where non-teachers might not expect it—in the A-stream—and a greater tendency not to accept what the teacher says in the C-stream. This kind of critical 'noise' in C-streams is entirely convincing and familiar to any teacher with a little experience. But Keddie proceeds—without any evidence whatsoever—to explain what is not in any case a problem (the teacher's firm stand) in terms of the distribution of power in society. The argument seems to be this: the teacher of social science, when challenged by C-stream pupils (for instance over the definition of 'family'), is able to stand his ground because social power is on his side. If the challenge were of any real magnitude or gravity and the teacher actually felt intellectually threatened there might be some sense in advancing this ponderous and unlikely 'explanation'. What Keddie has accepted wholly uncritically is Pierre Bourdieu's latest theories and the surface significance of C-stream pupils' awkward questions.

The 'defiance' of working-class pupils is almost certainly confined to a very small minority (as Jencks concluded from American evidence)[77] and does not amount to fundamental criticism or rejection of the 'taken-for-granted' and the status quo; the 'docility' of middle-class pupils (and all intelligent pupils, whatever their 'class') is often more apparent than real: short-term and tactical, often concealing strategic subversion and radical doubts. When we look beyond 'classroom interaction' to the behaviour of pupils on a wider stage, it is the A-stream (often middle and skilled working-class) pupils who offer a serious challenge to current assumptions. This was apparent when I investigated the truly radical National Union of School Students in the mid-nineteen-seventies: weak C-stream (and ghetto comprehensive) participation; strong A-stream (and upper-class suburban comprehensive) participation. Support was especially strong from the 'new' middle class.[78] In fact the NUSS of the nineteen-seventies was, in its social and intellectual composition, a children's version of the CND movement of twenty years before.

To summarize: until the mid-nineteen-seventies Marxists said that schooling made the working classes docile so that they would fit smoothly into subordinate positions in the capitalist system, but made the upper classes self-confident so that they could control it. By the late-nineteen-seventies they were saying that the working classes were not docile after all but the middle classes were. This was not because of their schools but their early upbringing at home. The system rewarded the middle classes for their compliance and punished the working classes for their defiance. Thus schools exercise social control and perpetuate inequality from generation to generation. This is a slight, but not serious, oversimplication. And this *volte-face* makes it very difficult to take the Marxist enterprise very seriously.

The evidence presented in this chapter suggests that 'mass schooling' since the early nineteenth century has enormously strengthened the competitive position of the working class; it has not made them servile but has made a vital contribution to their 'respectability', morale, and sense of order and control over their own lives and destinies. It was not forced on them; it was largely a response to their own felt needs and demands. But it never really reached the lower, unskilled working class until it was made compulsory at the end of the century. It is most accurately seen as a crucial element in the making of a capable and confident skilled working class.

In contrast, the upper classes refashioned the Public Schools and in many ways crippled themselves. It is true that they moralized themselves, standardized themselves, and generally cleaned themselves up; but the picture presented by Correlli Barnett (in his book, *The Collapse of British Power*) is broadly true. The obsessive concern with ball games, the school chapel, character, and pluck was really a self-inflicted wound in an age calling for less juvenile values, a wider vision, a harder sense of social priorities and realities. But the upper classes made themselves sufficiently respectable to occupy public office without obvious discredit. They did this in spite of, rather than because of, the long years of terror and humiliation they suffered at school, and their much acclaimed 'self-confidence' must find an explanation—insofar as it existed at all—in a background of social support and (often outrageous) privilege rather than the absurdly glamorized Prefect system. It was the eleven-year-old working-class Monitor in the elementary school, and not the eighteen-year-old Monitor at Harrow, who learnt self-confidence, cool judgement, and the power of command.

NOTES

1. Paulo Freire has popularized the notion of education as 'domestication': see *Pedagogy of the Oppressed*, Penguin Books, Harmondsworth, 1972.
2. Paul Willis, 'The class significance of school counter-culture', in Martyn Hammersley and Peter Woods (Eds.), *The Process of Schooling*, Routledge and Kegan Paul, London, 1976.
3. Everett Reimer, *School Is Dead*, Penguin Books, Harmondsworth, 1971.
4. R. H. Kanter, 'The organization child: experience management in a nursery school', *Sociology of Education*, **45** (1972).
5. Herbert Gintis, 'Towards a political economy of education: a radical critique of Ivan Illich's *Deschooling Society*', *Harvard Educational Review*, **42** (1972).
6. Samuel Bowles and Herbert Gintis, *Schooling in Capitalist America*, Basic Books (U.S.A.) and Routledge and Kegan Paul, London, 1976; reprinted 1977. Prescribed as a set book for the Open University's new (1977–78) course on 'Schooling and society'.
7. S. Bowles and H. Gintis, 'The problem with human capital theory—a Marxist critique', *American Economic Review*, **65** (1975).

> The model is not wrong—individuals and families do make choices, and may even make educational choices roughly as described by the human capital theorists. We reject the individual choice framework because it is so superficial as to be virtually irrelevant to the task of understanding why we have the kinds of schools and the amount of schooling that we do.

8. S. Bowles and H. Gintis, *Schooling in Capitalist America*, Routledge and Kegan Paul, London, 1976, p. 114.
9. *Ibid.*, pp. 130–131.
10. Herbert Gintis, 'Towards a political economy of education: a radical critique of Ivan Illich's *Deschooling Society*,' *Harvard Educational Review*, **42** (1972).
11. S. Bowles and H. Gintis, *Schooling in Capitalist America*, Routledge and Kegan Paul, London, 1976, pp. 231–238.
12. David B. Tyack, 'Ways of seeing: an essay on the history of compulsory schooling', *Harvard Educational Review*, **46** (1976).
13. Lawrence Stone, 'Literacy and education in England 1640—1900', *Past and Present*, February **1969**, No. 42.
14. Michael Sanderson, 'Literacy and social mobility in the Industrial Revolution', *Past and Present*, **1972**, No. 56.
15. T. W. Laqueur, 'Debate: literacy and social mobility in the Industrial Revolution in England', and M. Sanderson, 'A rejoinder', *Past and Present*, **1974**, No. 64.
16. W. B. Stephens, 'Illiteracy and schooling in the provincial towns 1640–1870: a comparative approach', in D. A. Reeder (Ed.), *Urban Education in the Nineteenth Century*, Taylor & Francis, London, 1977.
17. William Landes and Lewis Solmon, 'Compulsory schooling legislation: an economic analysis of law and social change in the nineteenth century', *Journal of Economic History*, **32** (1972).
18. E. Brotherton, 'The state of popular education', *Transactions of the National Association for the Promotion of Social Science*, **1865.**
19. J. McCosh, 'On compulsory education', *Transactions of the National Association for the Promotion of Social Science*, **1867.**
20. R. Johnson, 'Educational policy and social control in early Victorian England', *Past and Present*, **49** (1970). 'The idea that the school and the teacher could and should take over many of the responsibilities of the parent was a key concept in Kay's educational thought and a guide-line of his policies.'
21. J. F. C. Harrison, *Learning and Living 1790–1860*, Routledge and Kegan Paul, London, 1961, p. 40.
22. Richard Johnson, 'Notes on the schooling of the English working class 1780–1850', in Roger Dale *et al.* (Eds.), *Schooling and Capitalism*, Routledge and Kegan Paul, London, 1976.
23. *Ibid.*, p. 49.
24. For some discussion of this contradiction see Ted Benton, *Philosophical Foundations of the Three Sociologies*, Routledge and Kegan Paul, London, 1977, pp. 161–165.
25. R. Martin Goodridge, 'The ages of faith—romance or reality?', *Sociological Review*, **23** (1975).
26. Geoffrey Crossick, *An Artisan Elite in Victorian Society: Kentish London 1840–1880*, Croom Helm, 1978.
27. Nicholas Abercrombie and Bryan S. Turner, 'The dominant ideology thesis', *British Journal of Sociology*, **29** (1978).
28. Thomas Walker Laqueur, *Religion and Respectability. Sunday Schools and Working Class Culture 1780–1850*, Yale University Press, New Haven, Conn., 1976. Laqueur says that in Thompson's study 'Religion generally, Methodism and Sunday schools in particular, are seen as agents of the middle class in this struggle to remould the innermost feelings and desires of the working people', and that his own work '... began as an attempt to confirm Thompson's interpretation in one corner of nineteenth-century history' (pp. xii–xiii).
29. E. P. Thompson, 'Time, work-discipline and industrial capitalism', *Past and Present*, **1967**, No. 38.
30. Sidney Pollard, 'Factory discipline in the Industrial Revolution', *Economic History Review*, **16** (1963–64). 'Almost everywhere, churches, chapels and Sunday schools were

90

supported by employers, both to encourage moral education in its more usual sense, and to inculcate obedience.'

31. E. P. Thompson, *The Making of the English Working Class*, Penguin Books, Hamondsworth, 1968. 'But the Methodists—or many of them—*were* the poor. Many of their tracts were confessions of redeemed sinners from among the poor; many of their preachers were humble men who found their figures of speech (as one said) "behind my spinning-jenny" ' (p. 386).

32. Ibid., p. 441.

33. This 'diversionary' aspect is singled out by Chambers in his review of Thompson's book: '... vainly thirsting for the blood of the bourgeois, they consoled themselves by bawling about the Blood of the Lamb'. See J. D. Chambers, 'The making of the English working class', *History*, **51** (1966).

34. E. G. Currie and R. M. Hartwell, 'The making of the English working class?', *Economic History Review*, **18** (1965).

35. T. W. Laqueur, *Religion and Respectability. Sunday Schools and Working Class Culture 1780–1850*, Yale University Press, New Haven, Conn., 1976, p. 216.

36. *Ibid.*, p. 147.

37. See Sidney Pollard, 'Factory discipline in the Industrial Revolution', *Economic History Review*, **16** (1963–64).

38. T. W. Laqueur, *Religion and Respectability. Sunday Schools and Working Class Culture 1780–1850*, Yale University Press, New Haven, Conn., 1976, p. 189. 'Working men and women in hundreds of communities throughout England were at least as important in building this educational patchwork as were the Hannah Mores, Sarah Trimmers or Robert Raikes on whom exclusive credit is usually bestowed' (p. 21).

39. Beryl Madoc-Jones, *Social Implications of Elementary Education 1800–1850, with Particular Reference to the Work of Monitorial Schools*, Unpublished Ph.D. thesis, University of Exeter, 1977, pp. 91–93.

40. Andrew Ure, *The Philosophy of Manufactures*, Knight, London, 1836, p. 420.

41. M. B. Katz, *Class, Bureaucracy and Schools*, Praeger Press, New York, 1971, p. 11.

42. This picture of the monitorial classroom is taken from Beryl Madoc-Jones, *Social Implications of Elementary Education 1800–1850*, Unpublished Ph.D. thesis, University of Exeter, 1977, p. 141.

43. *Ibid.*, p. 271.

44. *Ibid.*, pp. 133–134.

45. See W. Ashworth, 'British industrial villages in the nineteenth century', *Economic History Review*, **1951,** and E. Akroyd, 'On the relations betwixt employers and employed', *Transactions of the National Association for the Promotion of Social Science*, **1857**: 'The works (at Copley) may be called self-contained—that is, they are shut in and form a small hamlet in themselves, in which there are no residents save those in my employ. ... About a thousand persons are employed in the mill, and every effort is made to secure their comfort and the education of their families.'

46. R. M. Hartwell, *The Industrial Revolution and Economic Growth*, Methuen, London, 1971, p. 244.

47. T. W. Laqueur, *Religion and Respectability. Sunday Schools and Working Class Culture 1780–1850*, Yale University Press, New Haven, Conn., 1976, p. 151.

48. T. W. Laqueur, 'Working-class demand and growth of English elementary education', in Lawrence Stone (Ed.), *Schooling and Society*, The Johns Hopkins University Press, Baltimore, Md., 1976, p. 202.

49. David Stow, *The Training System*, Blackie, Glasgow, 1850, p. 50.

50. L. Stone, 'Literacy and education in England 1640–1900', *Past and Present*, **1969,** No. 42.

51. J. S. Howson, 'Report on popular education in Liverpool', *Transactions of the National Association for the Promotion of Social Science*, **1859.**

52. J. Hole, *The Homes of the Working Classes*, London 1866, p. 117.

53. Mary Carpenter, 'Our neglected and destitute children', *Transactions of the National Association for the Promotion of Social Science*, **1865**.
54. J. M. Goldstrom, *The Social Context of Education 1808–1870*, Irish University Press, Shannon, 1972, pp. 177–179.
55. See A. H. Body, *John Wesley and Education*, Epworth Press, London, 1936.
56. N. B. G. James, *The History of Mill Hill School*, Melrose, London, 1909, p. 87.
57. J. T. Slugg, *Woodhouse Grove School*, T. Woolmer, London, 1885, p. 188.
58. Graham Allan, 'A theory of millennialism: the Irvingite movement as an illustration', *British Journal of Sociology*, **25** (1974).
59. F. D. How, *Six Great Schoolmasters*, Methuen, London, 1904, p. 75.
60. John de S. Honey, *Tom Brown's Universe*, Millington, London, 1977, pp. 104–110.
61. E. B. Hugh-Jones, 'The moral aspect of athletics', *Journal of Education*, **22** (1900).
62. A. Ponsonby, *The Decline of the Aristocracy*, Fisher and Unwin, 1912, pp. 207–208.
63. *Ibid.*, pp. 213 and 219.
64. Cyril Connolly, *Enemies of Promise*, Andre Deutsch, London, 1938.
65. Alice Heritage, *Public Schools as Presented by the Clarendon and Taunton Commissions and by Contemporary Novelists 1825–75*, Unpublished Ph.D. thesis, University of Manchester, 1977, Chap. Five: 'Power and authority'.
66. Anthony Trollope, *An Autobiography*, Oxford University Press, London, 1953, pp. 136–137 and 145.
67. See Margery Perham, *Lugard. The Years of Adventure 1858–1898*, Collins, London, 1956, pp. 27–35.
68. T. J. H. Bishop, *Winchester and the Public School Elite*, Faber, London, 1967, p. 18.
69. Cecil King, *Strictly Personal*, Weidenfeld and Nicolson, London, 1969, p. 30.
70. Anita Leslie, *Francis Chichester*, Hutchinson, London, 1975, p. 26. See also Francis Chichester, *The Lonely Sea and the Sky*, Brockampton Press, 1964, pp. 12–13.
71. A. H. Halsey, 'Towards meritocracy? The case of Britain', in J. Karabel and A. H. Halsey (Eds.), *Power and Ideology in Education*, Oxford University Press, New York, 1977. 'Nevertheless, what has happened is the weighting of the dice of social opportunity according to class and "the game" is increasingly played through strategies of child rearing refereed by schools through their certifying arrangements' (p. 184).
72. The notion of imposed upper-class 'rules of the game' is that of Samuel Bowles: 'The power of the upper class is hypothesized as existing in its capacity to define and maintain a set of rules of operation or decision criteria—"rules of the game"—which ... have the effect of maintaining the unequal system.' See Samuel Bowles, 'Unequal education and the reproduction of social division of labor', in Karabel and Halsey (Eds.), *Ibid.*
73. Allison Davis, *Social Class Influences upon Learning*, Harvard University Press, Cambridge, Mass., 1949, p. 30.
74. Jules Henry, 'Docility, or giving the teacher what she wants', *Journal of Social Issues*, **11** (1955).
75. Paul Willis, 'The class significance of school counter-culture', in M. Hammersley and P. Woods (Eds.), *The Process of Schooling*, Routledge and Kegan Paul, 1976.
76. Nell Keddie, 'Classroom knowledge', in M. F. D. Young (Ed.), *Knowledge and Control*, Routledge and Kegan Paul, London, 1971.
77. C. Jencks, *Inequality*, Penguin Books, Harmondsworth, 1975: 'While a few lower-class and working-class children behave in ways that schools find unacceptable and try to punish, the great majority evidently do not' (p. 139).
78. F. Musgrove, *Ecstasy and Holiness: Counter Culture and the Open Society*, Methuen, London, 1974, pp. 160–163.

CHAPTER 5

Grammar Schools, Public Schools, Class, and Elites

The English working class has been betrayed twice in my lifetime: first in the General Strike of 1926 and then forty years later when the grammar schools 'went comprehensive'. In 1926 the working class was betrayed by the capitalists; forty years later by the sociologists. The first betrayal makes perfectly good political sense: there is no great difficulty in understanding self-interest and greed. The second is more puzzling: a revolution that practically nobody wanted. The Labour Party did not abolish the great Public Schools, the obvious strongholds of upper-class privilege; with unbelievable perversity they extinguished the only serious hope of working-class parity. The remarkable social revolution of post-war socialist Britain was this: the upper classes kept their Public Schools; the working classes lost theirs. Ironically, the most serious charge levelled against this supreme working-class institution, the free, academically selective grammar school, was that it was 'middle class'.

With quite astonishing speed and zeal, a small band of youthful and dedicated sociologists had subverted the 1944 Education Act before butter had come off the ration and the last intake of fee-payers had left the system. The groundwork was done in the three years 1949 to 1952; the books and reports which killed the grammar schools were published in the two years 1954 to 1956. Even before our ill-fated Suez 'adventure' the Mason Plan had been launched in Leicestershire and the scholarship boy revealed as none other than the uncouth 'Lucky Jim'.

The essential charges against the selective grammar schools were two: that clever working-class boys and girls could not as a rule succeed in them and that in any event they did not make a significant contribution to England's elites. Two kinds of study went hand in hand: of the fate of working-class scholarship boys in grammar schools and of the educational and social background of recruits to top professions and national elites. The grammar school was under a cloud both for being 'elitist' and for its signal failure to get its ex-pupils into any elites.

Neither of these charges is in fact true; neither was true in 1950 or 1956. But both were made to stick. As a result working-class scholarship boys are now an extinct race. They were actually withdrawn from the field. Power, wealth, and privilege were left with a severely emasculated opposition.

The books which were thought to place a large question mark over the fairness and effectiveness of the selective grammar school were the following: in 1954 the report, *Early Leaving*,[1] and *Social Mobility in Britain*, a collection of empirical studies and surveys edited by D. V. Glass;[2] in 1955 important chapters (for instance by Floud) in *Looking Forward in Education* edited by A. V. Judges;[3] and in 1956 *Social Class and Educational Opportunity* by Floud, Halsey, and Martin.[4] The middle nineteen-fifties also saw the publication of two books of quite a different kind, which were of unparallelled virulence: in 1954 Amis's novel *Lucky Jim* and in 1958 Young's satire *The Rise of the Meritocracy*. They made a powerful and popular impact: they discredited the grammar school and the scholarship boy and made merit a term of abuse. The first may have done this inadvertently. The second did it with carefully calculated malice. *The Rise of the Meritocracy* is not an argument; it is a sneer.[5] It has done incalculable harm to social justice (and perhaps social efficiency) in post-war Britain.

In the six years after the appearance of *The Rise of the Meritocracy*, between 1959 and 1964, three further publications seemed to drive home the lessons of 1954 to 1956: the 'Crowther Report', *15 to 18*, which was published in 1959; Jackson and Marsden's *Education and the Working Class*, which was published in 1962; and Douglas's *The Home and the School*, which was published in 1964. The 1944 Act was implemented in 1945, but it takes seven years for an intake of pupils to show its paces and complete the full grammar school course. None of the studies listed above, including the last three, tells us anything about children and their secondary schools after the middle nineteen-fifties. The 'Crowther Report' is based on children who left school between 1954 and 1955; *Social Mobility in Britain* is basically about education and social status up to 1949; the report, *Early Leaving*, tells us about children who entered secondary schools in 1946; *Education and the Working Class* is about people born in the early nineteen-thirties who went to grammar schools early in the war and left their Sixth Forms round about 1950. For England's new-style free, selective, post-war grammar schools, fortune did indeed turn rotten before it was ripe.

The 'Robbins Report', *Higher Education*, published in 1963, must be included in this second wave of assaults on the grammar school. The report devoted a good deal of attention to the flow of pupils through grammar schools to universities. Information on the relative performance of working-class and middle-class schoolchildren was made available to the Robbins committee for incorporation in its final report. It came from Douglas. There was a specially expedited delivery. *Higher Education* appeared in 1963; Douglas's book, with an introduction by D. V. Glass, was published in 1964. His data were provided ahead of publication. No comment was made on his circular and essentially meaningless use of 'class' (see Chapter 3 above). Douglas's data are uncritically accepted and reaffirmed as the unassailable truth about 'class' and grammar schools.[6] And so the high authority of the 'Robbins Report' is added to the view that the free, selective post-war grammar school works against the interests of clever working-class boys and girls and is, after all, a middle-class institution.

The real demolition job was done in the two years 1954 to 1956; but it was heralded as early as 1950. Early warnings appeared in the *Year Book of Education* for 1950 and in the timely launching, in 1950, of the *British Journal of Sociology*. Here we see elites being cast in a very unfavourable, even sinister, light (for instance by Raymond Aron); and the demonstration that working-class scholarship boys who go to grammar schools do not in any case get into them.

Nicholas Hans provided the 1950 *Year Book* with a preview of his work on elites and the apparently impregnable position of the great Public Schools, undiminished over more than two centuries;[7] Jenkins and Jones showed (in the first volume of the *British Journal of Sociology*) how the grammar schools lost ground at Cambridge, contributing 16 per cent. of the students in 1750, 11 per cent. a century later, and a derisory 7 per cent. in 1900.[8] Floud concluded in her chapter in the *Year Book of Education*: 'There has been no such striking challenge as might have been expected from the products of the maintained secondary (grammar) schools to the hold of the sons of the public day and boarding schools on the leading positions in professional and business life.'[9] The grammar schools seemed incapable of projecting anyone beyond black-coated clerical work in the ranks of the lower middle class. It seemed clear by 1950 that the grammar school had made a negligible impact on the class structure of English society and seemed foredoomed never to do so.

A WORKING-CLASS INSTITUTION

By 1953 two-thirds of grammar school pupils were working class. This figure is based on a very stringent definition of working class as manual workers, and it refers to the country's direct-grant grammar schools as well as those wholly maintained by local education authorities.[10] In 1926 one-third of the boys in maintained secondary (grammar) schools were working class (if the sons of domestic servants are included),[11] but at that date more than 60 per cent. of the places were reserved for fee-payers. A working-class majority seems to have been reached before the Education Act of 1944, even by the late nineteen-thirties, although fee-payers still took some 50 per cent. of all places. It is true that in South-West Hertfordshire only about 30 per cent. of places were occupied by the children of manual workers in 1943.[12] However, in Middlesbrough children from the homes of manual workers were more than 50 per cent. of secondary (grammar) school pupils by 1935 to 1938,[13] and in the rather superior London grammar school (formerly a proprietary school) described by King, manual workers' sons exceeded half the intake for the first time in 1938.[14]

A more realistic definition of working class might include manual workers who are in charge of other manual workers (foremen), shop assistants, routine clerical workers, perhaps postmen, police constables, and even jobbing builders. If such people of minimal educational qualifications and modest circumstances in life were included, the working-class percentages cited above would have to be raised by between 20 and 30 per cent.; the nation's secondary grammar schools would have to be seen as having a preponderance of working-class pupils by the middle nineteen-twenties. Even Watford Grammar School was working class on such criteria by the late nineteen-thirties. But this chapter will not attempt to introduce a more sensible notion of 'working class'. Working class means manual workers.

Three post-war books give us good trend data on the social class composition of particular grammar schools since the beginning of this century; four national surveys give us good, comprehensive snapshots without the same historical depth. From these seven publications it is possible to put together a reasonably accurate picture of the changing participation of England's manual working class in secondary grammar school education.

Particulars of grammar school pupils in South-West Hertfordshire for the period 1884 to 1953, and in Middlesborough between 1905 and 1953, are provided in *Social Class and Educational Opportunity* (by Floud, Halsey, and Martin); in a rather superior London grammar school between 1907 and 1957 in King's *Values and Involvement in a Grammar School*; and in a grammar school in a rather seedy part of Greater Manchester between 1905 and 1965 in Lacey's *Hightown Grammar*.

The four surveys which provide a national picture are Floud's report on the educational experience of the adult population as at July 1949 (published in Glass's *Social Mobility in Britain*); the report, *Early Leaving*, based on the 1946 intake into grammar schools; the 'Crowther Report', *15 to 18*, based on 4,000 children who left school in 1954–55 and a survey of 9,000 National Servicemen from 1956 to 1958; and a survey of 3,000 twenty-one-year-old ex-grammar school pupils which was made in 1962 for the 'Robbins Report', *Higher Education*. An eighth source of some interest and value might be added: Tawney's *Equality*, published in 1931, which compared the social background of pupils in secondary (grammar) schools in 1926 with the position thirteen years earlier.

There is a ninth publication that has been extensively used. It must be treated with great caution. That is the picture provided by Douglas in *The Home and the School*. Based on the children born in one week of March 1946 who took their grammar school selection tests eleven years later, this should give valuable data. It does not. There is not only the problem of defining 'class', which has already been discussed; there is also the problem of the remarkable 'shape' of Douglas's population. Approximately 3,400 of the original survey children are included in this study, and only 40 per cent. of them are 'working class'. In a representative national sample we should expect almost twice this proportion. For some reason that is not altogether clear, Douglas's study is based on a massive working-class underrepresentation. It is true that when his tables give actual numbers of pupils, as distinct from average scores and percentages—which happens in the Appendices, but not in the twenty-four tables in the main text—he has 'weighted' his working-class children by multiplying them by four. The fact remains that when 'Number of Children' in the working class is given as 5,615,[15] this means approximately 1,400 actual children; and that is roughly four-tenths of the total. It would be unwise to regard Douglas's 'sample', in which 60 per cent. are middle class, as telling us anything about the population at large.

The basic national picture for the nineteen-fifties is quite clear. The proportion of grammar school pupils from manual workers' homes in the report, *Early Leaving*, is 65 per cent. (44 per cent. from the homes of skilled workers, 21 per cent. from the homes of unskilled workers); the Crowther Report, *15 to 18*, found that 59 per cent. of the National Servicemen who had attended grammar schools were from the homes of manual workers (45 per cent. from 'skilled' homes, 14 per cent. from 'unskilled'), and 60 per cent. of grammar school leavers in the mid-nineteen-fifties;[16]

the Robbins survey of twenty-one-year-olds similarly found that 62 per cent. of those who had attended grammar schools were the children of manual workers (44 per cent. were from the homes of skilled workers, 18 per cent. from unskilled workers' homes).[17]

It would be unwise to attach too much importance in survey work of this sort to variations of two or three percentage points, but the figure of 44 or 45 per cent. of grammar school pupils from the homes of skilled manual workers is a remarkable constant in diverse surveys at different points in time since 1945. What also seems reasonably clear from these surveys is that the contribution of unskilled workers' families was not constant. It seems to have fallen throughout the nineteen-fifties from a little over 20 per cent. to not much more than 14 or 15 per cent. (12 per cent. inthe Crowther Report's leavers' survey). Other government statistics included in the Robbins Report again show the 'skilled' constant of 44 per cent. (intake in 1946, leavers in 1961), but a drop from 21 to 16 per cent. in the contribution of unskilled workers' homes.[18]

It would be difficult to exaggerate the distinction between the large, skilled manual working class (who from the very early days of this century have commonly bought their own houses and whose daughters have not been pregnant when they married) and the small (and diminishing and perhaps deteriorating) semi-skilled and unskilled manual working class. Any meaningful study of grammar schools and universities and 'class' must make this distinction crystal clear and focus upon it. Usually they do not. This crucial distinction is lost in a broad, simple, and highly misleading division into non-manual workers ('middle class') and manual workers ('working class'). The skilled manual working class always performs at least as well as the children of white-collar workers at any stage of the educational system. It is quite fatal to a true understanding of 'class' and education simply to lump together skilled workers and unskilled workers and label them 'working class', as many studies do. Thus the Robbins Report, for example, lumps them together at critical points in its analysis: it never separates them for analytical purposes when presenting the results of its survey of twenty-one-year-olds and it does not separate them before A-level (at eighteen years of age) when presenting the results of the Ministry of Education's survey of school leavers in 1960–61. Grossly misleading statements are made in consequence about 'the working class' when what is at issue is the special (and worsening) problem of the minority of unskilled labourers.

The twentieth-century grammar school has been the great success story of England's large skilled manual working class. On the basis of her 1949 national survey data Floud pointed to the remarkable success of her 'status category' 5. (This fifth and by far the largest of seven status categories comprised skilled manual workers and routine non-manual workers.) Indeed, among the adult population alive in July 1949, the proportion of status 5 males who had attended secondary grammar schools had multiplied by five from the very oldest to those most recently at school.[19] Floud refers to the 'substantial increase' in the proportions of children coming from categories 5, 6, and 7 over the period from 1900 to 1940: '... the *absolute* numbers of such children found in the secondary schools were substantial. Indeed, in absolute numbers the largest single group of individuals achieving secondary education were those whose fathers were in status category 5. ...'[20] It is not only the absolute numbers that are impressive. Over the first forty years of the twentieth century 'category 5' children are not significantly underrepresented among those holding free-place scholarships in secondary grammar schools: during this period status 5 adult males were 41 per cent. of all workers;[21] their children were 38 per cent. of all free-place holders (but only 28 per cent. of all children in secondary grammar schools).[22]

In South-West Hertfordshire the children of manual workers (skilled and unskilled) were 11 per cent. of grammar school children before 1900 and 44 per cent. in 1953; the children of clerical workers were the same proportion at both dates (16 per cent.), although they had been over 30 per cent. in the nineteen-thirties; the children of foremen and small shopkeepers fell away dramatically, from 48 per cent. in 1900 to 19 per cent. in 1953.[23] In Middlesbrough the children of clerical workers similarly remained a 'constant' (8 per cent. in 1905 and again in 1953); manual workers' families contributed 18 per cent. of the grammar school boys in the first two decades of the century, 50 per cent. by the mid-nineteen-thirties, and 54 per cent. by 1948. The shopkeeper and foreman contribution also slumped at Middlesborough, from around 40 to 24 per cent. over half a century.[24] The broad picture is of clerks maintaining their steady minority hold on the grammar schools and a massive displacement of shopkeepers by the manual working class.

In the London grammar school described by Ronald King the sons of manual workers were roughly a fifth of the pupils in 1907, 40 per cent. as early as 1928, an actual majority before the Second World War, and comfortably in excess of 50 per cent. in the nineteen-fifties.[25] 'Hightown' in Greater Manchester appears at first sight to be anomalous: '... by 1957 Hightown Grammar School was recruiting almost the same proportions of working-class boys as in 1905.'[26] For sixty years (1905 to 1965) the proportion of boys from the homes of manual workers remained virtually unchanging at around 37 per cent. But in fact the post-war selective Technical High School in Hightown recruited 67 per cent. of its pupils from the manual working class and the overall figure for the town in the early nineteen-sixties was 49 per cent.[27]

Of course the proportion of grammar school pupils who are the sons and daughters of manual workers has varied throughout the country. In 1951 Himmelweit found that 67 per cent. of the Third Form of one London grammar school were from manual workers' homes, but only 41 per cent. in a suburban area.[28] But the general, overall predominance of working-class pupils by 1950 is clear. Two things are surprising: the remarkable progress that had been made long before the 1944 Education Act was conceived and passed; and the hiccup that occurred in the late nineteen-fifties.

The central theme of Tawney's treatise, *Equality*, was that the educational system since the 1902 Education Act had done little to help the working class. He assembled Board of Education statistics to prove it. What the figures show is that in 1913 a quarter of the boys in maintained secondary (grammar) schools came from working-class homes (stringently defined to exclude clerks and shop assistants); in 1926 the proportion was a third.[29] This is remarkable in view of the fact that after 1907 only a quarter of the places were free, by 1920 just under a third, and by 1928 just over.[30] The striking improvement in the position of the manual working class between the wars was achieved while more than half the places in secondary grammar schools were reserved for fee-payers.

Skilled manual workers have been exactly 'represented' among free-place scholarship holders in secondary grammar schools throughout this century; this means that since all places were made free after the Second World War, they have been exactly represented in the total grammar school population. Three entirely independent post-war studies (published in 1954, 1960, and 1963) which actually used five quite different national samples give exactly the same result.

The children in these five national samples entered their selective grammar schools between 1946 and 1956; their fathers were mainly in the age range from 35 to 45 at the time of the 1951 Census, which shows that 43 per cent. of men of that age were skilled manual workers and 22 per cent. were unskilled. Thus England's manual working class was 65 per cent. of all workers. The contribution of the two levels of the manual working class to these five national samples of grammar school pupils is summarized in the following table:

Manual workers' children in grammar schools from late nineteen-forties to early nineteen-sixties

Sample	Entered grammar school	Percentage of grammar school pupils		
		Skilled manual	Unskilled manual	Total manual
1. Report: *Early Leaving*[31]	1946	44	21	65
2. Crowther Report: *15 to 18*[32] School leavers 1954–55	1947–51	48	12	60
3. Crowther Report: *15 to 18*[33] National Servicemen Survey	1947–49	45	14	59
4. Robbins Report: *Higher Education*[34] Survey of twenty-one-year-olds	1951–52	44	18	62
5. Robbins Report: *Higher Education*[35] Ministry of Education Leavers' Survey	1953–56	45	16	61

Thus England's large skilled manual working class was 'perfectly' represented in post-war selective grammar schools (as, indeed, was the other middle status group, the 12 per cent. or so of clerical workers). Unskilled labourers were not underrepresented in the late nineteen-forties, but have been since. 'The working class'—in the sense of all manual workers—constituted 65 per cent. of the adult population; these five surveys give the total working-class percentage of grammar school pupils as: 65, 60, 59, 62, 61. The extent to which the manual working class was 'underrepresented' was entirely accounted for by a shortfall in its unskilled fringe.

ATTAINMENT IN THE GRAMMAR SCHOOL AND THE SPECIAL PROBLEM OF THE UNSKILLED LABOURER'S CHILD

A major part of the case against the post-1944 maintained grammar school was that working-class children did badly in it in three respects: they did not get their fair share of places in the first place; they left early; and they did relatively badly scholastically. There is some truth in the second charge: in the Sixth Forms of the nineteen-fifties skilled workers' children were somewhat underrepresented (between 35 and 40 per cent. of all Sixth Formers) and unskilled workers' children very considerably so (between 4 and 7 or 8 per cent. of all Sixth Formers). Nevertheless, the preoccupation with 'wastage' and early leaving in the pinched nineteen-fifties was rather foolish and shortsighted: this problem would be cured semi-automatically by rising affluence and Act of Parliament.

The charge regarding scholastic performance and examination success seems to have substance only when the minority of unskilled labourers' children are included in an undifferentiated working class. The Robbins Report on higher education, which is particularly shrill and insistent on the issue of social-class differences, is singularly unhelpful at this point. There are 'social-class' differences when examination results and scholastic levels and attainments are presented simply in two categories: manual versus non-manual workers' children.[36] The differences disappear (except for unskilled labourers' children) in the one table which distinguishes different levels of the manual (and non-manual) class.

Thus the table of A-level examination results (based on particulars of 1960-61 school leavers supplied by the Ministry of Education) tells us this about pupils who stay on till they are eighteen years of age to take the grammar school Sixth Form's A-level course: 65 per cent. of the children of skilled manual workers got at least two A-level passes, 64 per cent. of the children of clerical workers, and 67 per cent. of the children of professional and managerial workers; but only 56 per cent. of unskilled workers' children.[37] And yet, on the basis of the four tables which had presented results in a simple two-column form, the Report of the Robbins Committee felt able to say quite firmly: '... working class children are progressively less successful than children of the same 11 + grading in other social groups.'[38]

Data on eleven-plus grading (by intelligence level) which the Report provides, really gives the probable answer to this problem: the children of unskilled workers—even those selected for grammar schools—are rather more stupid than other grammar school children. The children of skilled manual workers are not. Thus the children from 'unskilled' homes were 16.4 per cent. of all the grammar school children in the survey, but only 10.6 per cent. of the most intelligent third, and 21 per cent. of the least intelligent third. The children of skilled manual workers, 44.5 per cent. of the total, were more 'fairly' represented at all intelligence levels (they were 46.6 per cent. of the top third).[39]

Lacey makes much of the comparative scholastic failure of working-class boys at Hightown Grammar: indeed, his book is devoted to explaining '... the disappointing performance of working-class boys in grammar schools since the 1944 Education Act'.[40] The table of examination results for the years 1962 to 1965 which tells against working-class pupils[41] makes no distinction between the sons of skilled and unskilled manual workers. In fact the book says nothing about this very important distinction within the working class, but the differentiation is made in two tables which show the class composition of the school at different dates. It seems clear that while the proportion of working-class pupils remained roughly constant, the quality of the working-class intake deteriorated. Between 1917 and 1920 the sons of unskilled workers were 24.7 per cent. of all working-class boys in the school;[42] between 1962 and 1965 they were 34.5 per cent.[43] Although the percentage of manual working-class children at the Hightown School was substantially below the average for the nation's grammar schools, the proportion of unskilled workers' children (14 per cent. of all the pupils) was not. Lacey devotes his book to 'laying bare the social mechanisms' that account for relative working-class failure and offers a generally unconvincing explanation in terms of anti-school working-class subcultures. The explanation is probably very much simpler: the working-class pupils were now of poor quality.

The 'hiccup' that occurred in the mid to late nineteen fifties in working-class participation in the grammar schools can probably be explained in terms of the small minority of children from unskilled workers' homes. King's London grammar school detected the hiccup in 1957: the working-class intake was down to 45.5 per cent. (compared with 53.5 per cent, in 1949); but King does not distinguish between different levels of the working class. Neither does Floud in her examination of the hiccup in South-West Hertfordshire between 1952 and 1954; she sees the explanation lying at least in part with the abolition of intelligence tests in selection procedures.[44] But the problem generally was probably not their abolition but their use. The hiccup had also occurred early in Middlesbrough, and here we have data which show how it was constituted. In 1948 working-class boys were 54 per cent. of those entering the grammar schools; in 1953 this had slumped to 44.6. But the contribution of the skilled working class was virtually unchanged: 31.6 per cent. in 1948 and 30.8 per cent. in 1953. The slump was wholly in the contribution of unskilled workers' families, which fell from 22.4 to 13.8 per cent.[45]

The data that have been used to 'demonstrate' the relative academic failure of working-class children in post-war grammar schools are more ramshackle than most. The first overzealous attempt was made by social psychologist Himmelweit as early as 1951. Her evaluation of the operation of grammar schools under the 1944 Education Act was carried out six years after the Act was implemented with children who had been two years in the schools.[46] It was a before-and-after study which included no 'before' data whatsoever. This does not prevent Himmelweit from making firm statements about trends.

The thirteen-year-old boys in London grammar schools who were the subject of this study had taken no public, externally set, marked, and moderated examinations. They took the usual end-of-year examinations in seven different subjects. They were being taught (and examined) in eleven different forms in four different schools. The top five and the bottom five in each subject in each form were compared for 'social class'. On this basis the middle-class boys were judged superior: Himmelweit says the result shows a 'marked difference in academic attainments'. She quotes an unnamed author and source on the 'failure of the grammar school' and says that her work confirms this failure.

Middle-class boys did best in these terms in forty-two examinations, working-class boys did best in twenty-three, and in ten there was no difference. Himmelweit concedes the need for caution: 'Such small units make a statistical evaluation of the significance of differences meaningless. ...' Nevertheless, her entire case rests on these differences not being meaningless. What in fact is reasonably clear is that in the one school in which working-class pupils outnumbered middle-class pupils they were more often found in the top positions in end-of-year examinations; in the three schools in which working-class children were heavily outnumbered, middle-class children were more often in top positions. But even this trend probably means very little.

This kind of comparison is in fact extremely hazardous and difficult to make; it must be done only by people who actually know how to do it. When so much hangs on it, it is really very important to get it right. And the results must be statistically significant beyond any shadow of doubt. In their follow-up study of 'Plowden children' Ainsworth and Batten did a technically faultless job with a full understanding of all the pitfalls that await the unwary; they did not find connexions between social class and academic attainment in the nine maintained grammar schools and the three direct-grant grammar schools included in their study.[47]

Having obtained a result that was statistically meaningless, Himmelweit then proceeded with inquiries to explain what had never been proved. A number of remarkable questions were put to 332 thirteen-year-old grammar school boys, such as: 'How much do you worry about your school work compared with other boys?' Thirty-three per cent. of the middle-class boys but only 21 per cent. of the working-class boys said: 'More'. It is difficult to know what even the most perceptive social psychologist could make of answers to this unanswerable question. If the percentages have any meaning, it is presumably that middle-class children lack the robust self-confidence that characterizes working-class scholarship boys. This is probably true. It may also indicate the kind of stupidity that a willingness to answer unanswerable questions implies. Himmelweit says it indicated 'socialized anxiety'. This is apparently an excellent thing to have; it is a great middle-class asset because it makes them work hard.

This study, of little intrinsic worth, would not normally merit much attention; but in it we see the early stages of the making of one of the most potent and mischievous myths of our time. Since 1950 the view has found a place in highly prestigious journals and books that the grammar school is not a fit place for working-class children; it is so bad for them that they can not as a rule succeed in it. This view is false.

But there remains a persistent and perhaps worsening fringe problem of the unskilled labourer's child. Often he does well; he is certainly not doomed to fail. But he is rather more likely to fall by the wayside than other children. It is curious that the official reports of the nineteen-fifties were quite clear that this was where the real problem lay; and yet the 'failure of the grammar school' was in general perversely interpreted as failure for the entire working class. The Crowther Report, *15 to 18*, underlined the fact that the children of skilled manual workers were 'nearly half the school population' in grammar as well as secondary modern schools, but went on to emphasize the contrary fortunes of unskilled workers' children: '... boys from the homes of semi-skilled or unskilled workers are much under-represented in the composition of the selective schools, proportionately to the size of the parental occupation group from which they come.'[48] The report *Early Leaving* had made precisely the same point but more forcefully and at greater length: 'One of the significant findings to which we wish particularly to call attention concerns the children of semi-skilled and unskilled workers. ... So many of the unskilled workers' children achieved little that it will be worth while considering them separately.' The Report could only speculate, but thought that the character and atmosphere of particular working-class streets was one source of the difficulty. The Report concluded that it would be 'wrong to adjust the machinery of selection' to deal with this special problem.

A quarter of a century later we can still only speculate; but we have not simply adjusted the machinery—we have totally dismantled it. The problem remains. The reasons for the relative failure of the unskilled worker's child are probably three: genetics, poverty, and community. He was, in the days of eleven-plus selection, more often at the borderline of intelligence for grammar school admission; he was poorer than other pupils and needed to earn money; and he lived in a highly intolerant community which still savagely punishes anyone who shows signs of getting above himself. The unskilled labourer's family is not insulated and protected by 'privatization'; it is exposed to the punishment that is especially severe for those who show an incipient interest in 'culture'. This is the 'social mechanism', rather than allegedly polarized subcultures in schools, that needs study. The answer to the problem is certainly not the astonishing one we have now devised: the neighbourhood school. It is the opposite. There is no solution in institutionalizing— and sentimentalizing—ghetto education.

THE MIDDLE-CLASS ANTI-SCHOOL SUBCULTURE

The problem of the grammar school was not to get middle-class children out, but to get them in. The problem was so great by 1860 that a Royal Commission had to be set up to solve it. And for seventy years after the Taunton Commission reported in 1868 the problem was tackled and partially solved. In fact, the middle classes were curiously reluctant to come in; they were suspicious of an education that was abstract, literary, and non-applied, and they escaped for a time into the Higher Grade Schools. (Only the Cockerton Judgement got them back.) And yet the inducements they were offered were very considerable: a nominal entrance examination and fees infinitely beyond a miner's family but comfortably within the reach of the local ironmonger. The problem of the grammar school was to show that it had the confidence of the backbone of the nation. The endowed grammar schools had clearly lost it even before Victoria ascended the throne.

The normal relationship between social class and attainment in grammar schools was modified but not reversed in the nineteen-fifties, and the normal relationship was the superior performance of the working-class pupil. The fate of the middle-class child was to leave early and fail scholastically. After 1944 the middle classes saw that they must fight, and they did so with some success. But the bogey of the grammar school's 'middle-class traditions and ethos' which are foreign to working-class children, so successfully presented by Floud, Halsey, and Martin,[49] is meaningless. We must be quite clear that what this middle-class tradition meant in the inter-war years and before was that of the proprietor of the high street shoe shop and grocer's shop and the manager of the local brickworks and of the Odeon cinema. They were not people of great wealth or power; they were unremarkable for their culture; they were distinguished only by owning Morris Minors and Austin Sevens and being able to buy their child a place in the C-stream for twelve or fifteen pounds a year. These C-form middle-class fee-payers were held in contempt by the working-class scholarship boys in the A and B forms; they commonly left early; and if they stayed to the age of sixteen might conceivably get a School Certificate but were unlikely to get a 'Matric'. 'Matrics'—as distinguished from School Certificates—distinguished the aristocracy of talent; and the aristocracy was working class.

By the eighteen sixties only a hundred of England's 820 endowed grammar schools were 'first grade' schools providing a classical education to the age of eighteen. The average size was 94 pupils of whom 48 were boarders. Fifty endowed grammar schools were wholly in abeyance; 198 functioned only as elementary schools; the rest (248) were small (average size 64) and losing middle-class pupils to private and proprietary schools. The trouble with the endowed grammar schools, said the Schools Inquiry (the 'Taunton') Commission, was the 'social difficulty'. And by the social difficulty they meant that most of the schools were now wholly working class.

The commissioners who, from the various regions of England, sent their magnificent detailed surveys and reports to Lord Taunton's Committee all told the same story: the middle classes found the traditional grammar schools alien institutions and were everywhere deserting them for private and proprietary schools which taught practical, applied, and, above all, commercial subjects. Stanton reported from the South West that 'Successful tradesmen do not as a rule patronize the grammar school of their town';[50] headmasters of grammar schools were resigning and establishing private schools which would have the confidence of the middle class (which often included the local trustees of the grammar school itself). Fitch reported in exactly the same vein from Yorkshire: 'Of the fact of the general decadence of the endowed grammar schools within the county there can be no doubt. These schools are not popular; they do not possess the confidence of the parents.' In Yorkshire the landed gentry had used the grammar schools but the urban middle classes looked on them with suspicion or contempt. Keighley Grammar School had experienced 'a steady deterioration in the social rank of the children and with it a steady decline in the numbers and reputation of the school', and at Batley Grammar School 'the poor multiplied, gentlemen's sons were withdrawn, and the school being the only one in the place, served the purpose of an elementary school'.[51] The lesser gentry (often, indeed, the aristocracy) had found the endowed grammar schools to their taste; the great Public Schools, which enshrined and sustained the same traditions, now had their patronage. The grammar school was never a middle-class institution; its traditions are gentry traditions. Berkhamsted was an endowed grammar school for 144 pupils; in 1865 it had only 48. The middle classes did not like the classical curriculum; they wanted for their children a course of studies that might actually have a job at the end of it.

It was in the private and lesser proprietary schools, with their book-keeping and commercial studies, that the middle classes of England were at home. Lord Taunton's commissioners investigated middle-class private schools and were impressed by their efficiency. Bryce found five private schools in Bolton, four in Wigan, two in Accrington, three in Rochdale, and three in Oldham; Fitch inquired into 116 in Yorkshire, received detailed information from seventy-four, and himself visited forty-four. 'They pursue with very little energy any but directly practical branches of knowledge,' said Bryce. Fitch reported: 'Much stress in often laid on book-keeping. Some parents make a special stipulation that this subject shall be taught.' Bryce's main criticism was that the private school master had to teach Classics 'almost by stealth'; Fitch's was that parental interference was excessive: 'The condition on which a private school exists is, that it shall please the parents. ... The end they (the parents) contemplate in sending a boy to school is that he shall be prepared to "get on" in life.' Bryce was aghast. Certainly no grammar school master worth his salt has ever subscribed to such vulgarity.

The aim of the Taunton Commission was to restore confidence in the endowed grammar schools so that they could effectively serve all classes of the nation. For this it was essential to enlist the support of the substantial middle class and to get their children in significant numbers into the schools. Only then would the endowed grammar schools have the efficiency and the standing to provide the service for poor boys which their founders intended. The schools would be really worth going to. And so the central recommendation was that indiscriminite gratuitous instruction should be abolished and free places awarded for merit only.[52] There should be open competition for a small number of places in first-grade classical schools; the tests should be principally in arithmetic, since the well-to-do had no special advantage in this subject, and they should not normally be taken before the age of thirteen:

> For boys under 13 there is reason to fear that this might prove too severe a strain. Whenever it is desirable to give gratuitous schooling to children so young as this, it would seem best to select them from particular schools after a careful observation of their industry and progress for a year preceding.

This was the dawn of the meritocracy that was destined to be destroyed within a hundred years.

The Taunton Commission underestimated the distaste of the middle class for the grammar school tradition. Thirty years after the commission published its report, middle-class abstention from the grammar schools was a major source of concern for the Bryce Commission on secondary education. The Higher Grade Schools provided under the Elementary Code now offered precisely the applied and vocationally oriented education that the middle classes wanted and understood; so whereas the Taunton Commission, reporting in 1868, lamented their addiction to private schools, the Bryce Commission, reporting in 1895, lamented their massive presence in Higher Grade Schools and 'Higher Tops'. Simon has pointed out how grammar schools of great standing, like Manchester Grammar School, were threatened by this middle-class defection and how informed observers thought the grammar schools were bound to lose: 'The competition between the two is as unequal as that between Nelson's *Victory* and an ironclad.'[53]

The Higher Grade Elementary Schools were preponderantly middle class. (Simon refers to an estimate of 1897 which would put middle class pupils at approximately two-thirds.)[54] And they were full, even over-full. The grammar schools of England, by contrast, had a quarter of their places unfilled.[55] There was some regional variation: in London only some 10 per cent. (1,500 out of some 17,000) were vacant. And yet the Hon. Edward Lyulph Stanley, giving evidence for the London School Board to the Bryce Commission, thought that people with middle-class incomes of around 200 pounds a year would rush to fill as many as eighteen new Higher Grade Schools if they were built.[56]

In Birmingham, Sheffield, Leeds, and Newcastle it was clear that the middle classes—even very prosperous professional families—saw the advantages of this new type of applied education that was being provided within the Elementary Code and preferred it to the grammar schools. At Sheffield the Grammar School, with 160 pupils, was far from full; in the Higher Grade School there were 1,000 and from it went boys 'who turn their superior knowledge to good practical account in the manufactures. A very considerable proportion of the boys really go to useful careers in the large works.'[57] At Leeds the Grammar School was 'not particularly prosperous': solicitors, merchants, manufacturers, 'persons of good social position, enjoying large incomes' were sending their children to the Higher Grade School. The vice-chairman of the Birmingham School Board gave evidence of a similar situation in his own city. Only the 'Cockerton Judgement' (which ruled School Board expenditure on 'higher grade' subjects illegal) and the consequent demise of the Higher Grade Elementary Schools brought a reluctant middle class in the twentieth century into the alien grammar school tradition.

The damaging cliché of our times, that the grammar school was a middle-class institution which embodied middle-class traditions and enshrined the 'middle-class ethos', is absurd. When the middle classes eventually, with reluctance, came in (on highly favoured terms) they fared badly. But working-class scholarship boys found in the grammar school a natural home: they were its Prefects and their names were thick on the honours boards. To middle-class pupils it remained an alien, unnatural, unworldly place.

His Majesty's Inspectors of Schools were keenly aware of this and always feared that the middle classes would be pushed out (to the detriment of the standing of the schools and so of their working-class pupils). A Board of Education report on maintained secondary (grammar) schools for the year 1923–24 said: 'It is the common experience both that they (the free place holders) stay longer at school than other pupils and that they form a large portion of the able pupils, with the result that in the higher forms they tend to predominate.'[58] In Ronald King's London grammar school only 28 per cent. of the fee-payers got School Certificates in 1928, but 79 per cent. of manual workers' sons with free places did so; in 1938 the gap was still wide: 40 and 79 per cent. respectively.[59] Lacey's examination data for Hightown Grammar in the nineteen-thirties point in the same direction and show that 'in every category (school certificate, Matriculation and Higher School Certificate) working-class boys have a higher proportion of passes'.[60] Scholarship boys and fee-payers are not distinguished, but 20 per cent. of working-class pupils, for example, got 'Matrics' in the years 1934 to 1939, while only 15 per cent. of lower middle-class pupils did so (although the small 'upper middle class', with 30 per cent., did better than both).[61]

The superiority of working-class scholarship boys over middle-class fee-payers is not especially remarkable; what is more puzzling is the superiority of working-class scholarship boys over middle-class scholarship boys. At King's London School in 1913 all scholarship boys from manual workers' homes obtained School Certificates, only 69 per cent. of the scholarship boys from non-manual homes did so. There were fluctuating fortunes in the inter-war years, but the percentages for 1938 were 79 and 68, for 1945, 51 and 48, and for 1949, 58 and 54 respectively. Lacey provides similar evidence about scholarship-holders in the different social classes at Hightown in the nineteen-thirties;[62] sums up in a similar sense and points to comparable evidence of working-class superiority in Middlesbrough.[63] He also provides evidence on early leaving which shows, for instance, that only 42 per cent. of the upper middle-class scholarship boys even completed the course in the years 1934 to 1939, but 57 per cent. of working-class scholarship boys did so.[64]

Lacey devoted an appendix to explaining this pattern of pre-war performance (which, curiously, he refers to as a reversal of the normal) and yet failed to do so.[65] The explanation almost certainly lies in the middle-class anti-school subculture which he refers to elsewhere ('an important middle-class fee-payer contingent associated with anti-school attitudes').[66] 'Old Boy' informants stressed their consciousness of their (superior) working-class scholar status and their contempt for weak and inadequate middle-class pupils: 'In their eyes, many of the middle-class fee-payers were lazy and badly behaved because they were supported by well-off parents who could secure their children's future.'

So bad was the middle-class record that one of two explanations seems likely: the anti-school subculture of the middle-class was so powerful (perhaps like the American middle-class anti-school culture described by James Coleman) that it undermined academic effort; or the middle class simply was not trying. (Perhaps these are not two explanations but one.) In South-West Hertfordshire working-class boys did so well in the free-place competition in relation to their abilities (getting more than a half of the free places between 1904 and 1945 when they 'ought' to have got only a quarter),[67] that the only possible conclusion is that the middle classes had not seriously entered into competition. It was only when fees were abolished, and in other respects the meritocracy began to bite in post-war England, that the middle-class decided to fight. Neither father's money nor connexions would any longer see you all right if you left school early without even a School Certificate. It was precisely when the middle classes were for the first time under serious pressure that meritocratic systems were abused and finally destroyed and the pressure removed.

The inter-war and immediately post-war free, selective grammar school triumphantly celebrated the high abilities and intellectual excitement of England's skilled manual working class. Jackson and Marsden's Huddersfield study is the great celebratory record of the glories of the grammar school as a working-class institution. What bothered Jackson and Marsden was not that working-class boys did not fit in and succeed, but that they did: 'Most (of the 88 selected for study) accepted the new school with its different values and became its most hard working and worthwhile members. In turn they became its prefects and its leaders.'[68]

The trouble was 'another side to the orthodoxy': they fitted in all too well, perhaps became 'over accommodating', even 'emollient', and most regrettable of all rejected ('at conscious or unconscious levels') the life of the neighbourhood. They looked back on their schools with satisfaction and approval, and what appears to have been their unpardonable offence was that '... they wanted the system that produced them preserved intact'.[69]

The Prefect system, reviled in the general nineteen-fifties campaign against merit and the meritocracy, was the pinnacle and supreme expression of the English grammar school. By the time we have reliable statistics, in the immediate post-war period, the grammar school Prefect system was an established working-class institution. The report *Early Leaving* found that 47 per cent. of the sons of unskilled workers in the Sixth Forms became Prefects, 43 per cent. of skilled workers' sons, 40 per cent. of the sons of professional and managerial workers, and 35 per cent. of the sons of clerical workers.[70] King had dropped 'social class' by the time he came to look at his London Prefects, but found no bias in terms of the categories he used: 31 per cent. of first-generation pupils became Prefects and 33 per cent. of second-generation pupils. Jackson and Marsden found no middle-class bias in the appointment of Prefects: 'Bias, if any, runs the other way.'[71] Fifty-four per cent. (48 out of 88) of the working-class pupils in their study necame Prefects. It is true they try to play down, in impenetrable prose, the significance of this arithmetic. In King's study Prefects did not hold 'school-approved values' more strongly than non-Prefects, but there is no doubt that in all these studies the (largely working-class) Prefects were the crown and glory of the school.

PUBLIC SCHOOLS VERSUS GRAMMAR SCHOOLS

Correlli Barnett has painted a very convincing picture of the naivete and innocence of England's early twentieth-century ruling class: the product of late-Victorian Public Schools, they had spent much of their youth steeped in a suitably purified classical curriculum listening to their headmasters preaching about honour and service and sin.[72] Incapacitated by an overmoralized education, England's ruling class made a major contribution to the collapse of British power. There is great force in this argument. But while England was ill-served by this immaculate conception of education, the individuals who experienced it reaped high rewards. So deeply entrenched and 'overrepresented' were they in England's mid-twentieth-century elites that they seemed virtually unassailable.

There seemed almost to be an iron law that sixty leading Public Schools would always contribute two-thirds of the members of England's elites: the nine great 'Clarendon' schools,[73] it seemed, would always contribute about a quarter, and fifty other leading schools around 40 per cent. When Nicholas Hans studied a national sample of 3,500 eminent Britons (2,300 Englishmen) born between 1685 and 1785, taken from the *Dictionary of National Biography*, he found that 22 per cent. of the Britons and 28 per cent. of the Englishmen were educated at the nine Clarendon schools: 'They (the figures) prove indisputably that these schools supplied almost one-third of the elite in England of the eighteenth century and that of this amount the two schools Eton and Westminster had the lion's share.'[74] Westminster and Eton together contributed almost 60 per cent. of the share of these nine schools, Winchester only some 10 per cent. A further 28 per cent. of all these eminent men had not attended school at all: they had been educated at home by private tutors. Thus 56 per cent. of the eighteenth-century elite had received a privileged education.

For comparative purposes Nicholas Hans took a sample of 2,500 eminent contemporaries from the *Authors' Who's Who* (1948). Twenty-four per cent. had been educated at the nine 'Clarendon' schools and 42 per cent. had attended fifty-one other Public Schools (including Sedbergh, Uppingham, Clifton, Oundle, and Marlborough).[75] Thus the essential change in two centuries seemed to be that private tutors were replaced by new Public Schools. The contribution of the great nine Clarendon schools was a constant. Hans summed up his essential conclusion when he said: 'Two-thirds of selected Englishmen are provided by a small group of schools and private tutors in the eighteenth century and by sixty schools at the Headmasters' Conference in our time. In spite of all changes in population and educational provisions the percentages remained stationary.'

Other studies published in the ten years after the Second World War emphasized the high degree of 'self-recruitment' in English elites and the major professions. In the second half of the nineteenth century 29 per cent. of Cambridge students who were the sons of doctors themselves became doctors; in the late nineteen-thirties 56 per cent. did so. In the legal profession the respective proportions were 33 and 48.[76] The difficulty with any study of elites is that the subjects are usually at least in middle life and reflect educational circumstance at least twenty and probably thirty or forty years earlier. Such studies are likely to give a far more conservative picture of society than contemporary facts warrant. Attention needs to be focused on the younger entrants into occupational elites from whom leaders will be drawn.

One of the first discouraging studies of the contribution of the maintained secondary (grammar) schools to superior positions in life was Tawney's *Equality*. This set the tone for many years to come. It drew evidence from Ginsberg's surveys in the nineteen-twenties and quoted his observation that 'the social ladder so far lifts relatively small numbers'. But when we read Ginsberg we find that he emphasizes the new degree of opportunity. He divided his survey population into three social classes and found that two-thirds of the present generation in Class I had come up from below. Unlike some later surveys, he found very little downward movement.

His final words are: 'It would seem that there has been an increase in mobility upwards in the present generation, whilst the downward movement is slight and nearly constant during three generations.'[77] Ginsberg's study shows a dawning of opportunity; even the sons of 'skilled wage earners' were now—though in very small numbers—being admitted to Lincoln's Inn: 'There are signs of the working class beginning to creep in.'

The discussion of elites, like the discussion of classes, is beset by problems of definition. Elites are not classes; in many respects they are the opposite. Giddens follows Weber in defining class as an aggregate of individuals who share the same market position; he restricts 'elite' to people who occupy formally defined positions of authority in organizations or institutions.[78] This seems too narrow, at least in relation to a study of education. Pareto, on the other hand, used the term too widely, to embrace the foremost in any field—so that there could be, as he said, en elite (or 'aristocracy') of brigands no less than an elite of saints. 'Elite' will be used here to refer to people who have reached a position of consequence in all walks of life which are honourable and carry social approval. Particular attention will be given to the higher civil service because it has been fully and carefully studied and can be regarded as the 'model' of the post-1860 meritocratic society.

Noel Annan has described the Trevelyan–Northcote Report of 1853 on the reform of the civil service as the Bill of Rights of the intellectuals, its implementation in the eighteen-seventies as their Glorious Revolution: 'Then it was ordained that men of good intellect should prosper through open competitive examination. ...'[79] The *Quarterly Review* at that time took a more disparaging view, complaining that overeducated young men would go into the Post Office 'and other departments of inferior dignity' and claiming that: 'The object, in point of fact, is to turn the sixteen thousand places in the Civil Service of the empire into so many exhibitions for poor scholars.'[80] That is in fact an excellent definition of meritocracy and needs no apology.

The proportion of high-ranking civil servants with manual worker fathers trebled (from 7 to 20 per cent.) in the twenty years from 1930 to 1950. Of course, this was still a massive 'underrepresentation' of the manual working class, but it represents a remarkable triumph for 'merit' after what were perhaps setbacks in the nineteen-thirties (through the operation of interviews in the selection process), and a considerable boost during and after the Second World War through promotion from the ranks (which meant that grammar school boys who had proceeded no further than their 'Matric' still had an opportunity to rise to the top).

In the inter-war years, when an interview was used as well as written examinations, there was a 25 per cent. 'error' in selection for the higher civil service at the expense of grammar school boys. During these years candidates who had attended schools administered by local education authorities obtained significantly higher marks in the written examinations and significantly lower marks in the interviews.[81] Kelsall considers that it is reasonable to infer that in the inter-war period the interview favoured candidates from the Clarendon schools and other major boarding schools. When he studied the eighteen borderline candidates among the seventy-six who were successful, with eighteen who had just missed a place, he concluded that a quarter of those who were successful in 1938 would not have been without interview. Those who just got in were mainly from boarding schools; those who just failed to do so were mainly from day schools maintained by local education authorities.[82]

In the early years of this century boys who had attended maintained secondary (grammar) schools were 6 per cent. of those entering the higher (administrative) civil service; they were almost a half in the nineteen-fifties.[83] The nine Clarendon schools contributed 30 per cent. of the entrants in the years immediately preceding the First World War and only 8.5 per cent. in the years from 1949 to 1952. (Their contribution as a proportion of male recruits has remained steady at this figure into the nineteen-seventies.)

This massive decline in the contribution of the nine Clarendon schools to England's 'mandarins' in the course of less than half a century was one major change; another was that twenty other high-status Public Schools (including Fettes, Uppingham, and Sedbergh) 'changed places' with maintained secondary (grammar) schools after the Second World War. In the three decades before 1939 these twenty schools produced some 26 per cent. of the recruits while the maintained secondary schools produced 15 per cent.; in the years 1949 and 1950 the positions were reversed: the twenty schools provided 11 per cent. of the recruits and 27 per cent. were grammar school boys.

Kelsall underlines the negligible proportions of men from top-ranking Public Schools among the higher civil servants of 1950: 'It is surprising to find that little more than 2 per cent. of higher civil servants are Wykehamists, and that Rugbeians form a similar proportion, with Etonians nearer one per cent.'[84] This is part of what Anthony Sampson (in *The New Anatomy of Britain*) refers to as the 'failure of Public School leadership'.

When he was writing about leading politicians and public servants in 1971 Anthony Sampson emphasized not the persistent influence of the great Public Schools but the strong and effective competition they faced from the state secondary grammar schools. The big-city direct-grant grammar schools had done even better: Peter Walker went to Latymer Upper and Dennis Healey to Bradford Grammar School; but James Callaghan went to Portsmouth Northern Secondary (Grammar) School, Harold Wilson to Wirral Grammar School, Roy Jenkins to Abersychan Grammar School, and Margaret Thatcher to Kesteven and Grantham Grammar School for Girls.

Most remarkable of those local authority grammar schools, perhaps, was Quarry Bank School, Liverpool. In the late nineteen-thirties the future Cabinet Minister, Peter Shore, was a pupil (before proceeding to King's College, Cambridge); Bill Rodgers, another future Minister, was there at the same time (before going on to Magdalen College, Oxford). And exactly contemporary with Peter Shore was David Basnett, the future trade union leader.

It is the supreme self-confidence of the successful grammar school boy (or girl), especially if he has proceeded to a degree at Oxford or Cambridge, that has been particularly impressive. Anthony Sampson underscores this point: 'Once at university, the confidence gap between the public-school and grammar-school boys has visibly diminished, and clothes and accent no longer distinguish public-school undergraduates: in later life men like Roy Jenkins, Denis Healey and Anthony Barber show no sign of lack of confidence behind their ambition.'[85]

Twenty-one heads of major civil service departments were listed by Sampson. All were born between 1912 and 1918; they were attending secondary schools in the nineteen-twenties or early nineteen-thirties; and in the early nineteen-seventies were at the height (and near the end) of their careers. Only four had been to 'Clarendon' schools (Eton, Harrow, Charterhouse, and St. Paul's);[86] eight had been to maintained, local authority secondary (grammar) schools; and nine had been to direct-grant grammar schools mainly (like Edinburgh Academy) in large cities. The three top command posts were occupied by Sir William Armstrong (Head of the Civil Service), Sir Douglas Allen (Treasury), and Sir Philip Allen (Home Office). Sir William Armstrong, whose father was an officer in the Salvation Army, attended a London secondary school (Bec School) before going up to Exeter College, Oxford; Sir Douglas Allen, whose father was killed in the First World War, was brought up in some poverty[87] and attended Wallington Grammar School before proceeding to the London School of Economics; Sir Philip Allen went to King Edward VII School, Sheffield, before Queen's College, Cambridge.

'The enormous and increasing success of the grammar schools' to which Jonathan Gathorne-Hardy refers in his recent book, *The Public School Phenomenon*,[88] was apparent precisely when they were destroyed. A scrutiny of men in elite positions then in their late fifties gives a wholly inadequate idea of their triumph. The lower echelons of elite groups and organizations, from which future leaders will be drawn, show the success of grammar school boys which has not yet had time to show at the top. It is true that some highly visible top positions have been vacated by Public School men and occupied by others educated at maintained grammar schools: Sir Hugh Carleton Greene was educated at Berkhamsted (and Merton College, Oxford); his successor as Director-General of the BBC, Sir Charles Curran, at Wath-on-Dearne Grammar School (and Magdalene College, Cambridge). But the real promise around the year 1970 was to be seen among the younger men. Thus in 1967 although only 7 per cent. of our Admirals had been educated at grammar schools, at the level of lieutenant nearly 60 per cent. had been educated at grammar schools and only 30 per cent. at Public Schools. It is possible that this Public School minority will supply most of our Admirals in the future, but it seems more likely that the new top leadership of the future will be of 'an entirely different type', provided by a new race of career-minded 'military managers' recruited far more heavily than in the past from grammar school boys.[89]

Anthony Sampson concluded that the Public Schools could only survive if they became more like grammar schools. There were signs that they had the good sense to realize this. But Sampson was not too confident of the outcome: 'Whether the public schools will be able to maintain their confident position in the power-structure of the nineteen-eighties must be very doubtful.[90] He stressed their vulnerability, although they were more concerned with intellect and less obsessed with character than formerly. As the Public Schools aped the grammar schools their prospects improved, but: 'The grammar schoolboys are making deeper marks on the British power-structure. ... The grammar schools appear to be less prone to dropouts, pot-smokers and general *ennui*.' Grammar schoolboys had 'a more straightforward ambition for success'; they were more interested in power and probably more capable of wielding it. Miss Joan Hills, Registrar of the Independent Schools Careers Service said something very similar in 1973: Public Schoolboys had lost their taste for power. They preferred art.[91]

In the mid-nineteen-seventies the Headmaster of Eton, Michael McCrum, told Jonathan Gathorne-Hardy that it was plain to him that the already shrinking Public School dominance would shrink still more. 'There is no doubt,' concluded Gathorne-Hardy, 'that he was right.'[92] Both the Headmaster of Eton and Jonathan Gathorne-Hardy are wrong. Neither had reckoned with the Labour Party. And in fact Gathorne-Hardy, venturing somewhat outside his own sphere of high professional competence as a historian, points with good reason to the different pedagogies of the Public Schools and the state comprehensives: the efficient, rather old-fashioned, formal teaching in the former, and the more 'open', less pressurized teaching in the latter, which may deprive them of their competitive edge.[93] We have some alarming reports of torpor in big-city grammar schools turned comprehensive, where once there was pace and zest.[94]

While the grammar schools were being undermined and finally destroyed in post-war Britain, the Public Schools experienced a rebirth. They modelled themselves on the grammar schools with telling effect. They have repeatedly performed this feat of renewal. They have not suffered the fate of classical schools elsewhere, like those of French Canada, for example, which failed to adapt to the modern industrial world and crippled French Canadians by remaining true to their cultural heritage. John Porter says of the persistence of this system of classical schools: 'It was an outstanding example of institutional failure.'[95]

The English Public Schools do not provide an example of institutional failure or misguided fidelity. They are a case study in institutional survival and success. In the eighteen-sixties the Clarendon Commission on the Public Schools was astute enough to coopt the very architect of the modern meritocracy and competitive examination—Sir Stafford Northcote. A century later, in the face of competition from the grammar schools, death duties, the collapse of Empire, and a more egalitarian ethic, they achieved a near-magical transformation: 'The academic prejudices and obsessions of centuries dissolved in moments. Laboratories were built, science masters engaged, workshops and lathes and model furnaces became common.'[96] Marlborough, Sevenoaks, and Dauntsey's were especially notable in the nineteen-sixties for their pioneering work in the field of technological studies and activities in schools.[97]

The abolition of both maintained and direct-grant grammar schools in the mid-nineteen-seventies has been an astounding windfall for the independent Public Schools. As late as 1971 Anthony Sampson saw the maintained grammar schools as advancing upon and in some respects moving ahead of the great Public Schools: they were not as well connected with the world of power, but they had taken over the ethos of *noblesse oblige* without losing their sense of down-to-earth realism: 'The ideals of self-help and self-improvement rank higher in practice; and in the Tory cabinet Heath, Barber, Walker and Thatcher are appropriate symbols of this ambition.'[98] Jonathan Gathorne-Hardy's very impressive study of 'the Public School phenomenon'—impressive not only in its vast erudition but its imaginative grasp of essentials—led him to concur with the diagnosis that Anthony Sampson had made. And yet in his final judgement he cannot in fact support it. In the mid-nineteen-seventies the Labour Government falsified the optimism of Anthony Sampson and Michael McCrum for a more just and egalitarian society. Jonathan Gathorne-Hardy's final verdict, which is indubitably correct, is this:

> The position today, therefore, is that the public schools continue to provide a very large number of people for the positions of comfort, status and (arguably) power than would be expected from the proportion they form of secondary schools; and this will increase and not, as seemed likely only a short time ago, diminish.[99]

CONCLUSION

In his 1964 election campaign Harold Wilson declared himself in favour of grammar schools for all. The logic was faulty, but the instinct was right. As Maurice Kogan has recently emphasized: 'For a long time (after 1945) the leading theme of Labour Party policy was meritocratic.'[100] Ellen Wilkinson and George Tomlinson, the Ministers of Education in the first post-war government, defended the selective, tripartite system of education. Technical difficulties in methods of selection, which educational psychologists began to concede, seemed capable of technical solutions.

In the immediate post-war world sociologists attacked elitism and elites; they seemed comparatively unconcerned about social classes and in some notable instances supported them not only as bulwarks of culture but of liberty. Curiously, the grammar school was equated with elites and attacked as the bastion of privilege (often by men who had been educated at expensive, independent boarding schools). Young, in *The Rise of the Meritocracy*, sneered at the High Master of Manchester Grammar School's support for meritocratic distinctions and sympathized with local education committees thwarted in their plans for comprehensive education: 'But they were up against grammar-school masters ... and, to the country's undying credit, this has usually been sufficient to condemn anything.'[101] The meritocracy and the grammar school are synonymous: 'The workshop of the world became the grammar school of the world.'[102]

Elites are not classes: if their recruitment is open they may substantially circumscribe social-class power. (Pareto grasped this point; Marx did not.) Classes, as T. S. Eliot knew, are produced and perpetuated by families; elites are the natural products of schools. For this reason Eliot mistrusted schools and was against spreading them.[103] A powerful and widespread argument in the post-war Western world (perhaps with Russia in mind) was that we needed protection from elites (however meritocratic) and classes would provide it.

Daniel Bell has never faltered in his support for elites and a meritocratic organization of 'post-industrial' societies; but the attack since the nineteen-forties has come from many sides. Raymond Aron argued that classes protect ordinary people from the oppression of elites: 'A classless society leaves the mass of the population without any possible means of defence against the elite.'[104] Wright Mills also distinguished sharply between classes and elites (and even between the power elite and the ruling class, although his unified power elite looks uncannily like the upper class of America's East Coast). Mills also saw elites as a threat to individual liberty, especially in a so-called 'mass society' which no longer had what he called 'publics' capable of resisting centralized power.[105]

In more recent years the neo-Marxists renewed the attack on elites (and selective grammar schools) claiming that they are still tied to class, but hide this fact behind a facade of meritocratic, educational credentials. It is curious that the neo-Marxists focus their attack on the very meritocracy that has circumscribed class power; the attack centres on 'IQ-ism' and 'credentialism' as providing the criteria for elite recruitment. These are supposed to be merely 'legitimating ideologies' which sustain middle-class 'hegemony'.

This kind of argument, as advanced for instance by Paul Henderson in England[106] (and by Bowles and Gintis in America[107]), simply misses the target (and shows a very real ignorance of English society above small shopkeeper levels). Clerks and teachers are not 'hegemonic', and it is a patent logical absurdity to put the middle at the top. Henderson says: 'My argument is that because of their dominance in the class structure, the middle class are able to select and define those behavioural characteristics which are to be considered "intelligent".'

The imagined 'dominance' of ironmongers and commercial travellers simply diverts attention from the great, commanding heights of power, wealth, and privilege. And the almost incredible irony is that this facile, ill-conceived, and really very foolish social analysis undermines the only serious opposition that real power and dominance have recently faced.

The way to put these matters right will be outlined in the final chapter of this book. (Of course, there can be no question of simply putting the clock back; we need more selection than formerly, not less; a much richer and more varied provision for diverse talents as and when these are detected.) But at this point the aim is analysis rather than prescription. What still remains very elusive is the politics of the campaign against the grammar school. Only a minority of the English people approve of comprehensive schools—Gallop Polls of the mid-nineteen-seventies showed some 40 per cent. of the population approving (41 per cent. of the manual working class).[108]

If a think-tank had been established to consider how the recent spectacular advance of the manual working class in competition with the upper classes could be halted and preferably reversed, it could hardly have failed to recommend the sovereign remedy—the dissolution of the grammar schools. If the think-tank had wanted to make doubly sure that progress would be not only halted but reversed, it would have added a strong recommendation for mixed-ability teaching. The real and persistent problem of the unskilled worker's family has led to totally erroneous conclusions about 'the working class' and the grammar schools that served them well. What has happened is perhaps just another illustration and example of 'hegemony'.

NOTES

1. *Early Leaving: A Report of the Central Advisory Council for Education (England)*, HMSO, London, 1954.
2. D. V. Glass (Ed.), *Social Mobility in Britain*, Routledge and Kegan Paul, London, 1954.
3. J. Floud, 'Education and social class in the welfare state', in A. V. Judges (Ed.), *Looking Forward in Education*, Faber, London, 1955.
4. J. Floud, A. H. Halsey, and F. M. Martin, *Social Class and Educational Opportunity*, Heinemann, London, 1956.
5. M. Young, *The Rise of the Meritocracy 1870–2033*, Penguin Books, Harmondsworth, 1961. The 'meritocracy' and grammar schools are more or less equated in this book: see pp. 46 and 49.
6. *Higher Education* (the 'Robbins Report'), HMSO, London, 1963, App. One, pp. 46–51.
7. Nicholas Hans, 'The independent schools and the liberal professions', in J. A. Lauwerys and N. Hans (Eds.), *The Year Book of Education*, Evans Bros., London, 1950.
8. H. Jenkins and D. Caradog Jones, 'Social class of Cambridge alumni', *British Journal of Sociology*, **1** (1950).
9. J. Floud, 'Educational opportunity and social mobility', in *The Year Book of Education*, Evans Bros., 1950.
10. *Early Leaving: A Report of the Central Advisory Council for Education (England)*, HMSO, 1954, p. 17, Table J.
11. R. H. Tawney, *Equality*, Allen and Unwin, London, 1931, p. 296. Skilled workmen (1926): 21.0 per cent.; unskilled: 4.0 per cent.; no occupation: 1.0 per cent.; domestic servants: 2.2 per cent.; seamen, soldiers, etc.: 3.8 per cent.
12. J. Floud, A. H. Halsey, and F. M. Martin, *Social Class and Educational Opportunity*, Heinemann, 1956, p. 29, Table 1. Skilled manual fathers (1943): 20.6 per cent.; unskilled manual: 4.8 per cent.; unclassified: 2.4 per cent.
13. *Ibid.*, p. 30, Table 2.
14. Ronald King, *Values and Involvement in a Grammar School*, Routledge and Kegan Paul, London, 1969, p. 20, Table 1.
15. J. W. B. Douglas, *The Home and the School*, MacGibbon and Kee, 1964, p. 150, Table VI(a).
16. *15 to 18: Report of the Central Advisory Council for Education*, Vol. 2 (Surveys), HMSO, London, 1960, p. 112, Table viii.
17. *Higher Education*, HMSO, 1963, App. One, p. 40, Table 2. These percentages are calculated from the unweighted sample numbers.
18. *Ibid.*, p. 231, Table K1.
19. J. Floud, 'The educational experience of the adult population of England and Wales', in D. V. Glass (Ed.), *Social Mobility in Britain*, Routledge and Kegan Paul, 1954, p. 129, Table 7(b).
20. *Ibid.*, p. 107.
21. D. V. Glass and J. R. Hall, 'A description of a sample inquiry into social mobility in Great Britain', in Glass (Ed.), *ibid.*, p. 93, Table 3.
22. Calculated from J. Floud, 'The educational experience of the adult population of England and Wales', Glass (Ed.), *ibid.*, p. 130, Table 9.
23. J. Floud, A. H. Halsey, and F. M. Martin, *Social Class and Educational Opportunity*, Heinemann, 1956, p. 29, Table 1.
24. *Ibid.*, p. 30, Table 2.
25. R. King, *Values and Involvement in a Grammar School*, Routledge and Kegan Paul, 1969, p. 20, Table 1.
26. C. Lacey, *Hightown Grammar*, Manchester University Press, 1970, p. 27.
27. *Ibid.*, p. 28.
28. H. Himmelweit, 'Social status and secondary education since the 1944 Act: some data

for London', in D. V. Glass (Ed.), *Social Mobility in Britain*, Routledge and Kegan Paul, 1954.

29. R. H. Tawney, *Equality*, Allen and Unwin, London, 1931, p. 296.
30. These figures are taken from O. Banks, *Parity and Prestige in English Education*, Routledge and Kegan Paul, London, 1955.
31. See *Early Leaving: A Report of the Central Advisory Council for Education (England)*, HMSO, 1954, p. 17, Table J.
32. *15 to 18*, Vol. 2 (Surveys), HMSO, 1960, p. 112, Table viii.
33. *Ibid.*
34. These percentages are calculated from the raw data in *Higher Education*, HMSO, 1963, App. One, p. 40, Table 2. Out of 2,696 children, 1,176 were from skilled manual homes and 479 from unskilled.
35. *Ibid.*, these percentages are calculated from the raw data in App. One, p. 45, Table 7. Out of 92,010 leavers whose fathers' occupations were known, 40,820 were from skilled homes and 15,120 from unskilled.
36. *Ibid.*, App. One, Tables 3, 4, 5, and 6, pp. 41–44.
37. *Ibid.*, Table 7, p. 45.
38. *Ibid.*, para 10, p. 45.
39. *Ibid.*, calculations based on data in App. One, Table 7, p. 45.
40. C. Lacey, *Hightown Grammar*, Manchester University Press, 1970, p. xi.
41. *Ibid.*, Table 19, p. 30.
42. *Ibid.*, Appendix 2, p. 198. The percentages are calculated from the figures in this table.
43. *Ibid.*, Table 15, p. 27. The percentages are calculated from the figures in this table.
44. J. Floud and A. H. Halsey, 'Intelligence tests, social class and selection for secondary schools', *British Journal of Sociology*, **8** (1957).
45. J. Floud, A. H. Halsey, and F. M. Martin, *Social Class and Educational Opportunity*, Heinemann, 1956, Table 2, p. 30.
46. H. Himmelweit, 'Social status and secondary education since the 1944 Act: some data for London', in D. V. Glass (Ed.), *Social Mobility in Britain*, Routledge and Kegan Paul, 1954.
47. Marjorie E. Ainsworth and Eric J. Batten, *The Effects of Environmental Factors on Secondary Educational Attainment in Manchester: A Plowden Follow-Up*, Macmillan, London 1974. The method of ensuring the comparability of the raw marks obtained by 1,544 pupils in the various school subjects in fifty-three schools is described (pp. 13–14).
48. *15 to 18*, Vol. 2 (Surveys), HMSO, 1960, p. x.
49. J. Floud, A. H. Halsey, and F. M. Martin, *Social Class and Educational Opportunity*, Heinemann, 1956, p. 148.
50. *Report of the Schools Inquiry (Taunton) Commission (1868)*, Vol. 3, p. 43.
51. The 'Taunton Report', Vol. 9, p. 151.
52. The 'Taunton Report', Vol. 5, p. 594.
53. Brian Simon, *Education and the Labour Movement 1870–1920*, Lawrence and Wishart, 1965, p. 181.
54. *Ibid.*, p. 185. Simon is citing a reference in Banks to a not altogether convincing, and not very expert, private-enterprise survey: see O. Banks, *Parity and Prestige in English Secondary Education*, Routledge and Kegan Paul, 1955, p. 29. Simon's purpose in doing so is to advance the altogether implausible argument that the Higher Grade School was really the precursor of his cherished 'common school' which was nipped in the bud and superseded in the interests of class-dominated and socially divisive educational system intended to exclude the working classes from superior forms of education (pp. 238–239). The truth is the precise opposite of this: political strategy aimed to provide superior schools which were really worth while for working-class children to go to.
55. F. Musgrove, 'Middle class education and employment in the nineteenth century; *Economic History Review*, **14** (1961).

56. *Report of the Royal Commission on Secondary Education (1895)* Vol. 4, Question 16, 943.
57. *Ibid.*, p. 89.
58. Quoted in Brian Simon, *Education and the Labour Movement 1870–1920*, Lawrence and Wishart, 1965, p. 272.
59. R. King, *Values and Involvement in a Grammar School*, Routledge and Kegan Paul, 1969, Table 1, p. 20.
60. C. Lacey, *Hightown Grammar*, Manchester University Press, 1970, p. 24.
61. *Ibid.*, Table 13, p. 23.
62. *Ibid.*, Table 67, p. 200.
63. *Ibid.*, p. 187.
64. *Ibid.*, Table 66, p. 199.
65. *Ibid.*, App. 3, pp. 199–203.
66. *Ibid.*, p. 168.
67. J. E. Floud *et al.*, 'Social class and educational opportunity', in Harold Silver (Ed.), *Equal Opportunity in Education*, Methuen, London, 1973, pp. 150–156.
68. Brian Jackson and Dennis Marsden, *Education and the Working Class*, Routledge and Kegan Paul, London, 1962, p. 152.
69. *Ibid.*, p. 197.
70. *Early Leaving*, HMSO, London, 1954, App. 2, Table 9.
71. B. Jackson and D. Marsden, *Education and the Working Class*, Routledge and Kegan Paul, 1962, p. 132.
72. Correlli Barnett, *The Collapse of British Power*, Eyre Methuen, 1972, p. 33.
73. Eton, Charterhouse, Harrow, Merchant Taylor's, Rugby, St. Paul's, Shrewsbury, Westminster, Winchester: the nine schools included in the 'Clarendon Report' on the Public Schools (1864).
74. Nicholas Hans, *New Trends in Education in the Eighteenth Century*, Routledge and Kegan Paul, London, 1951, p. 19.
75. Nicholas Hans, 'The independent schools and the liberal professions', *Year Book of Education*, Evans Bros., London, 1950.
76. R. K. Kelsall, 'Self-recruitment in four professions', in D. V. Glass (Ed.), *Social Mobility in Britain*, Routledge and Kegan Paul, London, 1954, p. 310, Table 2.
77. Morris Ginsberg, 'Interchange between social classes', *Economic Journal*, December **1929.**
78. A. Giddens, 'Elites in the British class structure', *Sociological Review*, **20** (1972).
79. Noel Annan, 'The intellectual aristocracy', in J. H. Plumb (Ed.), *Studies in Social History*, Longmans, Green and Co., London, 1955, p. 247.
80. 'Competitive examinations', *Quarterly Review*, **108** (1860), No. 216.
81. R. K. Kelsall, *Higher Civil Servants in Britain*, Routledge and Kegan Paul, London, 1955, Table 5, p. 78.
82. *Ibid.*, pp. 84–85.
83. R. K. Kelsall, 'Recruitment to the higher civil service: how has the pattern changed?', in P. Stanworth and A. Giddens (Eds.), *Elites and Power in British Society*, Cambridge University Press, 1974, p. 176.
84. R. K. Kelsall, *Higher Civil Servants in Britain*, Routledge and Kegan Paul, 1955, p. 124.
85. Anthony Sampson, *The New Anatomy of Britain*, Hodder and Stoughton, London, 1971, p. 140.
86. Sir Michael Cary (Environment), Eton; Sir Antony Part (Trade and Industry), Harrow; Sir Ronald Melville (Aviation Supply), Charterhouse; Sir Martin Flett (Defence), St. Paul's.
87. See A. Sampson, *The New Anatomy of Britain*, Hodder and Stoughton, 1971, p. 279.
88. Jonathan Gathorne-Hardy, *The Public School Phenomenon*, Hodder and Stoughton, London, 1977, p. 382.

89. Oscar Grusky, 'Career patterns and characteristics of British naval officers', *British Journal of Sociology*, **26** (1975).
90. A. Sampson, *The New Anatomy of Britain*, Hodder and Stoughton, 1971, p. 139.
91. See *The Director*, September 1973.
92. J. Gathorne-Hardy, *The Public School Phenomenon*, Hodder and Stoughton, 1977, p. 382.
93. *Ibid.*, p. 378.
94. For a singularly depressing account of the Sheffield comprehensive school that was formerly King Edward VII Grammar School, see Graham Turner, 'Two schools, two worlds: who wins?', *Sunday Telegraph*, 2 July 1978. The headmaster concedes the possibility of 'a colossal blunder' in going comprehensive.
95. John Porter, *The Vertical Mosaic*, University of Toronto Press, 1975, p. 92.
96. J. Gathorne-Hardy, *The Public School Phenomenon*, Hodder and Stoughton, 1977, p. 371.
97. G. T. Page, *Engineering Among the Schools*, Institution of Mechanical Engineers, 1965.
98. A. Sampson, *The New Anatomy of Britain*, Hodder and Stoughton, 1971, p. 145.
99. J. Gathorne-Hardy, *The Public School Phenomenon*, Hodder and Stoughton, 1977, p. 383.
100. Maurice Kogan, *The Politics of Educational Change*, Manchester University Press, 1978, p. 31.
101. M. Young, *The Rise of the Meritocracy 1870–2033*, Penguin Books, Harmondsworth, 1961, p. 49.
102. *Ibid.*, p. 46.
103. T. S. Eliot, *Notes Towards a Definition of Culture*, Faber, London, 1948, pp. 35–49.
104. Raymond Aron, 'Social structure and the ruling class', *British Journal of Sociology*, **I** (1950).
105. C. Wright Mills, *The Power Elite*, Oxford University Press, New York, 1956, pp. 298–299, 324.
106. Paul Henderson, 'Class structure and the concept of intelligence', in R. Dale *et al.* (Eds.), *Schooling and Capitalism*, Routledge and Kegan Paul, London, 1976.
107. Samuel Bowles and Herbert Gintis, 'I.Q. in the U.S. class structure', in J. Karabel and A. H. Halsey (Eds.), *Power and Ideology in Education*, Oxford University Press, New York, 1977.
108. Ivan Reid, *Social Class Differences in Britain*, Open Books, 1977, Table 7.30, p. 230.

CHAPTER 6

Educational Opportunity, Equality, and Social Mobility

The development of equality of educational opportunity was one of the most hopeful and civilized features of Western industrialized societies in the first half of this century. It was discredited by the early nineteen-sixties. The charge was conservatism: it did not promote social equality but subverted it. It legitimated and reinforced the status quo. Equality of educational opportunity made the unacceptable acceptable: marked and persistent differences of power and position in a deeply unequal society. The pursuit of equality, on the one hand, and of equality of educational opportunity, on the other, are now widely seen as representing traditions of thought which are fundamentally and perhaps irreconcilably opposed.[1]

The French sociologist Raymond Boudon writes about 'IEO' and 'ISO' and the gap between them. IEO is inequality of educational opportunity, and this, says Boudon, has been declining in Western industrial societies since 1945; ISO is inequality of social opportunity, and this, says Boudon, has been increasing. IEO fell off steadily after the Second World War, but 'this decrease in IEO apparently had no effect on economic inequality'. It entirely escapes Boudon that it was never intended to do so. He proceeds: 'Indeed, the educational growth witnessed in all Western industrial countries since 1945 has been accompanied by an increase rather than a decrease in economic inequality. ...'[2] While educational systems have become more egalitarian, the societies they serve have become less.

THE OPPORTUNITY MODEL OVERTHROWN

The opportunity model is a simple open-competition model. Equality of educational opportunity in post-war England meant basically open competition for the limited number of grammar school places. It also meant getting an education appropriate to your abilities, but that was really the same thing. The competition was a sorting process; the only problems were technical ones of test efficiency. This open competition for grammar school places was seen as the basis not only of a just educational system but of a just society: those who won places could be expected to win prizes against all-comers for the rest of their lives.

The just society would be promoted through the destruction of 'status inheritance'. There would ideally be a purely chance or random connexion between a father's social position and his sons': the five sons of the high court judge would end up 'randomly distributed', one each in the Registrar General's five 'social

119

classes', and so would the five dustman's sons. These were the 'expected frequencies', and sociologists began to scrutinize 'observed' or actual frequencies to see if they were markedly different. The educational system would secure social justice because it was a means of randomizing the association between paternal and filial status. This ideal is easy to ridicule, but it remains a high conception of social justice and we lose sight of it at our peril.

The opportunity model, whatever its deficiencies, was easy to understand. The same cannot be said of the 'equality model' which is now superseding it. A 'weak' concept of equality has now been challenged by a 'strong' concept, we are told. Anthony Crosland made the distinction in 1962 in his book, *The Conservative Enemy*, and the British Labour Party slowly and reluctantly moved from the weak concept to the strong.[3] The difficulty in the ensuing debate on education is to know: equality of what? There are various contenders: 'inputs', 'outputs'; treatments, results; pupils, schools; educational systems, societies. James Coleman, whose work in this field in America has been monumental, concedes in a recent article that he now finds the terms of the debate virtually meaningless.[4]

There is a straightforward sense in which greater social equality furthers equality of opportunity: it makes the competition from the very outset fairer and more efficient. In the classical post-war opportunity model the competition was clearly loaded when children entered it from widely different social positions of weakness and strength. The use of relatively culture-free intelligence tests was no answer for children who were so radically disadvantaged that they could not reach first base.

There have been two principal attempts to make the contenders more equal: one is compensatory education (i.e. unequal educational treatments); the other (mainly in America) is the 'quota'. The first, unfortunately, has not proved very effective; the second, equally unfortunately, has. The first is difficult; the second immoral. In 1967 the 'Plowden Report' on primary schools saw compensation ('unequally generous treatment') not as an alternative to equality of educational opportunity but, quite explicitly, as a way of promoting it.[5] So ineffective have compensatory education programmes been that their directors may now recommend that the beneficiaries should not even enter the race.[6]

The difficulty of making children roughly equal at the start is exceeded only by the difficulty of making them roughly equal at the end. This is one of the strongest conceptions of equality of all: there should at the end of the day be equality of results. This, it is now abundantly clear, is wholly impossible without massive and unprecedented intervention in family life and the lives of very young children. As Coleman has said: 'No one except an advocate of state omnipotence with full power to extract a child from its unequalizing family environment could consistently maintain a definition of equality of educational opportunity in terms of results.'[7] Far-reaching 'ecological intervention' would be needed, as Urie Bronfenbrenner recognizes. It would require nothing less than 'major changes in the institutions of our (American) society'.[8]

It was the well-substantiated difficulties encountered by early-intervention programmes in America, like 'Headstart', that led Arthur Jensen to write his celebrated paper 'How much can we boost IQ?' for the *Harvard Educational Review* in 1969. The aim of compensatory education, said Jensen, 'had been utterly unrealized on any of the large compensatory programs that have been evaluated so far'. His paper set out to offer a psychologist's interpretation of 'the uniform failure of compensatory programs wherever they have been tried'. Some small-scale, intensive experiments, usually focused on specific abilities (rather than global 'cognitive development'), seemed to have had more success. Jensen's careful and painstaking consideration of the evidence leads him to emphasize the diversity of mental abilities, the need to cater in schools for this wide range, and the folly of defining equality as uniformity.[9]

If people cannot be made equal, they can be treated as if they were. The short-cut solution to the obstinate problem of human inequality is the quota. This, as Daniel Bell points out, introduces an entirely new, and thoroughly objectionable, principle of rights into American society.[10] (Actually it is a very old one: it is the ancient ascriptive principle of 'birth'.) To circumvent allegedly inequitable competitive processes, the winners are declared in advance. The sociologist's vocabulary of 'overrepresentation' and 'underrepresentation' is now deeply entrenched in the equality debate. Quotas have been applied most openly and systematically in recent years to black Americans (for an account and discussion of these developments, see below, Chapter 8). Quotas are a standing temptation in all highly plural societies. They may have value as a short-term expedient (for instance, to help a backward group to 'take off'); but in the end they will promote neither justice nor equality in any meaningful sense. They will destroy both.

Equality either at the starting line or the finishing line of schooling is impossible; so is equality of opportunity in the sense of completely random association between parental and filial status. But that is no reason for not working towards the impossible, even though it is finally unattainable. The real problem that has arisen in recent years is the pursuit of equality as an alternative to, or even in opposition to, equality of opportunity. The strong and the weak forms of equality are not necessarily enemies, although they can be made so. Greater equality can be the handmaiden of equality of opportunity and help to convert the promise into reality. Both have at the centre of their concern those who are the victims of their social inheritance. Coleman put the two concepts together in harness, and not in opposition, when he wrote after directing the major study of education and equality of opportunity in America: 'Schools are successful only in so far as they reduce the dependence of a child's opportunities upon his social origins. ... Equality of educational opportunity implies, not merely "equal" schools, but equally effective schools, whose influence will overcome the differences in starting point of children from different social groups.'[11] There are no wholly successful schools in these terms; but within the classical opportunity model they had steady and increasing (and actually measurable) success in neutralizing parents. There is no doubt that for the disadvantaged school matters and that a de-schooling policy which seriously eroded the first five or six years of school life would have one principal consequence: still more advantage to the already advantaged.

SOCIAL MOBILITY: PRELIMINARY CONSIDERATIONS AND THE 1949 MOBILITY STUDY

The sign of opportunity is mobility. Children are able to 'better themselves' and improve on the social position of their parents. Opportunity is indicated by reduced 'status inheritance' and influence of 'class'. By this indicator England has been outstandingly successful in promoting equality of opportunity—significantly more so than America. In England education has more influence on occupation and income; class has less. Indeed, class seems to have significantly less influence in England than in 'new' countries like Canada and Australia.

A few simple preliminary points have to be made before considering the often highly technical findings of inquiries into social mobility. These studies make use of mathematical measures such as correlation coefficients, indices of association, path analysis, and indices of inequality: these show the strength of connexions (for instance between the status of fathers and sons) and the relative power of different influences (for instance education compared with social origins) in particular populations and make international and cross-cultural comparisons possible. Path analysis is at present very modish. It is a form of regression analysis popularized by Christopher Jencks and his colleagues in *Inequality* which purports to show the relative weight of different influences that may underlie or contribute to a simple correlation coefficient.

But there are certain basic simplicities that should not be lost sight of. The first one is this: what goes up must come down. If the society is not expanding its opportunities and making more room at the top (through sophisticated economic growth, imperialism, declining fertility, or military conquest), movement up is possible only if there is corresponding movement down. This is variously known as 'exchange', 'circulation', or 'pure' mobility.

There is an obvious corollary: if there has been more movement down than up (net downward mobility), there must have been some expansion at the bottom to accommodate it. That means a growth in relatively low-level jobs. (It is crucially important to keep this very clearly in mind when considering the remarkable evidence produced by the famous British mobility study of 1949 conducted by Glass.) The movement that arises from expansion of positions at any level is over and above the movement based on exchange: it is 'structural mobility'.[12] It is also virtually irresistible mobility; it will tend to happen whether there are people 'really qualified' for it or not.

Logically there is no limit to the amount of exchange or circulation mobility (except the smaller numbers 'up' than 'down'). Under conditions of perfect competition everybody in every generation who is born 'upstairs' could change position with somebody from below. (The actual picture is never quite so tidy; 'generations' overlap. They are not cohorts which stand end-on.) But structural mobility is a 'plus'. It is sometimes said that it should be discounted in studies of education and mobility. It is not entirely clear why. Another simple preliminary point is this: education cannot create opportunities; it can only help you to seize them. There will usually be competition to seize structural no less than exchange opportunities.

There are particular pitfalls in international comparisons. One concerns the elementary issue of the 'amount' of mobility (and a related problem, its 'distance'). The amount depends on the number of layers, classes, or status levels that have been used. The safest procedure is to compare movement simply between manual and non-manual employment. This makes for reliability (but with some loss of validity). A final point is this: the variable 'education' can mean different and non-comparable things in different national studies. Often it is 'measured' in terms of years spent at school. This is a meaningful measure in America, but much less so in England, where type of education is a more effective discriminator. Some recent comparative studies have been sensitive to this. These will receive particular attention in this chapter.

There have been four post-war social mobility surveys in Britain based on national samples: the first was the 1949 London School of Economics study by Glass (sample size 3,500);[13] the second was a subsidiary part of a political study (of voting) carried out in 1963 by Butler and Stokes (sample size 2,000);[14] the third was the Nuffield College, Oxford, study of 1972 (sample size 10,000);[15] the fourth is George Psacharopoulos's study also of 1972 (sample size 8,000).[16] They are not all directly comparable in all respects. The last is the most technically accomplished of the four.

The difficulty is the 1949 (Glass) survey. It is renowned. It has been a massive international sociological datum for three decades, and it has done incalculable harm. It offers an authoritative image of Britain which shapes inquiry and social policy; important and influential books are written which draw on the evidence of 'a rigid, relatively closed and stable society which the book presented'.[17] It offers a (highly statistical) picture of Britain in the first half of the twentieth century, not as a land of increasing but actually diminishing opportunity in spite of its expanding educational provision. Of course the work is thirty years old, but it is not even a good historical document; it is a serious distortion of the past. The picture of opportunity in Britain which it offers is not only empirically implausible; it is a logical absurdity and an arithmetical impossibility. It is the cornerstone of post-war British sociology.

The essential and basic difficulty can be stated very simply: the national sample of men investigated in 1949 had experienced more downward than upward social mobility over a period when the relative number of superior opportunities had certainly not contracted and had almost certainly significantly increased. Although it is quite extraordinarily difficult to get the basic arithmetic of mobility out of Glass's statistical tables, the following calculations can be made from data in *Social Mobility in Britain*: by putting together the information in Tables 3 and 4 (p. 184) we can calculate that 35 per cent (1,228) of the total sample of 3,497 men were at the same social level as their fathers; 29 per cent (1,026) had moved to a higher position but 36 per cent (1,243) had moved down. The net downward mobility was therefore 7 per cent. This is not a statistic that Glass actually computes or to which he draws our attention. He emphasizes stability: 'In general the picture of rather high stability over time is confirmed.'

A more detailed examination of a subsample of 513 men gives the same essential picture of net downward mobility. It is possible to work out from other tables which give a breakdown by decade since the eighteen-nineties (e.g. Table 8, p. 188) that there was no improvement during the first half of this century. Net downward mobility was apparently greater at the end of the period than at the beginning.

The investigation carried out by Stokes and Butler was fourteen years later, but the overlap is substantial. They calculated net mobility rates very simply by dividing their population into a manual working class and a non-manual middle class and noting the movement of sons between the two. When routine non-manual workers were put 'below the line', in the working class, 15.7 per cent. of the sample had moved 'up' and 10.1 per cent. had moved 'down'. When the routine non-manual workers were placed above the line, in the middle class, 18.8 per cent. of the sample had gone up and 10.8 per cent. had gone down.[18]

Total mobility is substantially understated by using only two status levels (Glass used seven): movement within rather than between these two broad categories is missed, and so this study indicates that less than 30 per cent. of sons had 'moved'; in the Glass study it is 65 per cent. But in the inquiry by Stokes and Butler they moved in the right direction. On the basis of the first breakdown there was 5.6 per cent. net upward mobility; in the second 8.0 per cent. Glass's study has 7.0 per cent. in the opposite direction. There is no doubt that Glass has given us a picture of British society which is the precise opposite of the truth.

Of course the oddities of Glass's study have not passed unnoticed. But what is quite remarkable is the extraordinarily muted comment that has been made over the past quarter of a century on what must rank high among this century's more serious sociological blunders. This near-silence is no credit to British scholarship.

The American sociologist, C. Arnold Anderson, made a restrained comment in a footnote in 1961: 'The downward drift of net mobility in the sample is puzzling; it may arise from the mixed "occupational" and "status" categories used or there may be deficiencies in the sample or the scale of status.'[19] These reservations did not deter Anderson from using Glass's statistics in a major comparative study; indeed, he states in the main text: 'Since the data for Britain are more detailed, we make them the main object of analysis.'

Westergaard, writing in 1975, clearly understands the only conditions under which net downward mobility can occur. He refers to structural changes such as 'shifts in occupational structure' and changes in class differences in fertility: 'That apart, however, there must be as many people coming down the ladder as there are people going up it, from one generation to the next. ...' But then in a footnote he completely endorses the opportunity picture presented by Glass. He refers to comment that has been made on 'the large volume of downward mobility recorded in the 1949 survey as a notable feature of the pattern of social circulation in Britain'. He does not dissent from this view and adds his own gloss: 'The frequency of downward movement shown there follows, as an arithmetical necessity, from the frequency of upward movement (across the manual/non-manual line) in conjunction with the large and, as the occupational categories were defined, fairly stable share of manual workers in the male population over time.'[20] This is almost unbelievable rubbish. It is precisely the alleged stability of the proportion of manual workers that makes net downward mobility impossible. Arithmetic, even of the most elementary kind, knows no such necessity as Westergaard claims. The most rudimentary logic requires precisely the opposite.

Since the mid-nineteen-seventies a little more critical attention has been directed to the anomalies of the 1949 LSE mobility inquiry. Ridge points out that the original investigators showed some sign of unease about the occupational changes in Britain that their study implied. 'They too seem to have been somewhat surprised, and attempted by manipulations of census statistics to show that the same trend can be observed on a status scale other than that of Hall and Jones.'[21] It is true that Glass tried to square his picture of English society with the picture to be found in Census data and Bowley's studies of population and income.[22] Geoff Payne and his colleagues have also pointed to Glass's footnote which considers without resolving the inconsistencies between Bowley's data and his own. Payne's very technical and expert reappraisal of the 1949 survey leads him to the conclusion that 'there are major factual inaccuracies and logical improbabilities in the LSE study which call for explanation, and for which no adequate explanation currently exists'. He has no tidy explanation to offer and it may be at this date there is none: 'It is still an open question as to what went wrong.'[23]

Amidst all the involved technicalities there is one basic and quite simple issue: did the proportion of manual workers grow, remain constant, or contract? Only if it expanded does the Glass study make logical or arithmetical sense. The overlap of the generations studied, as Noble points out, raises problems of comparison with the national context at any given point in time. 'Despite this it nevertheless remains important to keep the occupational structure in mind when evaluating social mobility data.'[24] When evaluating Glass the national 'occupational structure' is central.

Goldthorpe, like Westergaard, writes of social mobility as an 'arithmetical requirement' of particular circumstances; but he gets the equation right. When there is expansion at the top, people of lower rank are in effect 'forced' to move up. Goldthorpe is writing about the 'Nuffield' mobility survey of 1972 and draws particular attention to structural changes since 1940. He points to the tendency in modern industrial societies for the proportion of non-manual occupations to expand and manual ones to contract; such changes mean that: '... a large measure of intergenerational stability at the higher levels of the class structure can, of course, coexist with much upward movement into these levels.'[25] This is precisely the picture painted by Blau and Duncan of mid-twentieth-century America: there has been extensive movement 'up' but 'no compensatory increase in downward mobility from white-collar origins; on the contrary, increasing proportions of those originating at this level remained there'.[26]

Glass gives precisely the opposite picture for Britain in the first half of the twentieth century. Of course, he is dealing with an earlier period than Goldthorpe. It is possible that Britain's experience was the opposite of other highly developed industrial countries. Wright Mills has demonstrated a spectacular growth of middle-class compared with working-class occupations in America in the period 1870 to 1950.[27] Britain may not have had such an extreme experience; it would be altogether remarkable if it were the reverse.

The Registrar General's occupational returns for the first half of this century have received intensive scrutiny and his various categories have been regrouped and recombined. Goldthorpe[28] and Giddens[29] stress the relative stability but nevertheless moderate decline in the proportion of male manual workers; Noble shows a steady fall in the proportion of male manual workers between 1911 and 1951 (with a sharp acceleration after that);[30] Marsh emphasizes the decline during this period of semi-skilled and unskilled manual workers;[31] Payne shows a significant decline in 'blue collar' workers (again accelerating sharply after 1951).[32] Only the French Marxist theorist, Poulantzas, claims that England's working class has actually increased, and he locates the major increase precisely where everybody else says it most rapidly declined. With the loss of Empire, says Poulantzas, Britain's administrative superstructure shrank; only America had an expanding middle class, as she became an imperial power and the administrative capital of the world.[33]

Glass makes adjustments to the Registrar General's data and concludes that the early decades of this century saw '... some increase in the proportion of "manual" as compared with "non-manual" occupations'.[34] This is almost certainly wrong. Robert Havighurst drew the only possible conclusion from Glass's picture: that it '... must be due to an actual decrease of middle and higher status positions in the past half century'.[35] But in any event only a massive increase in the size of the manual working class compared with the non-manual middle class would have made possible the high rate of net downward mobility implicit in his data.

There are, indeed, phases of industrial development (and 'modernization') in which net downward social mobility will almost certainly occur. Studies of early nineteenth-century industrial Lancashire show a vast expansion of low-level jobs requiring little skill; they were taken by young people whose fathers had often served long appreticeships to highly skilled trades which were now obsolescent. There was, at this early stage of industrialization, a high rate of net downward mobility.[36]

Early stages in the modernization of pre-literate societies show similar characteristics. There was substantial net downward mobility in Western Uganda (Toro) in the nineteen-forties and -fifties as the sons of cattlemen and large-scale Batoro cultivators moved (via an elementary mission-school education) into low-level wage employment as 'porters': messengers, routine clerks, post-boys, and the like.[37] But late nineteenth-century and early twentieth-century Britain is a quite different story: a highly developed, elaborate, mature capitalist system in which the balance was entirely the other way, with jobs of high sophistication rapidly increasing and relatively unskilled manual jobs diminishing. Glass has given us a picture of a backward, retrogressive society. His blunder has been extremely damaging. It was of a very high order of magnitude.

OPPORTUNITY IN BRITAIN AND ELSEWHERE

The Glass mobility study is not a set of scientific facts; it is a legitimating ideology for the destruction of opportunity in Britain. It fits tidily into the left-wing view of

Britain as socially rigid and class-ridden. It legitimates the destruction of precisely those institutions which have made that picture false.

Two especially striking facts are emerging from the Nuffield College study of social mobility. The first is the very high rate of intragenerational mobility. For the national sample of British adults investigated in 1972 opportunities had been life-long. The second is the large amount of long-distance social movement and the openness at the very top. Sixteen per cent. of the sons of unskilled workers (class VII) had made it to the highest occupational levels (classes I and II); 34 per cent. (815 out of 2,373) of the men in classes I and II had originated in the two manual occupational classes VI and VII.[38]

These patterns of recruitment to the highest ranks of administrative and managerial work over recent decades are, as Goldthorpe says, '... inconsistent with any idea of "closure" '. A very high proportion have come, whether intergenerationally or intragenerationally, 'from below'. What is especially notable in the Nuffield College data is that the service class of administrators and managers 'has recruited to a major extent, and regardless largely of class of origin, via worklife advancement'.[39] People growing up and making their careers in Britain since the nineteen-twenties have not been frustrated by the rigidities of a class society. Even taking a job on the factory floor at the age of fourteen proved not to be a life-sentence.

All this is another way of saying that 'status inheritance' in Britain, although far from random, has for some decades been low. And it has been decreasing. Britain has experienced in the past half century a significant shift from ascribed to achieved social status.

All mature capitalist societies have probably had a similar experience. There is good evidence that status inheritance tends to be greater in less developed than in highly developed capitalist economies.[40] Mobility data for Chicago in 1950 show a significant fall in status inheritance compared even with data for 1940.[41] In Britain there are similar, perhaps stronger, indications. When the LSE study of 1949 is compared with the Nuffield College study of 1972 and when different age levels within the 1972 study itself are compared, the decline in status inheritance is clear. The correlation between the status levels of fathers and sons in the 1949 data was 0.46; in the 1972 data it was only 0.36.[42]

In France in 1964 it was 0.469;[43] in America in 1962 it was 0.405. This degree of occupational status inheritance in America is given in the authoritative study of Blau and Duncan.[44] Jencks has corrected it for 'measurement error' and says the true coefficient is higher: 0.482.[45] He rounds this off to 0.50 and describes it as 'surprisingly small'.[46] Compared with British results in the past few years it is astonishingly large. George Psacharopoulos's recent national study yields a coefficient of only 0.265.[47]

Class in Australia seems to be at least as powerful an influence as in England—probably greater. An Australian National University study in 1967 showed the same degree of status inheritance as England: the correlation between the occupational levels of fathers and sons was 0.36. But a Melbourne survey of 1974–75 yields a coefficient very much higher: 0.44. The correlation of father's status with survey subjects' 'subjective class' (self-assigned status) was higher still: 0.48.[48] This suggests that class influence in Australia might be nearer the relatively high level in America than the relatively low English level.

There are two main problems that have to be kept in mind when making these comparisons: the first is that different studies may not be based on fathers of the same age or at the same point in their careers; the second is that a father's status may make a concealed or indirect contribution to his son's via education. When education is bought in an open market this is more likely; today most civilized countries have controlled this market. A more ingenious argument is that schooling is in any event constructed and conducted to reward children with a particular ('superior') kind of family upbringing. Those who are really determined to see England as a class-ridden society will search out all such devious connexions. But what is impressive is the consistent superiority of Britain whatever statistical measure or other systematic form of analysis and description is used. It is not possible to describe England in the terms that Porter applied to Canada in the mid-nineteen-sixties: immigration had been used as an alternative to educational reform and enterprise and so 'mobility deprivation continues'.[49] Canada remained in the grip of a '... class-bound education as exemplified by the classical college system in Quebec and the academic collegiate system in Ontario'.[50] His picture of status inheritance in Canada is confirmed rather than challenged by Wallace Clement's more recent study.[51] England comes well out of all international comparisons. Miller's 'index of inequality' places England as the most 'open' of the eighteen nations included in his comparative study;[52] when 'pure' social mobility (using Q-values) has been computed, England has come out ahead of a range of countries including Sweden, Denmark, and the United States.[53] Any particular study may leave doubts in the mind. What is impressive is their unanimity.

Twenty years ago there was a wave of scepticism about the ability of education to help very much in personal advancement and social mobility. Lipset and Bendix concluded in a famous book which they published in 1959 that industrial societies differed little in their rates of social mobility 'as measured by the shift across the manual–non-manual line'.[54] Different educational systems and provisions, it seemed, made no significant difference. Apparently unchanging rates over time in some industrial countries seemed to point to a similar conclusion.

The most prominent sceptics were Gosta Carrlson in Sweden and C. Arnold Anderson in America. On the basis of a study of men born in Sweden between 1899 and 1923 Carrlson concluded in a book he published in 1958: 'The factor of education does not come out of the analysis in the impressive manner we might have expected.'[55] Anderson put together surveys from a number of countries to test the view that 'in complex societies vertical mobility is closely dependent upon formal education'. He concluded that it was not. He found that while many children got a higher education than their fathers had enjoyed a much smaller number achieved higher social positions.[56]

Education is in fact much more efficient than these analysis of the nineteen-fifties suggested. Of course it is not an overwhelming determinant of social position; if it were, it would take the heart out of life as much as 'class'—and the high levels of intragenerational mobility that we enjoy in England would be impossible. But its efficiency is high and at the moment rising. It needs to rise somewhat higher still if we are to eliminate the considerable delayed or 'lagged' effects of class.

Countries are generally likely to be more 'open' if their educational and communications systems are developed; and individuals are more likely to 'get on' with education than without. These relationships are strong and 'significant'. But many influences other than education have a bearing on opportunity, and when all have been taken into account there is always a good deal of 'unexplained variance'. This may be social science's new term for luck.

In an ambitious thirteen-nation comparison Cutright found the highest rates of 'pure' or exchange social mobility where there was a high level of technological development and high intensity of 'communications' (education in a wide sense as indicated not only by literacy rates and schooling levels but the consumption of newsprint and the volume of domestic mail). The correlation between mobility rates and education thus conceived was higher than the correlation with technology: 'The higher the level of communications, the lower the occupational inheritance ($r = -0.83$).' The correlation with technology (energy consumption) was -0.74.[57] Other similarly extensive studies have shown school enrollment correlating with social mobility to a much higher degree than political stability, urbanization, achievement motivation, and per capita GNP.[58]

Education has been firmly reinstated as a factor of great importance in the promotion of social mobility and the limitation of status inheritance. But its importance varies considerably even among advanced industrial nations. One particularly important study of education and mobility in Britain and America uses the 1963 English data of Butler and Stokes and 'measures' education in England by type of school rather than 'years of schooling'. Education has a stronger influence on occupation in England ($r = 0.63$) than in America ($r = 0.57$). It is consonant with this picture that education has more influence on earnings in England than America (a correlation of 0.585 compared with 0.406).[59]

The relationship between a person's education and his occupational level is stronger than the relationship between his father's occupational level and his own in both England and America. In this simple sense education counts for more than the direct influence of 'class'. In France it does not. Whereas in England—using only the most conservative estimates—the correlation between your occupation and your education is certainly not less than 0.47 (this is Psacharopoulos's figure) and the correlation between your occupation and your father's socioeconomic status is not more than 0.36 (this is the 'Nuffield' figure), in France the position is precisely the reverse: 0.37 and 0.47 respectively.[60] It is no doubt true that industrial societies tend, in the very long run, to 'converge' and exhibit similar rates of social mobility and related characteristics. But in the meantime they are far from uniform; their variations are rooted in different historical traditions of educational organization, religion, and family life. We can change social opportunities by changing the educational system: there is no universal, automatic, and inexorable process called 'industrialization' which takes care of our problems of justice and equality and absolves us from making the effort.

The accompanying table presents in summary form comparative correlational data which show the weaker social effects of education in America than in Britain and the more powerful effects of class.

Education, occupation, income, and social class: the United States and Britain

		Correlation coefficients	
		United States	Britain
I	Education and occupation		
	(Treiman and Terrell, 1975)	0.57	0.63
II	Education and income		
	(Psacharopoulos, 1977)	0.33	0.40
	(Treiman and Terrell, 1975)	0.40	0.59
III	Class of origin and education		
	(Jencks et al., 1975; Psacharopoulos,		
	1977)	0.50	0.29
IV	Class of origin and occupation		
	(Hope, 1975)		0.46 (1949)
	(Blau and Duncan, 1967)	0.41 (1962)	
	(Hope, 1975)		0.36 (1972)
	(Psacharopoulos, 1977)		0.27 (1972)

Sources: See note 61.

INTERNAL BARRIERS AND CIRCULATION MOBILITY

One of the more facile antitheses in modern sociological literature is Turner's extensively cited distinction between 'sponsored' (British) and 'contest' (American) social mobility.[62] As 'ideal types' they were never logically convincing, and they violate the empirical evidence and common observation. At least in Britain academic posts are openly advertised in the national press and it is not dishonourable to apply without being invited to do so. Contacts are useful, even in Britain, but they do not have the remarkable power that studies of academic life in America (for instance by Caplow and McGee[63] and by Hagstrom[64]) make abundantly clear. England is the land of the Civil Service Commission, America is the land of the 'spoils system'. There is little doubt that Turner arrived at the precise opposite of the truth: in Britain mobility is preeminently 'contest'; in America it is preeminently sponsored.

The distinction is particularly relevant to considerations of circulation or exchange, as distinct from structural, mobility. (But the distinction should not be overemphasized: structural opportunities, too, can be either competed for or occupied through sponsorship.) Various studies have indicated that circulation mobility is lower in America than in England[65] or even Australia (but somewhat higher than in Italy).[66] Contest or sponsorship is one aspect of internal barriers which influence the extent of social circulation.

The eminent French sociologist, Raymond Boudon, has constructed a 'model' (the 'IEO–ISO model') of social mobility. This enables him to explore and explain impediments to, and the promotion of, circulation mobility. His model, he tells us, has revealed that 'the rigidity of stratification' is the principal impediment.[67] His IEO–ISO model has enabled him to proclaim the self-evident as if it were one of the more recondite truths of modern science: if there are obstacles to mobility, we are likely to have less of it.

Exchange mobility will occur when bankruptcy is easy and so is credit or saving on a sufficient scale to set up a new business and when enterprises die with the owner—or would do if the widow did not marry the apprentice. It will occur when 'marrying out of your class' is not greatly hindered by law or convention and when people who want important work done seriously look around for the best man for the job. It will be low wherever the family (perhaps backed by the Church) maintains its public and private influence and it will be reduced wherever bribery and corruption are rife. Circulation mobility rises with the cleasing of public, institutional morality. Education is at least a latent influence in favour of circulation: it provides relatively uncontaminated measures of personal worth for those who are looking for them; but it can increase the 'rigidites of stratification' as well as surmount them. It may be simply the accompaniment of social status instead of its determinant.

Education is the handmaiden of opportunity. The century after 1540 has been described by Lawrence Stone as 'the great age of social mobility': during these years 'English society experienced a seismic upheaval of unprecedented magnitude'.[68] It was also the century of England's 'educational revolution'. The grammar schools and the universities expanded to meet an invasion from all levels of society: 'So great was the boom—much greater than has hitherto been recognized—that all classes above a certain level took their part. ... Everyone was included except the very poor.'[69] But education did not create these new opportunities; it simply helped some people take them.

They were created by an access of 'new' land. The basis of opportunity and unprecedented rates of social mobility was an economic transformation, under-pinned by population growth, but arising directly from 'new' land which came from the Crown and the Church after the dissolution of the monasteries. This was the essential 'structural' change which made net upward mobility (notably the rise of the gentry) possible. An effective addition to England's land supply was made when some 30 per cent. of the total acreage of England was released on to the private market between 1534 and 1660. This extensive addition to England's 'structure' meant more room at the top.

But there was very considerable exchange mobility as well as structural mobility. Stone has anatomized this 'seismic upheaval' and has shown, especially in the land transactions of the time, how extensive were changes of individual fortune. His evidence makes it clear that this was 'a phase of unprecedented individual mobility both upwards and downwards'. He places manipulation of the land market as the most important source of mobility; marriage was also a key to social advance; and education brought its rewards. But education was often used (especially by newly risen gentry) to signal a change of status rather than to secure one.

It did both. The remarkable number of 'plebs' at Oxford and Cambridge were there to advance their status—and in the late sixteenth century were generally able to do so. (The peak of university expansion was in the sixteen-thirties; on Stone's calculations some 40 per cent. of students were from country gentry families, but a clear majority were 'plebeian'.) Stone sees opportunities for graduates in the secularization and modernization of the late-Tudor state; Kearney thinks this source of opportunity exaggerated.[70] The universities produced parsons, and it is true that many graduates—perhaps a third—looked for a career in the Church.[71] But a clerical career had many rewards for the ambitious, not all of them spiritual: 'A young man in 1550,' says Kearney, 'could do a lot worse than take up an ecclesiastical career.'[72]

In early seventeenth-century England the expansion of education began to outstrip opportunities which arose from 'circulation', or structural change, or both. There is evidence of significant numbers of 'alienated intellectuals' before the Civil War (who in retrospect were seen as one of its causes).[73] Structural mobility declined when there was no more 'new' land; circulation mobility declined as those who had risen consolidated their position. Thus in Northamptonshire: 'Within a couple of generations ... the flowing lava of local society had solidified. The county of rapid change became increasingly the county of rigid caste.'[74]

Those who had benefited from a century of opportunity now married among themselves; in the seventeen-thirties they converted coffee houses into clubs; they used schools and universities (and cavalry regiments) to celebrate and signal their rank. In short, from the end of the seventeenth century there was 'closure'. And perhaps one of the most effective ways of protecting superior status, preventing circulation, and promoting closure is corruption. Bribery, never of course absent, was now institutionalized—given a place of honour in English life. That is what 'rigidity of social stratification' means; it is far more reliable than educational credentials.

It is the antithesis of open competition. Institutionalized forms of open competition were central ingredients of the new public morality of early Victorian England; it went with the abolition of rotten boroughs and of the purchase of army commissions. It has been the basis of rates of circulation mobility which until only yesterday were probably without equal among the industrial nations of the world.

STRATIFICATION AND INNATE ABILITY

Equality of educational opportunity, it is said, must lead to a caste society. Social levels will be based on intelligence levels and must be more rigid than anything known in the past because intelligence is largely inherited. This vision was popularized in 1958 when Young published *The Rise of the Meritocracy*. In recent years it has been more powerfully reaffirmed in North America by Carl Bereiter and by Richard Herrnstein. Curiously, Cyril Burt drew precisely the opposite conclusion from the hereditary nature of intellectual endownment. Only very high rates of intergenerational mobility (ideally around 60 per cent. but perhaps 30 per cent. would suffice) could ensure a reasonably 'steady state' in which abilities remained roughly matched to occupational needs. Stability and social efficiency called for constant change from generation to generation.

Herrnstein speculates on the reasons for the violence of the recent attack on the concept of 'intelligence' and the refusal by well-disposed people even to consider the evidence that it is to a considerable extent inherited. (Daniel Bell has engaged in similar dismayed speculation on the 'populist revolt': 'One sees this in the derogation of the IQ and the denunciation of theories espousing a genetic basis of intelligence.')[75] Herrnstein considers that 'the measurement of intelligence is one of psychology's most telling accomplishments to date' and the evidence that intelligence is highly heritable virtually unassailable.

He is probably right. The fact that intelligence tests are used to 'legitimate' inequality, as well as measure it, is doubtless correct, too. The concept of intelligence and the technology of testing are not invalidated because they may be abused. What is much more open to doubt is the inference for social structures that Herrnstein makes. We are he says replacing 'arbitrary barriers' between classes with biological barriers: '... our society may be sorting itself willynilly into inherited castes.'

As we eliminate crude environmental differences within a nation and equalize the circumstances of life, the more certainly, says Herrnstein, will intellectual differences be inherited. Moreover, intelligence becomes more important in work as routine jobs are done by machines. Biological stratification arises precisely from our success in achieving 'relatively unimpeded social mobility'; the data on IQ and social differences, Herrnstein believes, show that it has already arrived. The future will see genetically based social classes become increasingly rigid: 'Greater wealth, health, freedom, fairness, and educational opportunity are not going to give us the egalitarian society of our philosophical heritage. It will instead give us a society sharply graduated, with even greater innate separation between the top and the bottom.'

Bereiter would not disagree—except, perhaps, with the moderateness of Herrnstein's conclusions. Equality of opportunity means that already progress towards a caste system is well advanced. Modern marriage intensifies the process: it tends to occur among people of similar intelligence and so the inheritance of high or low intelligence is made more likely. But Bereiter focuses attention on the abilities required in 'our complex society': intelligence, he argues, is increasingly the only ability that really counts, and the importance of individual differences is not obliterated by machine performance but enhanced. The key tools of the future, he says, are intellectual tools which are mathematically based. These are not equalizers but amplifiers of individual differences: they magnify rather than nullify individual differences in ability.[77]

These predictions are falsified by three quite well-established correlation coefficients: between the intelligence of father and son (0.50); between children's intelligence and their 'social class' (0.35); and between intelligence and occupational level (0.55). These correlation coefficients are statistically significant but they are a very long way from unity. Their magnitude allows for a high degree of indeterminacy in these relationships. These 'structures' are loose enough for the unexpected be be constantly breaking in.

The debate about the 'true' nature of intelligence and its genetic base will continue. But if we cannot measure 'real' intelligence, we can measure intelligent behaviour. One fact, however interpreted, stands out from countless studies: that the correlation between a father's intelligence as measured by tests and his son's is around 0.50. This is the figure arrived at by Burt;[78] it is also Jensen's figure, derived from a dozen independent studies;[79] Jencks gives 0.48 based on 'the six best American studies', but would raise it to 0.55 after correcting for unreliability.[80]

There is also remarkable agreement about the correlation between children's measured intelligence and their 'social class' (or fathers' 'socioeconomic status'). In the course of a famous debate with Cyril Burt twenty years ago Halsey conceded innate differences in intelligence between individuals, but maintained that the social distribution of 'real' intelligence among social classes was approximately random.[81] Burt gave a correlation coefficient of 0.32 for children's intelligence and their social class, based on surveys in which he had been involved with the National Institute of Industrial Psychology.[82] Jensen has reviewed the studies in this area and shows that most of them give a range between 0.35 and 0.40.[83] Jencks has made a similar survey and concludes: 'Taking all the evidence together, however, we estimate that a family's economic status probably correlates about 0.35 with the children's test scores.'[84]

The correlation between intelligence and occupational level is around 0.55. This is Jensen's figure. Bowles arrives at a coefficient of 0.52.[85] The wide range of intelligence found in most occupations has been a subject of some speculative comment in recent years. Jensen points to 'a considerable dispersion of IQs within occupations' but observes that: 'The spread of IQ increases as one moves down the scale from more skilled to less skilled occupations.' Advancing an argument flatly contrary to Bereiter's, Jensen thinks it would be surprising if it were otherwise: 'Because intelligence is only one of a number of qualities making for merit in any given occupation, and since most occupations will tolerate a considerable range of abilities and criteria of passable performance, it would be surprising to find a very high correlation between occupational level and IQ.'[86]

Burt is now being attacked as fraudulent. He is also reviled because, it is said, in his work 'the class system appears as the economic reflection of a genetically-determined order of human merit'.[87] But far from giving undue emphasis to the genetic basis of intellectual abilities and the consequent rigidity of the class system Burt's thesis was precisely the opposite: he advanced an argument for continuing high rates of intergenerational mobility on the basis of '... the comparatively modest correlation that obtains between the intelligence of parents and their children'.[88]

Burt's paper on 'Intelligence and social mobility', published in 1961 is justly famous. It is an impressive piece of work. Burt was a psychologist and it is true that, like many sociologists who should know better, he uses an operational definition of social class which, from the point of view of educational research, is essentially circular: he does not define the 'class' of parents in terms of wealth, power, or even occupational prestige, but in terms of 'the degree of ability required for the work' they do. And so it is hardly surprising that a measure of parents' intellectual abilities correlates highly with their 'class'. But this is not central to Burt's argument—and, indeed, he himself dismisses this correlation as having 'little meaning'.

He focuses on the modest correlation (which many investigators on both sides of the Atlantic have found) between children's intelligence test scores and their parents' intelligence—of the order of 0.5. This means that in any social class a great many children will differ markedly from their parents in intelligence: 'The intelligence of the individual children within each class will vary over a far wider range than that of their fathers.' Burt points to some of his own data which show a few parents in unskilled occupations with above-average intelligence, but among their children four times as many. Burt's concern is not to underline the extent of inheritance but the discrepancy between one generation and the next.

These discrepancies are cumulative. Burt concludes not that genetically based class differences must increase, but that they must diminish; indeed, unless a good deal of re-sorting occurs, 'After about five generations the differences between the class-means would virtually vanish.' Burt is concerned with occupational efficiency and so thinks that the 'match' between job level and intelligence should not be worse than it is. Even now it is not an especially good match, but merely to maintain it would require a major re-sorting every generation: a social mobility rate of some 30 per cent.

Burt's only important error is to overstate the 'need' of high-level jobs for high intelligence. High rates of social mobility and open competition for superior jobs is desirable, not because the jobs are especially difficult but because they are not (although the pay is good). Even the modest correlation of 0.55 between intelligence and job level is unnecessary. The work of Bowles and Gintis in America convincingly demonstrates that within a particular 'class' or at a given educational level 'intelligence' makes virtually no independent contribution to occupational achievement: it does not distinguish those who are successful from those who are not.

This stands the arguments of Herrnstein and Bereiter precisely on their heads. Bowles and Gintis do not say that high intelligence is never important: '... for some individuals and for some jobs cognitive skills are economically important.' But they do maintain that 'for the majority of workers and jobs, selection, assessed job adequacy and promotion are based on attributes other than I.Q.'[88]

The upshot of all this is quite simple: the social structures in which we live are in fact less structured, far less determined, with larger amounts of 'unexplained variance', than social and behavioural scientists claim or imply. It is not quite true to say that anything can happen; but often it does. The quite weak connexions between different facets of our lives—which is what all these very modest correlation coefficients mean—are the basis of hope. Opportunity is what we have the political will to create.

CONCLUSION

In their notable book, *Inequality*, Christopher Jencks and his colleagues said that their principal concern was inequality of income;[90] but they devoted their book to the analysis of inequality of opportunity. The two meanings of inequality are conceptually distinct and a great deal of misunderstanding has arisen in recent years from confusing them. If the aim of social policy is to arrive at greater equality of income, it is more likely to achieve this through direct political action rather than through indirect means like manipulating the educational system.

To promote equality of educational opportunity may thwart the pursuit of equality of wealth, welfare, and income. Jencks (like Boudon) says that as educational levels have become more equal, incomes have become less.[91] Jencks (like Boudon) is wrong, and the facts about income that he produces refute this contention: there has been a more equal distribution of income in America over the past quarter of a century. Coleman has underlined this discrepancy between Jencks's facts and theories; but even he thinks that one possible (but by no means certain) explanation is that 'increasing equality of education does have a strong effect on increasing equality of income'.[92] The relationship is more likely to be the other way round: greater economic equality has made possible more equally matched contestants, a fairer fight, and greater equality in taking advantage of the educational opportunities that are available.

There is a further sense of equality that has entered the debate, especially in America: the equality of the effects of schooling. The analogy here seems to be medical (and to offer a possible basis of ligation): hospitals provide equal cures for the same disease; schools should provide equal cures for ignorance, illiteracy, and innumeracy (and incompetence in the higher mathematics). However different in ignorance and understanding pupils might be at the start, they should converge over the period of the school course and be roughly the same at the end.[93] The argument is also applied to groups as well as individuals: in the debate on race in America some have argued that equality of opportunity implies movement towards equal test-score means for different ethnic groups.

Equality of school effects is presumed to further social equality. If this unattainable result were ever achieved, the consequences would almost certainly be the opposite. Other influences (like 'class') would be taken into account to sort people out and assign them to different social and economic positions and roles.

More widespread educational opportunities doubtless have an equalizing effect in one respect: they diminish the special advantages that arise from a 'superior' education. Indeed, some Marxists argue that capitalists have encouraged (even endowed) a greatly expanded provision of higher education precisely to convert intellectuals into proletarians. There is no doubt that this process of proletarianization is implicit in the expansion of higher education, and the problem is to ensure that the able sons of proletarians are not promptly returned to the proletariat via doctoral programmes in arts and social science.

In England, as in America, education is a very important means of advancement in life. It is highly correlated with intergenerational social mobility. George Psacharopoulos looked specifically into this connexion in his recent study, because of the doubts that have sometimes been expressed about it. He looked at the 'distance' sons had travelled from their father's social level and found that this was closely connected with the amount of schooling. Part-time qualifications had been especially important in long-distance movement; higher degrees less so (but this was partly because people getting higher degrees often had not so far to travel).[95]

The amount of intergenerational mobility will depend on two kinds of opportunity: 'structural', which arises principally from economic change and growth and the expansion of superior jobs, and 'circulation', which arises when positions are 'exchanged'. Education will create neither kind of opportunity but may be important for taking advantage of both. Even though extensive structural opportunities arise, some individuals and sections of the community may receive little benefit because their education has not equipped them even to compete. Circulation mobility will depend on the positions that already exist being genuinely thrown open to talent.

Jencks concluded that in America '... occupational status is more directly related to educational attainment than anything else we can measure'.[96] The same is true in England. The influence of education on the first job is greater than on subsequent jobs, but even there it is increasing.[97] In the meantime the direct effect of father's status has been diminishing. But the correlation between job and education is far from 'perfect'; it allows for many people with little education in youth to make significant worklife advancement. The danger is that in later life the influence of education diminishes and the influence of class reasserts itself. There is ample evidence that this happens. The problem is to sustain, or at least renew, the influence of education throughout a career.

The bogey of a biologically based caste society arising from a system of equal educational opportunity has been deeply damaging to the prospects of able working-class children. It has legitimated their exclusion from the competition; it has made the contest itself immoral. It is a bogey that serves well the interests of the well-heeled who have enjoyed a privileged, expensive, private education. They invented it. They can be confidently expected to refurbish it. The danger lies not in new rigidities which arise from open contest, but the perpetuation of old rigidities through its suppression.

NOTES

1. The opposition between the two notions of equality is clear in a recent article by Halsey when he writes of:

   > ... the dangers of meritocracy, which carries the possibility of sanctifying new and greater divisions between the powerful and the common man. ... To put the matter positively, equality rather than equality of opportunity is the aim and there is a belief in this tradition of political thought that a more equal distribution of power and advantage is not only desirable but also possible.

   See A. H. Halsey, 'Towards meritocracy? The case of Britain', in Jerome Karabel and A. H. Halsey (Eds.), *Power and Ideology in Education*, Oxford University Press, New York, 1977. For an examination of changing notions of equality in education see Julia Evetts, 'Equality of educational opportunity: the recent history of a concept, *British Journal of Sociology*, **21** (1970).

2. Raymond Boudon, *Education, Opportunity and Social Inequality*, Wileys, New York, 1974, p. xiii.

3. Maurice Kogan, *The Politics of Educational Change*, Manchester University Press, 1978, pp. 29–33.

4. James S. Coleman, 'What is meant by "an equal educational opportunity"?', *Oxford Review of Education*, **1** (1975).

5. *Children and Their Primary Schools* (the Plowden Report), Vol. I, HMSO, London, 1967, para. 152, p. 57.
6. Eric Midwinter, *Priority Education*, Penguin Books, Harmondsworth, 1972, pp. 17–20.
7. J. S. Coleman, 'What is meant by "an equal educational opportunity"?', *Oxford Review of Education*, **1** (1975).
8. Urie Bronfenbrenner, 'Is early intervention effective?', *Teachers College Record*, **76** (1974).
9. Arthur R. Jensen, 'How much can we boost IQ and scholastic achievement?', *Harvard Educational Review*, **39** (1969).
10. Daniel Bell, *The Coming of Post-Industrial Society*, Penguin Books, Harmondsworth, 1976, p. 417.
11. J. S. Coleman, 'Equal schools or equal students?', *The Public Interest*, Summer **1966**.
12. For the methodological implications and the use of Yale's Q-coefficient to measure 'pure mobility' see Saburo Yasuda, 'A methodological inquiry into social mobility', *American Sociological Review*, **29** (1964). For studies which have been particularly concerned with the distinction between structural and exchange mobility see E. F. Jackson and H. J. Crockett, 'Occupational mobility in the United States: a point estimate and trend comparison', *American Sociological Review*, **29** (1964) (for evidence of an increased proportion of exchange mobility compared with structural mobility in America between 1945 and 1957), and Leonard Broom and F. L. Jones, 'Father-to-son mobility: Australia in comparative perspective', *American Journal of Sociology*, **74** (1969) (for evidence of more exchange, though less gross, mobility in Australia than America). The highest rates of exchange mobility appear to exist in Britain; see Phillips Cutright, 'Occupational inheritance: a cross-national analysis', *American Journal of Sociology*, **73** (1968).
13. Reported in D. V. Glass (Ed.), *Social Mobility in Britain*, Routledge and Kegan Paul, London, 1954.
14. David Butler and Donald Stokes, *Political Change in Britain*, Penguin Books, Harmondsworth, 1971, pp. 125–132. See also M. Kahan, David Butler, and Donald Stokes, 'On the analytical division of social class', *British Journal of Sociology*, **17** (1966).
15. See John H. Goldthorpe and Catriona Llewellyn, 'Class mobility: intergenerational and worklife patterns', *British Journal of Sociology*, **28** (1977).
16. George Psacharopoulos, 'Family background, education and achievement', *British Journal of Sociology*, **28** (1977).
17. G. Payne, G. Ford, and C. Robertson, 'A reappraisal of social mobility in Britain', *Sociology*, **11** (1977).
18. D. Butler and D. Stokes, *Political Change in Britain*, Penguin Books, 1971, p. 127.
19. C. Arnold Anderson, 'A skeptical note on education and mobility', in A. H. Halsey *et al.*, (Eds.) *Education, Economy and Society*, The Free Press of Glencoe, New York, 1964. See footnote 14. This article was first published in the *American Journal of Sociology*, in 1961.
20. John Westergaard and Henrietta Resler, *Class in a Capitalist Society*, Penguin Books, Harmondsworth, 1976, pp. 306–307. The note is at the foot of p. 307.
21. J. M. Ridge, 'Sibling rivalry', in J. M. Ridge, *Mobility in Britain Reconsidered*, Clarendon Press, Oxford, 1974, p. 91.
22. D. V. Glass (Ed.), *Social Mobility in Britain* Routledge and Kegan Paul, 1954, pp. 189–195.
23. G. Payne, G. Ford, and C. Robertson, 'A reappraisal of social mobility in Britain', *Sociology*, **11** (1977).
24. Trevor Noble, 'Social mobility and class relations in Britain', *British Journal of Sociology*, **23** (1972).
25. John H. Goldthorpe and Catriona Llewellyn, 'Class mobility in modern Britain: three theses examined', *Sociology*, **11** (1977).
26. P. Blau and O. D. Duncan, *The American Occupational Structure*, Wiley, New York, 1967, p. 103.

27. C. Wright Mills, *White Collar*, Oxford University Press, New York, 1951, p. 63.
28. See J. H. Goldthorpe and C. Llewellyn, 'Class mobility in modern Britain: three theses examined', *Sociology*, **11** (1977).
29. A. Giddens, *The Class Structure of the Advanced Societies*, Hutchinson, London, 1973, pp. 178–179.
30. Trevor Noble, 'Social mobility and class relations in Britain', *British Journal of Sociology*, **23** (1972). Manual occupations (male) were 78.2 per cent. of all occupations in 1911, 73.6 per cent. in 1951, 65.8 per cent. in 1966.
31. D. C. Marsh, *The Changing Social Structure of England and Wales*, Routledge nd Kegan Paul, London, 1965, Table 46, p. 198. 'The main positive trend is towards a reduction in class 5 and an increase in class 1 and 2 which is what could be expected from the changing pattern of occupational distribution' (p. 198). Marsh gives data for the thirty years from 1931 to 1961; for the same period see also R. Knight, 'Changes in the occupational structure of the working population', *Journal of the Royal Statistical Society*, **1967**, Part 3.
32. G. Payne, G. Ford, and C. Robertson, 'A reappraisal of social mobility in Britain', *Sociology*, **11** (1977). 'Blue Collar' workers were 70 per cent. of all male workers in 1921, 65 per cent. in 1951, and 54 per cent. in 1971. For trend data for 1911 to 1961 see also A. H. Halsey, *Trends in British Society since 1900*, Macmillan, London, 1971, Table 4.1, p. 113.
33. Nicos Poulantzas, *Classes in Contemporary Capitalism*, New Left Books, 1975, pp. 300–301.
34. D. V. Glass (Ed.), *Social Mobility in Britain*, Routledge and Kegan Paul, 1954, p. 192.
35. Robert Havighurst, 'Education, social mobility and social change in four societies', *International Review of Education*, **4** (1958).
36. M. Sanderson, 'Literacy and social mobility in the Industrial Revolution in England', *Past and Present*, **1972**, No. 56.
37. Jonathan Kelley and Melvin L. Perlman, 'Social mobility in Toro: some preliminary results from Western Uganda', *Economic Development and Cultural Change*, **19** (1971).
38. John H. Goldthorpe and Catriona Llewellyn, 'Class mobility in modern Britain: three theses examined', *Sociology*, **11** (1977), pp. 266–267. These calculations are based on the figure in Table 2 (p. 267).
39. John H. Goldthorpe and Catriona Llewellyn, 'Class mobility: intergenerational and worklife patters', *British Journal of Sociology*, **28** (1977).
40. Jonathan Kelley, 'Wealth and family background in the occupational career', *British Journal of Sociology*, **29** (1978).
41. See Otis Dudley Duncan and Robert W. Hodge, 'Education and occupational mobility: a regression analysis', *The American Journal of Sociology*, **68** (1963). The correlation between the status levels of sons and fathers had declined from 0.35 to 0.29. The authors point out that: 'We should, of course, expect a higher proportion of occupational inheritance and father–son occupational SES correlation exceeding 0.3 in a national sample.'
42. K. Hope, *Trends in the Openness of British Society in the Present Century*. Paper presented at SSRC Conference, University of Aberdeen, 1975.
43. Maurice Garnier and Lawrence E. Hazelrigg, 'Father-to-son occupational mobility in France: evidence from the 1960s', *American Journal of Sociology*, **80** (1974). This coefficient is based on a study in 1964 of a national sample of French males born after 1918 and therefore up to the age of forty-six when the enquiry was conducted.
44. Peter Blau and O. D. Duncan, *The American Occupational Structure*, Wiley, New York, 1967, p. 169.
45. Christopher Jencks *et al.*, *Inequality*, Penguin Books, Harmondsworth, 1975, p. 200, note 13.
46. *Ibid.*, p. 179.

140

47. George Psacharopoulos, 'Family background, education and achievement', *British Journal of Sociology*, **28** (1977).
48. Bruce Headey and Tim O'Loughlin, 'Transgenerational, "structured" inequality: social fact or fiction?', *British Journal of Sociology*, **29** (1978).
49 John Porter, *The Vertical Mosaic*, University of Toronto Press, 1965, p. 49.
50. *Ibid.*, p. 166.
51. Wallace Clement, *The Canadian Corporate Elite*, McClelland and Stewart, Toronto, 1975.
52. S. M. Miller, 'Comparative social mobility', *Current Sociology*, **9** (1960), Table IVa, p. 36.
53. Phillips Cutright, 'Occupational inheritance: a cross-national analysis', *American Journal of Sociology*, **73** (1968), Table 3, p. 412.
54. Seymour Martin Lipset and Reinhard Bendix, *Social Mobility in Industrial Society*, University of California Press, Berkeley and Los Angeles, 1964, p. 72.
55. Gosta Carrlson, *Social Mobility and Class Structure*, CWK Gleerup/Lund, Sweden, 1958, p. 137.
56. C. Arnold Anderson, 'A skeptical note on education and mobility', in A. H. Halsey *et al.* (Eds.), *Education, Economy and Society*, The Free Press of Glencoe, New York, 1964.
57. Phillips Cutright, 'Occupational inheritance: a cross-national analysis', *American Journal of Sociology*, **73** (1968).
58. Thomas G. Fox and S. M. Miller, 'Economic, political and social determinants of mobility: an international cross-sectional analysis', *Acta Sociologica*, **9** (1966).
59. Donald J. Treiman and Kermit Terrell, 'The process of status attainment in the United States and Great Britain', *American Journal of Sociology*, **81** (1975).
60. Maurice Garnier and Lawrence E. Hazelrigg, 'Father-to-son occupational mobility in France: evidence from the 1960s', *American Journal of Sociology*, **80** (1974).
61. I. (Education and occupation) see Donald J. Treinman and Kermit Terrell, 'The process of status attainment in the United States and Great Britain', *American Journal of Sociology*, **81** (1975).
    II. (Education and income) see George Psacharopoulos, 'Family background, education and achievement', *British Journal of Sociology*, **28** (1977), and Treiman and Terrell, *op.cit.* The correlation coefficient of 0.33 for America is taken from C. Jencks *et al.*, *Inequality*, Penguin Books, 1975. Jencks concluded from path analysis that the direct effect of education on income was much smaller and could for all practical purposes be discounted. Psacharopoulos (*op cit.*) also made a path analysis of his English data and concluded that the path was much higher in the United Kingdom and highly significant: 'Therefore, using as nearly as possible Jencks' technique and criteria of importance, we conclude that at least in the U.K., schooling matters in the earnings determining process.'
    III. (Class of origin and education) see Jencks *et al.*, *op cit.*, App. B, and Psacharopoulos, *op. cit.*
    IV. (Class of origin and occupation) see K. Hope, *Trends in the Openness of British Society in the Present Century.* Paper presented at SSRC Conference, University of Aberdeen, 1975 (his calculations for 1949 and 1972 are also given in A. H. Halsey, 'Towards meritocracy? The case of Britain', in J. Karabel and A. H. Halsey (Eds.), *Power and Ideology in Education*, Oxford University Press, New York, 1977; P. Blau and O. D. Duncan, *The American Occupational Structure*, Wiley, New York, 1967, and Psacharopoulos, *op. cit.*
62. Ralph H. Turner, 'Sponsored and contest mobility in the school system', *American Sociological Review*, **25** (1960).
63. See Theodore Caplow and Reece McGee, *The Academic Marketplace*, Doubleday, New York, 1965.
64. Lowell L. Hargreaves and Warren O. Hagstrom, 'Sponsored and contest mobility of American academic scientists, *Sociology of Education*, **40** (1967).
65. Phillips Cutright, 'Occupational inheritance: a cross-national analysis', *American Journal*

of Sociology, **73** (1968).
66. Leonard Broom and F. Lancaster Jones, 'Father-to-son mobility: Australia in comparative perspective', *American Journal of Sociology*, **74** (1969).
67. Raymond Boudon, *Education, Opportunity, and Social Inequality*, Wiley, New York, 1974, pp. 185 and 193.
68. L. Stone, 'Social mobility in England 1500–1700', *Past and Present*, **1966**, No. 33.
69. L. Stone, 'The educational revolution in England, 1560–1640', *Past and Present*, **1964**, No. 28.
70. Hugh Kearney, *Scholars and Gentlemen*, Faber, London, 1970, pp. 23–25.
71. Mark H. Curtis, 'The alienated intellectuals of early Stuart England', *Past and Present*, **1962**, No. 23.
72. Hugh Kearney, *Scholars and Gentleman*, Faber, 1970, p. 32.
73. M. H. Curtis, 'The alienated intellectuals of early Stuart England', *Past and Present*, **1962**, No. 23.
74. Alan Everitt, 'Social mobility in early modern England', *Past and Present*, **1966**, No. 33.
75. Daniel Bell, *The Coming of Post-Industrial Society*, Penguin Books, Harmondsworth, 1976, p. 140.
76. Richard Herrnstein, 'I.Q.', *The Atlantic Monthly*, **228**, (September 1971).
77. Carl Bereiter, 'The future of individual differences', *Harvard Educational Review* (Reprint series), **1969**, No. 2.
78. Cyril Burt, 'Intelligence and social mobility', *British Journal of Statistical Psychology*, **14** (1961).
79. Arthur R. Jensen, 'How much can we boost IQ and scholastic achievement?', *Harvard Educational Review*, **39** (1969), p. 49.
80. C. Jencks *et al.*, *Inequality*, Penguin Books, 1975, App. A, pp. 274–275.
81. A. H. Halsey, 'Class differences in general intelligence', *British Journal of Statistical Psychology*, **12** (1959).
82. Cyril Burt, 'Class differences in general intelligence: III', *British Journal of Statistical Psychology*, **12** (1959).
83. A. R. Jensen, 'How much can we boost IQ and scholastic achievement?' *Harvard Educational Review*, **39** (1969), p. 75.
84. C. Jencks *et al.*, *Inequality*, Penguin Books, 1975, p. 78.
85. Samuel Bowles and Herbert Gintis, 'I.Q. in the U.S. class structure', in Jerome Karabel and A. H. Halsey (Eds.), *Power and Ideology in Education*, Oxford University Press, New York, 1977, p. 219, Table I.
86. A. R. Jensen, 'How much can we boost IQ and scholastic achievement?', *Harvard Educational Review*, **39** (1969), p. 15.
87. 'Sir Cyril Burt and the great IQ fraud', *New Statesman*, 24 November 1978.
88. C. Burt, 'Intelligence and social mobility', *British Journal of Statistical Psychology*, **14** (1961).
89. S. Bowles and H. Gintis. 'I.Q. in the U.S. class structure', in J. Karabel and A. H. Halsey (Eds.), *Power and Ideology in Education*, Oxford University Press, New York, 1977.
90. C. Jencks *et al.*, *Inequality*, Penguin Books, 1975: 'The reader should by now have gathered that our primary concern is with equalizing the distribution of income' (p. 261).
91. *Ibid*.:

None of the evidence we have reviewed suggests that school reform can be expected to bring about significant social changes outside the schools. More specifically, the evidence suggests that equalizing educational opportunity would do very little to make adults more equal. ... Furthermore, the experience of the past 25 years suggests that even fairly substantial reductions in the range of educational attainments does not appreciably reduce economic inequality among adults (p. 255).

92. James S. Coleman, 'Equality of opportunity and equality of results', *Harvard Educational Review*, **43** (1975).
93. James S. Coleman, 'The concept of equality of educational opportunity', in *Equal Educational Opportunity*, Harvard University Press, Cambridge, Mass., 1969.
94. For a discussion of this issue see Gerald Lesser and Susan S. Stodolsky, 'Equal opportunity for maximum development', in *Equal Educational Opportunity*, Harvard University Press, Cambridge, Mass., 1969.
95. George Psacharopoulos, 'Family background, education and achievement', *British Journal of Sociology*, **28** (1977).
96. C. Jencks *et al.*, *Inequality*, Penguin Books, 1975, p. 91.
97. A. H. Halsey, 'Towards meritocracy? The case of Britain', in J. Karabel and A. H. Halsey (Eds.), *Power and Ideology in Education*, Oxford University Press, New York, 1977, p. 183.

CHAPTER 7

Gentry Hegemony and Ideology in English Education and Life

It would be difficult to exaggerate the past power and the continuing influence of the 'gentry' over English social life and institutions. Marxists who locate 'hegemony' in the ranks of industrial capitalists have simply failed to understand the structure of English society. (Joseph Schumpeter's analysis of modern capitalism and the protective role of Europe's gentry and aristocracy—the 'steel frame' of the social structure—is a better guide.)[1] It is the gentry ideology that pervades English society and finds its purest expression in such diverse strongholds of gentry culture as an Oxford Senior Common Room and a troop of Boy Scouts. The influence on English education has been profound—mediated especially by Her Majesty's Inspectors of schools. The core curriculum of the gentry culture has always been blood sports; and yet intellectuals (and the Anglican clergy) have since the sixteenth century been the gentry's cadet branch. This is crucial to an understanding of English education and intellectual life: intellectuals are embedded in the gentry hegemony. In America intellectuals have to be adversaries; in England they are part of the power structure.

In pre-industrial England 5 per cent. of the population were 'in' the rest were 'out'. Peter Laslett describes this as a 'one-class' society;[2] but it is the basic, underlying, binary structure of English life. The 5 per cent. who were 'in' were gentry (and above); the 95 per cent. who were 'out' were the mass of ordinary people below gentry rank. The Poll Tax of 1660 charged them sixpence a year; but a gentleman paid five pounds and an esquire paid ten.[3]

In the seventeenth century there were roughly 17,000 landed gentry (in a population of 5.5 million); today there are only some 6,000 (as listed in *Burke's Peerage*) in a population ten times as big. The earlier figure needs to be multiplied by three to take account of what Laslett calls a penumbra of 'self-reputed and locally recognized gentlemen'. (It is this augmented number that accounted for some 5 per cent. of English families.)[4] In the mid-nineteenth century the proportion was probably not dissimilar: thus the twelve-year-old sons of the landed gentry were roughly 4 per cent. of all twelve-year-old boys.[5] But in 1919 England changed hands. The transfer of land was probably greater than at any time since the Norman Conquest.[6] The landed gentry largely sold out. (Only one-third of the landed-gentry families in Essex, Oxford, and Shropshire in the late nineteenth century still survived in the nineteen-fifties.)[7] But it would be a mistake to dismiss even their economic significance today. In a recent study of the rich Giddens observes: 'The "landed gentry", a distinctively English phenomenon, includes some very prosperous families, as well as many whose means are no greater than that of the average member of the urban white-collar middle class.'[8]

But they are still well connected with 'the City'; newly enriched men still like to join their ranks, and so 'the old money' still for the most part absorbs the 'new' and the life-style of the country gentleman 'comes to be sustained without serious signs of disintegration'.[9]

The deep binary structure of English society is today heavily overlaid with modern 'classes' and new status groups: it survives in its pristine purity only in the Army's basic structural division into officers and other ranks. But in pre-industrial society, says Laslett, 'The term gentleman marked the exact point at which the traditional social system divided up the population into two extremely unequal sections.'[10] There is remarkable unanimity among social historians about this dichotomous structure of pre-industrial England. 'In the sixteenth century,' writes Hugh Kearney, 'the division between gentleman and non-gentleman became the most important social distinction in English life.'[11] Of course there were different status groups above and below the line. Lawrence Stone says: 'Within the dual system of gentlemen and non-gentlemen contemporaries recognized a rough six-fold status division.'[12] There were peers, the county elite of squires, knights, and baronets, and then the lesser gentry, all 'above the line'; below it were yeomen, labourers, and finally servants who 'lived in'. But the essential and abiding discontinuity of English social life was between those who were of 'gentle' birth and breeding, and those who were not.

And yet the gentry were never a caste; nor did they impose the gentry ideology only on themselves. They shared it as widely as they could. Grammar schools, field sports (but not organized games), and late nineteenth-century youth movements were powerful agencies of 'incorporation'. It was not only clerks and the aspiring working class who were incorporated. Capitalists were incorporated too.

GENTRY HEGEMONY IN AN INDUSTRIAL SOCIETY

The 'rise of the gentry' was located by Tawney in the eighty years before the English Civil War.[13] His thesis has been vigorously debated, but his original views—strongly attacked by Trevor Roper but broadly supported by Stone[14]—are probably substantially correct. The gentry 'rose' in the sense that they acquired land when the Church, Crown, and nobility allowed it to slip from their grasp. This rise is only partly an optical illusion resulting from the temporary weakness of the aristocracy.[15] Their gains were solid; England's landed gentry became, deservedly, the envy of Europe: the bedrock of the social order.

They continued to rise. They did not decline as industrial capitalism rose in the nineteenth century; they rose further with it. Their rise was unchecked by the repeal in 1846 of the Corn Laws which protected landed interests, or by the alleged 'Great Depression' in agriculture after 1870. The reform of the franchise had some (delayed) effect; open competitive examinations had none. Their rise was checked only by death duties and the Great War. As industrial capitalism developed, the landed gentry moved steadily but massively forward into the higher ranks of the power elite. The capitalists who joined them had renounced industry, bought landed estates, and been elected to Boodle's or White's.

It is too flippant to say, as Stone has done, that even before the First World War the English aristocracy had abdicated their responsibilities: 'From looking after the tenantry and serving the Empire, they took to hunting and gaiety girls.'[16] Half of the Cabinet Ministers in the thirty years from 1886 to 1916 were aristocratic landowners, and so were a quarter in the twenty years from 1918 to 1935.[17] But the gentry—with perhaps two thousand acres, as distinct from an aristocrat with fifty thousand—were less obtrusive, less vulnerable, and their obligations (and debts) less burdensome. During Victoria's reign they quietly infiltrated the great Public Schools, the officer corps, and the peerage; their hold on the House of Commons was not significantly relaxed until the last fifteen years of Victoria's reign; and their junior branch, the sons of parsons, ruled India.

The gentry (baronets, esquires, and gentlemen) were less than 5 per cent. of the nation in the eighteenth century but they were 25 per cent. of England's elites. This spectacular overrepresentation was found in all walks of life. Nicholas Hans has given us the particulars of a sample of 3,000 eighteenth-century men whose distinction earned them eventually a place in the *Dictionary of National Biography*, and this percentage is based on his data.[18] The sons of parsons made another major and disproportionate contribution (20 per cent.); these should be bracketed with the gentry. (They were definitely 'above the line' that cut the nation in two: as Kearney says, 'The medieval priest had been a peasant among peasants. The parson in 1600 was a gentleman among gentlemen.')[19] If the contributions of peers, gentry, and clergy are put together, the minority aristocratic–gentry culture of eighteenth-century England is seen to produce 50 per cent. of her eminent men.

The contribution of the landed gentry to science is even more remarkable. In the seventeenth century this 5 per cent. of the nation produced 50 per cent. of the scientists sufficiently distinguished to be included in the *Dictionary of National Biography*. (The contribution of the clergy was a further 20 per cent.) The landed-gentry contribution declined to a quarter by the middle of the eighteenth century; but even at the end, this 5 per cent. of the nation produced 18 per cent. of the nation's distinguished scientists.[20] The contribution of capitalists' sons was never more than 16 per cent.

Between the end of the eighteenth century and Victoria's accession the landed gentry quietly took over the officer corps. In 1780 they were outnumbered by aristocrats: they contributed 16 per cent. of the officers in the British Home Army while the aristocracy contributed 24 per cent. By 1830 the positions were reversed: the aristocracy contributed 21 per cent. and the landed gentry 32 per cent. They held this position for the next eighty years. In 1912 their contribution was still precisely 32 per cent.; the aristocracy's contribution was now down to 9 per cent.[21]

Social order was thought, after the civil disorders of the seventeenth century, to be most effectively guaranteed if members of power elites were men of property (preferably in land) and could not live on their pay. The guarantee was still stronger if they actually purchased their positions (whether seats in Parliament or army commissions) and subsequent promotions. To rise to the rank of Lieutenant-Colonel in a cavalry regiment cost more than 10,000 pounds; such a sum invested wisely would enable a man to live in more than modest comfort and in idleness for life. The landed gentry invested in power. They were roughly a quarter of Sandhurst entrants in 1820, but more than a half by 1860;[22] they contributed a third of the Major-Generals and above in 1830, but 40 per cent. in 1912.[23] By the time purchase of commissions was abolished (1871) and open competitive entry to Sandhurst and Woolwich introduced, the landed gentry were so skilled in using the Public Schools that their competitiveness was assured: 'Clearly the introduction of open competitive entry to the army did not bring about a revolution in the nature of the officer intake.'[24]

As England industrialized herself, the great Public Schools increased the proportion of landed-gentry sons in their intake and reduced the proportion of capitalists' sons. They geared themselves to the army. They would probably have agreed with Joseph Schumpeter about the crippling disability of capitalism: 'The stock exchange is a poor substitute for the Holy Grail.'[25]

The eight great Public Schools of England—Eton, Harrow, Winchester, Rugby, Shrewsbury, Charterhouse, St. Paul's, and Westminster—received 32 per cent. of their new boys from the families of landed-gentry in the decade 1801–1810; 41 per cent. in the decade 1840–1850. (The proportions were highest at Rugby: 43 per cent. in the earlier period and 56 per cent. by the mid-century.) The aristocracy maintained a level contribution of 12 per cent. The contribution of the clergy also remained steady at about 12 per cent. While England industrialized and her cities experienced their most rapid growth of all time (their population increased by 30 per cent. in the decade after 1821), the landed-gentry's contribution to the great Public Schools rose from a third to two-fifths; the contribution of the 'middle class' (which included manufacturers, merchants, and shopkeepers of all kinds) sank from 6 per cent. to less than 2 per cent. Of course some sons of manufacturers were now sent to these schools (Wedgwood sons went to Rugby) and, as Bamford observes, '... there has been a persistent story that Rugby's success was built on the influx of sons of manufacturers.' His indefatigable researches, from which the above statistics are taken, do not substantiate this story.[26]

In the later nineteenth century the grandsons of some of the pioneer industrialists were being sent to Public Schools. Mathew Boulton's grandson went to Eton; Richard Arkwright's grandsons went to Eton or Harrow and then to Christ Church, Oxford, or Trinity, Cambridge. In the eighteen-eighties the Kenricks began to go to Rugby and Balliol.[27] But what is really impressive about the great schools is the small percentage of their boys with this kind of background throughout the nineteenth century and beyond. Bishop has made an exhaustive study of boys born between the eighteen-twenties and the nineteen-twenties who attended Winchester College. Throughout this century the contribution of business fathers was 11 per cent. For boys born in the early nineteen-hundreds it reached its highest level (15 per cent.); by the nineteen-twenties the level was the same as in the eighteen-fifties—7.5 per cent.

When manufacturing fathers specifically are extracted from the business group, their contribution throughout is derisory: it was not until the eighteen-fifties that it exceeded 1 per cent.; it never exceeded 6 per cent. (it was 5.8 per cent. for boys born in the early nineteen-hundreds). For boys born in the nineteen-twenties it again scarcely exceeded 1 per cent.[28] As Bishop observes, there is no statistical evidence that Winchester College, throughout England's great century of industrialization, was a mechanism for converting industrialists into gentlemen.

It remained close to the real centres of power in industrial England: like the other great schools it was first and foremost a projection of the officer corps. But it was not a professional military academy and it was not an institution of state. And so the officer corps was saved from professionalism (and politics) and preserved as a branch of the landed gentry.[29] (All officers were expected to hunt two days a week;[30] they took their hounds with them when they went to fight in the Crimea.)[31] The Public Schools were not demilitarized until after the Second World War. In 1900 they provided 85 per cent. of Sandhurst entrants and in 1936, 84 per cent. (but only 36 per cent. in 1967).[32] Their chapels were at the centre of their lives; by the end of Victoria's reign they were (as Otley says) mausoleums, part of the commemoratory subculture which celebrates death in battle and decoration for valour.[33] Eighteen per cent. of the fathers of Winchester boys were army officers during the century examined by Bishop (rising steeply from 15 per cent. in the case of boys born in the eighteen-seventies to no less than 50 per cent. in the case of those born in the nineteen-twenties). Twenty-four per cent. of the boys chose the army as a career, the largest single occupational choice. Only 7.3 per cent. went into civil government service.[34]

Open competitive examinations for government jobs at home and abroad were not invented to keep the upper classes out but to bring them in. Examinations were linked to greater differentiation and a tightening up of hierarchies in the public services which would prove attractive to the upper classes. It is true that Trollope feared what he called 'the perils of competitive examination' because 'There are places in life which can hardly be well filled except by "Gentlemen" ';[35] but the architects of reform like Sir Charles Trevelyan—and indeed Gladstone himself—believed that examinations would enable the gentry and aristocracy to show their superiority. In the case of the Indian Civil Service the landed-gentry intake was in fact diminished (from a quarter to a tenth) when patronage was abolished and examinations introduced; but parsons' sons did very well ('the abolition of patronage came as a gift to the clergy') and in the eighteen-seventies 60 per cent. of successful candidates were Public Schoolboys: 'The Service was hardly wide open to the sons of drapers, undertakers, and gamekeepers.'[36] There was some fear that 'competition wallahs' might prefer a desk to a saddle, but in the event they proved to be as fanatical as pig-stickers and as contemptuous of books as any officer in the Brigade of Guards.[37]

The first millowner to be given a peerage and enter the House of Lords was Edward Strutt, who became Lord Belper in 1856. *The Times* newspaper heralded this as a sign of the times. *The Times* was quite wrong. A quarter of a century was to pass before any more industrial capitalists became peers. (Two were elevated in

1880: Sir Henry Allsopp and Sir Michael Bass.) All these ennobled industrialists were now in fact a long way from industry. It was only after 1885 that persons connected with industry and commerce were a significant proportion of new peers—usually about 20 per cent. New titles for members of aristocratic families declined, from 40 per cent. of new peers in the mid-nineteenth century to 13 per cent. in 1911. But the gentry share was almost a half throughout the seventy-five years from 1837 to 1911. It was 45 per cent. in the years from 1837 to 1851; it fell as low as 43 per cent. at the end of the century; and it was 44 per cent. in the decade before 1911. Some of these gentry had commercial connexions, but all of them owned land. And so, indeed, did most of the 'industrialists'. Only a quarter of the 200 peerages granted in the twenty-five years before 1911 went to men without landed estates.[38]

By the end of the nineteenth century only some 15 per cent. of Members of Parliament were the sons of peers or baronets. After the first Reform Act in 1832 the percentage was 33; before the second Reform Act in 1867 it was 27. This remarkable resilience of the landed aristocratic–gentry interest is even more striking in the composition of the Cabinet down to the inter-war years.[39] And while the aristocratic–gentry hegemony is now undoubtedly destroyed, our social institutions—and in particular our prestigious educational institutions—remain impregnated with its deeply pervasive influence.

The accompanying table summarizes the most up-to-date research data on the high and often rising rates of participation of England's landed gentry in selected power elites.

GENTRIFICATION AND EFFICIENCY

One of the more foolish themes in contemporary social analysis is the charge that many, perhaps most, of Britain's present misfortunes can be laid at the door of 'gentrification'. An 'irrelevant' classical curriculum in elite schools is an important ingredient in this argument. In fact some of our troubles arise not from the success of gentrification, but from its failure; and with regard to the rest the issue is a total irrelevance.

The British army, British politics, and above all the British economy are said to have been undermined by gentrification and a classical curriculum. The army, politics and the economy (it is said) have been in the grip of gentlemanly amateurs who have lacked a professional sense and training: they have been thinking about Horace's Odes instead of the brutal facts of trade union power and overseas trade.

It is true that gentry values are different from those of the bureaucrat and of the capitalist of the Weberian canon. Important among gentry values is a 'leisure ethic' rather than a work ethic, generosity, even prodigality, and a taste for gambling rather than thrift and cautious frugality. (Lavish entertainment could make a significant contribution to the end of a great landed estate.)[47] Brutality has never in fact been far from the surface: cock-fighting, pugilism and the slaughter of 'game'. But too much should not be made of values in explaining conduct. And it is not demonstrable that

Landed gentry in nineteenth-century power elites

Institution	Date	Percentage of landed gentry	
Eight major Public Schools	1801–1810	32	
(Bamford, 1961)[40]	1841–1850	41	
Officers: British Home Army	1780	16	
(Razzell, 1963)[41]	1830	32	
	1912	32	
Sandhurst entrants	1820	27	
(Otley, 1970)[42]	1850	40	
	1910	20	
Major-Generals and above	1830	32	
(Razzell, 1963)[43]	1912	40	
Members of the House of Commons	1833	33	(Sons of
(Guttsman, 1951)[44]	1865	27	peers and
	1897	15	baronets)
Cabinet Ministers	1886–1916	47	(Land-
(Guttsman, 1951)[45]			owners)
New peers	1837–1851	45	
(Pumphrey, 1959)[46]	1867–1881	45	
	1897–1911	44	

our work is any the worse because at heart we are really interested in something else. This is the surest safeguard against the final inefficiency of the fanatic.

The case against England's early twentieth-century and inter-war 'ruling class' has been made by Correlli Barnett in his book, *The Decline of British Power*. The argument that our rulers had an astonishing innocence and a debilitating inclination to moralize all issues is persuasive. It is consistent with the picture of almost hysterically moralized Public Schools in late-Victorian England.

The gentrification case against the army is less plausible: complex issues of cause and effect and of appropriate criteria of effectiveness have still to be faced. But there is substantial agreement among contemporary military historians that the gentlemanly tradition has had generally unfortunate consequences. The army, they say, has staunchly resisted professionalization and officer 'training' has been a form of class socialization rather than the transmission of expertise. Simon Raven has given us a particularly compelling account of this process in the post-Second World War army;[48] Correlli Barnett concludes from his comparative studies of military education that in the British army alone the old battle between the technician of war and the gentleman continues;[49] Michael Howard thinks that in the matter of officer training we reverted by the late nineteen-seventies to our nineteenth-century practice of relying on getting 'the right sort of young man' rather than giving him a thorough professional training;[50] and Harries-Jenkins, at the end of a recent book on the army and Victorian society, which underscores the lack of professionalism, concludes rather limply that this merely mirrored society and that Britain got the army she deserved.[51] But all this begs too many questions. The British army—certainly in relation to its cost—has been extraordinarily good at killing our enemies.

The gentry culture is now being interpreted as an important cause of Britain's relative economic decline since the eighteen-seventies. The argument takes two forms: the sons and grandsons of pioneering industrial families were sent to Public Schools, became gentlemen, and so were lost to industry; those members of the upper classes who did turn to industry had been unfitted by a Public School education for the competitive, technical world they had entered. Both these circumstances are said to have led to entrepreneurial failure and the consequent poor performance of the British economy.

There was indeed a notable migration of newly enriched industrial families into the ranks of the landed gentry. That is one reason why the landed gentry continued to thrive. Well-known social migrants were the Darbys from iron, the Peels, Arkwrights, Fieldens, and Strutts from cotton, and the Whitbreads from brewing: 'By no means all successful business men sought to set themselves up as landed gentlemen. But that a good many of the most able and forceful could do so was a source of great strength to the landed interest.'[52] Industrial success did not invariably lead to defection: the Pilkingtons seemed never to lose their interest in glass. But the succession of successful industrial families has been accorded a key role in England's 'decline'.

Aldcroft has given pride of place to irrelevant values in his interpretation of England's economic performance in the years before 1914. Entrepreneurs were seduced by a debilitating gentry culture: 'As succeeding generations of businessmen began to acquire new interests and sought to advance themselves in society, the restless striving to maximize profits ceased.'[53] Others have advanced the same argument more strongly and vividly, and have given the Public Schools a prominent place in the alledgedly disastrous process of gentrification. Although David Ward has pointed to the high proportion of boys entering industry and commerce in the later nineteenth century from newly established Public Schools like Sedbergh, this was not a matter for congratulation but regret. Whether the Public Schools brought people into industry or kept them out, its disastrous consequences were apparently the same:

> The Public Schools facilitated the transmission of the culture of the landed and gentry classes to the industrial classes, a culture which virtually ignored the economic life of the country; and, by speeding up the transmission to a rate that would hitherto have been impossible, they produced a haemorrhage of talent, and perhaps of capital, in the older industries which could not be made good.[54]

Charles Wilson has given a very different picture. First of all the claim that England 'declined' is a matter of dispute; and the spectacular performance of a host of 'new' men like Lever, Beecham, and Ludwig Mond suggests a high level of enterprise in the late nineteenth century and beyond.[55] Coleman concedes that business leaders after the eighteen-sixties tended to come from a kind of 'extended club' based on family and school connexions, but questions whether they were in any way handicapped by having been through the 'gentlemanly mill'.[56] The aristocratic–gentry culture provided an especially appropriate training for a career in 'the city' and high finance.[57] The race courses of England have been among our better business schools.

Defectors cleared the way for new men who had been to night-school. As the professors of economics at Manchester University found in the early years of the twentieth century, between two-thirds and three-quarters of the manufacturers, company directors and managers in the Lancashire cotton industry were 'first generation'. They were not following in father's footsteps: they were mainly ambitious men still keen to maximize profits, who had risen from the ranks of wage-earners. These twentieth-century capitalists had not been to Public Schools: 'Generally speaking, the ablest of the young wage-earners attend in the evening at technical classes.'[58] The 'haemorrhage of talent' thesis gets the scale of the problem wrong and shows a total misunderstanding of the English gentry and their schools.

The classical curriculum saved the English gentry and upper classes from any serious interest in the life of the mind and confirmed their intense practicality. People who promoted and taught the Classics were not idiots: they knew quite well that these studies were generally disliked, even hated and feared; that they virtually guaranteed that most of their (upper-class) pupils would be academic failures who would leave school contemptuous of literature and ideas for the rest of their lives. The explanation is very simple: this was precisely the purpose of the exercise.

When Trollope left Harrow, Thackeray's 'Rawdon Crawley' Eton, Samuel Butler's 'Ernest Pontifex' Shrewsbury, barely literate and with a distaste bordering on revulsion for the studies they had pursued for a decade, the system had not failed: it had succeeded. The danger with science (apart from its lack of moral content) and the reason for keeping it out of the curriculum was that it might actually interest the boys. The curricula of the great Victorian Public Schools ensured that the vast majority of upper-class men would not be distracted by the delights of literature, science, and ideas from the practicalities of life. Few people—certainly few industrialists—imagined that scientific studies were 'applied'; they were an indulgence, a diversion from the serious business of making things work.

The landed gentry and aristocracy showed their practical, technical talents most clearly where their interests were most directly engaged: in England's greatest industry, agriculture. In the eighteenth century they revolutionized it. Sir Robert Walpole read his farm correspondence before he broke the seals of his letters on affairs of state; Queen Caroline took the periodical, *Horse-Hoeing Husbandry*.[59] They pioneered technological advance when it was relevant to estate development—notably in connexion with iron and coal.[60] They tended to regard scientific activity and discovery as private property: the great Lincolnshire landowner (and biologist), Joseph Banks, ran the Royal Society for forty-two years like his private estate; the eminent chemist, Henry Cavendish (grandson of the Duke of Devonshire and the

Duke of Kent, whose father, Lord Charles, received the Copley Medal for his work on thermometers), was very reluctant to publish his research: it was private property and the property rights were his alone.[61]

Francis Egerton, Duke of Bridgewater, was a Gold Medallist of the Royal Society of Arts. His paper on 'the inclined plane' (published in the Society's *Transactions* in 1800) shows the depth and extent of his independent, innovative talents. The 'Canal Duke' was an outstanding and original engineer in his own right. The half-illiterate genius, James Brindley, who is commonly given the credit for the Bridgewater Canal, appears in fact to have made a very limited contribution: none to its conception and comparatively little (three years out of seventeen) to its construction.[62]

Francis Egerton's intense practical interests stood on a basis of classical studies at Eton. He turned to the problems of canal construction while on the Grand Tour with an accomplished classical scholar, Robert Wood, author of books on Homer, as his tutor. He successfully evaded Wood's refined literary studies and classical archaeology for canals and actresses. He made a close study of the docks and locks of the famous Languedoc canal in the south of France and, although Wood threatened to resign, insisted on attending courses in Bourdeaux on 'Experimental Philosophy'.[63]

But for more than a century to come scientific studies ('natural philosophy') would be widely regarded as a serious threat to industrial development. Thomas Henry (a medical practitioner, a Fellow of the Royal Society, and industrial chemist) addressed the Manchester Literary and Philosophical Society in 1781 on the relevance of 'philosophical' studies to commercial pursuits. He argued strenuously that knowledge of air-pumps, electrical machines, and microscopes would not cause a businessman to neglect his commercial interests.[64] Manchester's business community was not convinced.

The Literary and Philosophical Society supported a new College of Arts and Sciences in Manchester (founded in 1783). It lasted five years. The teaching of chemistry was given prominence and was widely advertised as having particular relevance to bleaching, dyeing, and calico-printing. The causes of the College's early demise are said to have included 'a superstitious dread of the tendency of science to unfit young men for the ordinary details of business'.[65] There had never been any such danger of seduction from Classics as taught at the great Public Schools.

GENTRY IDEOLOGY AND SOCIAL CONTROL

The central value of the gentry culture was courage. The middle classes were soft and effeminate; they lived in cities and were almost certainly cowards. The gentry ideology has courage at its centre with *esprit de corps* very close. The gentry imposed this ideology on themselves in Public Schools; and on virtually everybody else through fox-hunting, lads' clubs, and the Boy Scouts. This is known technically as 'incorporation', and sometimes as 'social control'.

In his famous essay, *On Compromise*, John Morley discussed 'the possible utility of error'. By this he meant the deliberate teaching of falsehood to secure social control: '... that the more enlightened classes in a community ... should openly encourage a doctrine for the less enlightened classes which they do not believe to be true for themselves.' This was apparently a perfectly reasonable issue to weigh and consider in 1874. The gentry ideology was not an imposed falsehood. What they said quite explicitly to the Boy Scouts, and signalled more covertly on the hunting field, they regarded as entirely true for themselves.

The dominant ethic of the new industrial England was not a work ethic. 'Pip' (in *Great Expectations*) was an entirely credible and even sympathetic character to Victorian readers. When he had expectations of becoming a gentleman he immediately left the toil of the forge, an honourable apprenticeship to a skilled trade; he dressed the part; he lived in idleness; he incurred debts. And when he was sufficiently idle and in debt his former master, the good, industrious blacksmith, Joe Gargery, called him 'Sir'. But though plausible and recognizable, the gentry role of Pip was a debased role. For the gentry work was disgraceful but service (unpaid) was paramount.

A gentleman was 'spirited'; he had courage, 'breeding', and physical grace (the 'vigour, good looks, and fine complexion' of Mathew Arnold's 'Barbarians');[66] and although these qualities were often subsumed under the heading of 'manliness',[67] they were in fact the attributes of a horse. As England's new industrial civilization rose in great cities a significant measure of social control was exercised through neo-totemism. (The RSPCA, founded in 1824, is significant as a formal part of this control apparatus.) Social categories were transformed into animal categories; ubiquitous hunting prints communicated the social organization, the morality (and the humour) of the hunting field to the deepest and darkest recesses of city life.

Mary Douglas has given us a very perceptive account of the way men have replicated and reinforced their social divisions through classifications of animals embodied in dietary laws: the purity of social categories was guaranteed in every encounter with the animal kingdom and at every meal.[68] Claude Levi-Strauss has provided a kind of 'transformational grammar' for converting animal categories into social categories: he follows Rousseau in arguing that men use the diversity of species as conceptual support for social differentiation; they borrow the differences they see among animals to create differences among themselves.[69]

The game laws of England had always distinguished 'game' animals and birds from others: they were protected and incorporated into the aristocratic–gentry class. The binary structure of English society was replicated and reinforced in the animal kingdom: falcons and stags (like trout and salmon) have always been officer class. (Rabbits and roach have never achieved gentry status, although the hare, like the grayling, has come very close.)

The social organization of fox-hunting after Meynell's reforms at Quorn was revolutionary: it represented a realignment of men and animals, and social control not through coercion but incorporation. The fox was vermin. There were no valuable spoils at the end of the chase. Fox-hunting was vermin control. The fox had never been a 'protected' creature, to be killed only by gentry, privileged, 'above the line'. Fox-hunting, unlike the old game laws, did not keep social subordinates out; until the end of the nineteenth century, when many hunts became clubs, it effectively brought them in. But they came in on gentry terms. Fox-hunting (like fly fishing) is a pursuit of gentlemen in that rules are designed not to promote 'goal-attainment' (as in a rational-utilitarian bourgeois culture), but precisely to prevent it. To kill foxes 'efficiently' with a gun or a trap is as unthinkable as taking trout with a maggot. Trollope's 'Archdeacon Grantly', though not himself a hunting man, recoiled in horror at the news that foxes on Mr. Thorne's land had been trapped; but he knew that a gentleman of Mr. Thorne's breeding—for whom baronetcies were a new-fangled invention of King James I—would put a stop to the keeper's heinous efficiency as soon as he knew. Although Mr. Thorne had once for a short time given up hunting (we are told in *Barchester Towers*), 'He did not cut his covers, for that would not have been the act of a gentleman. He did not kill his foxes, for that according to his light would have been murder.'

The record of the RSPCA has been very closely inspected for class bias. It has not been found guilty. In fact its activities were not socially divisive but cohesive. It is true that the Society in its early years was less concerned to defend animals than to civilize the lower orders,[70] but its inspectors usually found wealthy farmers and army officers at cock-fights and similar sports.[71] Often, indeed, they were the organizers and referees. The different levels of society were pushed together by the Society's activities, rather than pulled apart. But the basic dualism underscored by the RSPCA was between wild and domestic animals. It took no action to defend the latter until the end of the century. For a time, at least, there was a common enemy outside, the divisions were somewhat softened within.

But participation in fox-hunting never erased social rank. It has been described as the most aristocratic and the most egalitarian of English institutions. At least until the later part of the nineteenth century, anyone could join. Hunting was open to all, and all classes participated. But it was no social leveller. Tradesmen, small farmers, and chimney-sweeps who were welcome in the field did not usually wear scarlet and would not expect an invitation to the hunt ball or hunt breakfast.[72] But any local man who could borrow a horse could enjoy a day with the local hunt.

It was not an ancient sport. It was only when Meynell in the later eighteenth century bred much faster hounds that could actually keep up with a fox that fox-hunting was transformed into a popular sport. It was between 1800 and 1830, as England industrialized, that fox-hunting became a national institution; it was not only hunting men who came to feel that it '... could be trifled with only at the risk of wide-ranging social consequences'.[73] Fox-hunting assumed high significance as '... the symbol of the uniquely British manliness that enabled the nation to maintain its world prestige in peace and war'.[74]

The social openness of fox-hunting was destroyed by the railways; the local hunt became exclusive to protect itself from an army of invaders from (often quite distant) cities. By the eighteen-eighties hunts commonly charged a compulsory minimum subscription, and (as the editor of *The Field* complained in 1881) to become a master of hounds was no longer a sign of high social rank but a means of acquiring it. But for almost a century fox-hunting was seen quite explicitly as a 'Public School' for all social ranks: 'It was considered to be one of the great benefits of the openness that even the lower classes could be imbued with gentlemanly ideals.'[75]

Charles Kingsley strongly advocated fox-hunting for clergymen because of the moral qualities that it fostered; in India its (somewhat more dangerous) counterpart, pig-sticking, produced the qualities required in imperial command. The historian of the men who ruled India says: '... the good pig-stickers were usually very good officers. The district officer who spent all his time with his nose in files on the other hand did not always have his district in good order.' From pig-sticking the Indian administrator gained 'the power of quick but cool judgment, a stout heart, a controlled but fiery ardour and a determination not to be beaten ...'.[76] Hardiness, temperance, coolness, and clear-headedness were also to be learned, it was strongly maintained, from the hunt in the English shires.[77] The qualities which made the English gentleman were on offer to anyone who had some time and was able to borrow a horse.

The gentry did not impose a special set of servile values on the lower classes; they tried to impose their own. They did so with a considerable measure of success, especially through the youth movements (both uniformed and non-uniformed) of late-Victorian and Edwardian England. These movements were neither a politicized arm of the status quo nor a subversive youth culture, but in a quiet and unobtrusive way they were part of the fabric of the social order.

The transmission of these 'rulling ideas' was not intended to make the lower classes more docile subordinates; it was intended to make them self-reliant and independent, and as far as possible to develop their leadership qualities. The new youth organizations were about pluck, clean living, woodcraft, stalking wild animals, resourcefulness, and being of service to those in need; and even their 'hidden curricula', when exposed, reveal a remarkable political innocence.[78] Marxist historians of education now see these gentry-inspired youth movements in a more sinister light as neo-feudalistic strategies of class domination.[79] A close scrutiny of their ideology, activities, and organization points to a conclusion which is precisely the opposite. The gentry saw the clubs quite explicitly—if somewhat unrealistically—as 'Public Schools' which would develop in working-class youth the very qualities of command that Eton had developed in them.

The key was *esprit de corps*. This is what upper-class parents wanted Public Schools to give their sons; they were not always sure that the grammar schools offered it—as the head of Lincoln Grammar School conceded in 1911.[80] Elementary schools were entirely without it, but the new clubs would remedy this deficiency. The working classes could now get *esprit de corps* too. When an Old Etonian, the Hon. T. W. H. Pelham, took the lead in setting up a London Federation of Working Boys' clubs in 1888, he said of the clubs: 'They can, if efficiently managed, be in some degree to the poor what the public schools and universities have been to the rich. They develop, as no other agency can, that *esprit de corps* in which the poor are for the most part, so lamentably deficient.'[81]

This theme runs through the advocacy of boys clubs, the Boys Brigade, and the Boy Scouts. Badges were of critical importance as symbols of group loyalty. Public School 'Houses' and Arnold's Prefect system were explicit organizational models which legitimated meritocratic promotion from the ranks. When William Alexander Smith established the Boys Brigade in the eighteen-eighties one of his aims was to promote 'true Christian Manliness'; but Smith also aimed, as he himself said, to foster 'that *esprit de corps* which public school boys acquire as a matter of course, but which is almost entirely lacking in elementary school boys'.[82]

Smith promoted the rank-and-file after giving them an examination (in writing and drill) and assessing their qualities. A future historian of the movement described this as 'a procedure which seems to us natural but which anticipated for many Associations the promotion of leaders from among a "gang" of working-class boys themselves'.[83] High command was also available to working-class boys in the Boys Clubs through the 'house' system that was widely adopted: 'The training in leadership, responsibility, initiative and organizing capacity given by the functions these boys have to perform is of extraordinary value.'[84]

The lads' clubs of late-Victorian and Edwardian England did not reinforce gentry and upper-class control; they provided for working-class boys a remarkable experience of assuming responsibility, power, and authority. The committee system gave them the rudiments of management training. The Warden of Brighton Boys' Club detailed the nature of this experience:

> For the boys who serve on the committee it is an educative experience, for it helps them to understand that running a club is not so straightforward and simple a matter as they had thought. They realise, too, that an eye must be kept on the needs of the club as a whole, not on the needs of their particular pals ... they learn that everyone must not speak at once; that a chairman must be respected; they learn the value of the individual vote, and the discipline of accepting a decision which they themselves have voted against.[85]

Committees no less than badges were a source of *esprit de corps*. The lower, unskilled working class have never been extensively reached by youth organizations—just as they were never reached by the National Schools while attendance was voluntary. (The YMCA in its early years was very distinctively and exclusively lower middle class.)[86] A survey of cubs and brownies in Stockport in the mid-nineteen-sixties shows a familiar pattern: the Registrar General's 'social classes' I and II contributed 27 per cent. of a cross-section of children but 33 per cent. of the cubs and brownies; the large skilled working class were exactly 'represented'—60 per cent. of the population and 60 per cent. of the organizations' members; the unskilled working class were 13 per cent. of all children but only 7 per cent. of the members.[87]

Some 60 per cent. of adult men alive in 1966 had belonged at some time to uniformed youth organizations; the survey which provides this figure gives no information about those who had belonged to clubs which had no uniforms.[88] The effectiveness of this 'ideological apparatus' for transmitting the gentry culture can scarcely be in doubt. The ideology, like that of the great Public Schools, centred on 'manliness'. It accorded high value to practical skills. It was about honour. And it was always fragrant with woodland and woodsmoke. From the start the Boy Scout Governing Council was dominated by Generals and Bishops; and Kitchener's New Army knew that it could depend not only on Etonian subalterns but on 'the dissemination of public school loyalties and values among lower middle-class and working-class men'.[89] Scouting stood staunchly for Empire. If we wish to understand the meaning of hegemony and ideology in the context of English education and social life in late-Victorian and Edwardian England, the basic text is *Scouting for Boys.*

GENTRY HEGEMONY AND THE INTELLECTUALS

Gramsci's writings in the nineteen-thirties on intellectuals, hegemony, and the ruling class have recently received a great deal of attention. Gramsci is unusual among Marxists in the crucial role he assigns to intellect and intellectuals in the process of social transformation. Intellectuals are all-important in shaping the consciousness of the masses and achieving and maintaining hegemony.[90]

It is not a particularly remarkable notion that the influence of intellectuals will depend on their location in society—their relationship to the ruling class as well as to 'the masses'. (Thomas Hobbes is well aware of this in the *Leviathan.*) In England intellectuals have been given power; in America they have had to seize it. American intellectuals are combative and nurse their 'alienation'; in England they have prospered with greater self-confidence—they are part of the gentry hegemony.

In his outstanding study of anti-intellectualism in America Richard Hofstadter perceptively relates the intellectual's outsider position to the decline of the gentry;[91] in England the insider position of intellectuals must be related to the gentry's rise. The end of the sixteenth century, says Stone, saw one of the really decisive moments in England's history: 'For the first time in history the intelligentsia became a branch of the propertied classes.'[92] The English aristocracy and gentry took advantage of the 'educational revolution' to equip themselves for civil office. The intellectuals were no longer the *castrati.* They joined society (in its top division): 'At last it was possible to be an intellectual without having to endure the intolerable hardships of celibacy.'[93]

American social scientists have shown a sharp awareness of the favoured position of England's intellectuals: Lipset has pointed to the shelter they enjoy from being included in the broad category of 'gentleman';[94] but the most perceptive observer is Edward Shils. He relocated the intellectuals of post-war England in the aristocratic–gentry culture based on 'the London–Oxford–Cambridge Axis'; correctly saw their close connexion with authority which 'rests ultimately on the Crown and on the land' and with political power which is able to disown its industrial base. 'Never has an intellectual class found its society and its culture so much to its satisfaction.' The provincial, bourgeois culture, which seemed for a brief Victorian moment to flourish, was in retreat. Shils is describing a re-conquest, a recovery. Writing in the mid-nineteen-fifties he claims with confidence: 'The aristocratic–gentry culture has now come back into the saddle with little to dispute its dominion.'[95]

It is now usual to contrast the 'clerisy' with the 'avant-garde'. The clerisy are near the centre of the social order and uphold it; the avant-garde are near the periphery and subvert it. The contrast is useful, both between nations and within nations; but these polar extremes are not the only positions that intellectuals occupy. There are other, limbo positions for intellectuals, of the kind John Porter has described in Canada. There, intellectuals are of no account; they are negligible in support of the social order; they are no less negligible in attack. Porter calls them a clerisy because of their generally conservative stance.[96] He is wrong. A clerisy counts. Canada's intellectuals do not.

The establishment of the Regius professorships and the royal colleges, Christ Church and Trinity, at Oxford and Cambridge was part of the centralizing policy of the Tudor state. Intellectuals were now enrolled within the royal order. 'The object of education within the colleges,' writes Kearney, 'was to produce intellectuals and gentlemen who could be relied upon in a world constantly threatened, it was thought, by revolution.'[97] This was precisely the view expressed by Thomas Hobbes. It is true that he thought that universities could go astray (they had once upheld the power of Popes against the commonwealth), but they were of crucial importance in a well-ordered state for producing men who, as divines or educated laity, would instruct the masses in 'the essential rights which are the natural and fundamental laws of sovereignty'. University men would teach the ordinary people law and obedience to God, parents, and the King: 'It is therefore manifest, that the instruction of the people, dependeth wholly, on the right teaching of youth in the universities.'[98]

The clerisy are not powerful because they are intellectuals: they are intellectuals because they are powerful. When he coined the term 'clerisy' Coleridge was getting back to the idea of the clergy as 'clerks', a secular no less than an ecclesiastical elite. Their duty was '... to form and train up the people of the country to be obedient, free, useful, organizable subjects, citizens and patriots ...'.[99] To be a member of the clerisy was an obligation of property and birth. F. D. Maurice considered that all people born to property and high social rank were 'bound to show cause' why they did not go to a university and so 'put themselves in the best position for becoming what Coleridge calls the *Clerisy* of the land'.[100]

The election of Davy Crockett to Congress in 1826 signalled, it is said, America's rejection of the intellectual in favour of the non-cerebral, practical man. In England intellectuals as an arm of the gentry have remained close to the centres of power. (They have perhaps been helped by not being overly theoretical in their intellectual pursuits—collectors of discrete facts, addicted to puzzles and conundrums: *The Times* crossword—no pigmy challenge—the summit of their endeavours.) The intellectuals who benefited from the reform of public institutions in the nineteenth century were still men with strong gentry connexions. The nobility lost their powers of patronage; a wide range of posts now growing rapidly in importance passed from their control into the hands of this intellectual elite.

Noel Annan has dissected this 'intellectual aristocracy' of nineteenth-century England. Though they were closely associated with the power structure and considered themselves gentlemen, they were not part of the 'ruling class' and had no wish to be. This intellectual elite was based on cousinship and Evangelical religion. Its members did not move—and did not wish to move—in circles of high fasion; their good manners appeared in their prose.

They were the headmasters of Shrewsbury and Harrow; they took posts in museums, became school inspectors, editors of periodicals, and secretaries of philanthropic societies; and 'they became the new professional civil servants at a time when government had become too complicated and technical to be handled by the ruling class'. They were the Arnolds, the Huxleys, the Butlers, the Venns, and the

Vaughans. They intermarried and bestrode the top command posts of the new professions. Some did not hunt, but they all regarded themselves as gentry. They tended to be the cadet branches of gentry families: but Babington was a squire who could appoint to a living; the Trevelyans and Stracheys were old West Country families with baronetcies created in the seventeenth and eighteenth centuries. They were never an adversary culture. 'The influence of these families,' says Annan, 'may partly explain a paradox which has puzzled European and American observers of English life: the paradox of an intelligentsia which appears to conform rather than rebel against the rest of society.'[101]

The embattled position of intellectuals in American life was brought into sharp focus by Senator McCarthy's post-war inquisition on un-American activities. Intellectuals now asked why American intellectuals had become so vulnerable; they looked back to the beginning of their nation which had been created by intellectuals. Political leaders—John Adams, John Dickinson, Benjamin Franklin, Thomas Jefferson, Alexander Hamilton—were sages, scientists, men of broad cultivation. As the new nation established itself, says Hofstadter, 'the control of its affairs still rested largely in a patrician elite: and within this elite men of intellect moved freely and spoke with enviable authority.'[102] Intellectuals became outsiders when the gentry were pushed from the centre of politics between 1820 and 1830. This is the crucial difference between England and America: in England intellectuals have retained the protection of a powerful gentry class.

Annan overstates the separateness of intellectuals from England's ruling class. They were in fact in close association with aristocrats at the very centre of political power in late-Victorian and Edwardian England. Often they were lawyers who came into politics after success at the Bar. (Bryce also occupied the Regius Chair of Civil Law at Oxford; Harcourt the Chair of International Law at Cambridge.) Intellectuals and aristocrats also belonged to 'The Souls', an intimate group which moved around country houses, played pencil-and-paper games, and included the Duchess of Sutherland, the Duchess of Rutland, Arthur Balfour, George Curzon, George Wyndham, and the editor of the *Pall Mall Gazette*, Harry Cust.[103] The intellectuals came into politics from successful professional careers partly, says Guttsman, for the aristocratic contacts that high office entailed: 'Social intercourse with the aristocracy, country house life, dinners.'[104] The aristocracy had their own intellectuals in politics, too, some of whom, like Rosebery and Balfour, reached the highest offices of state.

Asquith enjoyed country house life and was often at Alderley for the weekend with Lord Sheffield. The son of a small Yorkshire employer, he took a First in 'Greats' (and numerous prizes) at Balliol and went to the Bar. He had a passion for miscellaneous information and quizzes; his second wife was Margot Tennant, who was at the centre both of the Souls and the Melton hunting set. One of her supreme pleasures in life after fast horses was to have a seat at dinner next to the Master of the Quorn.[105] This unlikely marriage in fact catches the unique character of hegemony in English society: the mix of scholarship, reckless horsemanship, aristocratic connexions, and political power.

American intellectuals moved towards the centre of political power in the

160

Depression and the Kennedy Administration, but their essential posture is 'adversary'.[106] 'Intellectual' is often synonymous with 'literary intellectual'; and literary studies in America have been a vehicle of moral protest. In England, Mathew Arnold, T. S. Eliot, and Leavis have stood in a different tradition, no less moral, but with the emphasis on order and decorum.[107] But American intellectuals are not ineffectual outsiders: they are rebels who succeed. They led the effective opposition to the Vietnam War and they are taking powerful action against the great corporations on the issue of pollution. They have fought giants and have won.[108]

Intellectuals, it is widely claimed (not only by Marxists), are now being proletarianized. There is truth in this. An overripe capitalist system provides for their overproduction.[109] Daniel Bell says otherwise: the needs of a knowledge-based post-industrial society gives them importance and power.[110] This will be true for a minority of gifted science graduates with a grasp of highly sophisticated knowledge; it will not be true for the swollen army of arts and social science graduates, especially if they come from working-class homes.

In England the aristocratic–gentry connexion still extends protection to universities and signals that they are a clerisy rather than the avant-garde. The connexion is symbolized in the appointment of ceremonial heads, the university Chancellors. Between 1970 and 1980 there was little more than a token gesture towards modern sources of wealth and power. It is true that Loughborough got Lord Pilkington, but there were only three dukes (excluding royalty) where formerly there were six. The Duke of Kent became the Chancellor of Surrey, Prince Philip of Salford, the Duke of Abercorn of the University of Ulster at Coleraine. The Duke of Northumberland was still the Chancellor of Newcastle-upon-Tyne and the Duke of Devonshire of Manchester.

These ceremonial and frequently very active heads of British universities publicly signal the continuing royal and aristocratic connexions of higher learning. Degree Day at the Victoria University of Manchester is ducal in its pomp and splendour—redolent of pheasants and grouse moors, with no hint that cotton ever was king.

CONCLUSION

The gentry gained power after they bought land extensively in the late sixteenth century; they lost power when they sold it after 1918. But for three and a half centuries, and throughout the Industrial Revolution, England's landed gentry did not simply hold on to their power; they increased it.

They penetrated deeply into the key institutions of state and their ideas were the ruling ideas. They commanded a comprehensive ideological superstructure which embraced the ancient universities, the Anglican church, the Public Schools, field sports, youth clubs, and the Boy Scouts. The Royal Society was for long one of their private estates.

The 'ideological apparatuses' through which their values were expressed and disseminated did not produce abject and servile subordinate ranks. On the contrary, they prepared the lower ranks for the responsibilities of command. Field sports, youth clubs, and the Scouts did not promote docility (though they nurtured self-discipline): they encouraged enterprise, loyalty, self-reliance, a capable practicality, and courage. They were at least as important as Sunday schools in the making of the respectable, skilled working class.

The influence of England's landed gentry did not decline with their power. Fiscal policies drove them from the land, but their values have remained potent. Their values and influence survived even the collapse of Empire, which was a kind of tropical extension of the Quorn (with good rough shooting and abundant beaters, even in regions where the tsetse fly excluded the horse). Shils considered that their values were resurgent in post-second World War Oxford and Cambridge, their culture the dominant culture. It is a culture which retains its ancient pragmatism, which is hostile to specialization, and which delights in table-talk about Jane Austen and wild flowers.

It has a curiously perennial 'relevance' which guarantees its continuing influence if not its centrality. It is no longer seriously supported by the Public Schools: they have now sold out to the bourgeoisie who want their sons to become accountants and technical managers. As Otley says, after his study of Public Schools in the past as quasi-military academies: 'The old leadership/service/sacrifice ethos has undoubtedly weakened—perhaps almost to vanishing point.'[111]

The gentry culture has a commitment to three values which are of crucial and increasing importance in our day: to experience, to leisure, and to the environment. The landed gentry have always been conservationists (and scientific stock-breeders) without equal; they knew how to find significance in life without submission to work and careers; and they valued experience over ideas. (The intellectuals they have sheltered have generally been rather suspicious of abstract thought.)

The great scarcity of our times will not be knowledge and ideas: these are ubiquitous. There is no productivity problem in today's knowledge industry; there is no real problem about distributing its product—only in evading it. The great scarcity will not be knowledge and ideas; it will be action and experience. A highly pragmatic gentry culture has not ruined the nation; it may ensure its survival. The next chapter (Chapter 8) will suggest ways in which transmutations of the gentry culture still have a bearing on our times.

NOTES

1. Joseph A. Schumpeter, *Capitalism, Socialism and Democracy*, George Allen and Unwin, London, 1976, pp. 131–142.
2. Peter Laslett, *The World We have Lost*, Methuen, London, 1965, pp. 22–52.
3. *Ibid.*, pp. 34–35.
4. An estimate in the year 1600 put the number of gentlemen at 16,000 or thereabouts plus 500 knights: see R. H. Tawney, 'The rise of the gentry, 1558–1640', *The Economic History Review*, **40** (1941), p. 3 (footnote 1). Gregory King's estimates for 1688 are given by Peter Laslett in *The World We Have Lost*, Methuen, 1965, pp. 32–33. King gave 800 baronets, 600 knights, 3,000 esquires, and 12,000 gentlemen: a total of 16,400 gentry families out of a total of some 1.4 million families.
5. Calculated from data in T. W. Bamford, 'Public Schools and social class, 1801–1850',

British Journal of Sociology, **12** (1961). Out of a total of 6.6 million twelve-year-old boys in England and Wales 21,500 were from landed-gentry families (see Table 3).

6. F. M. L. Thompson, *English Landed Society in the Nineteenth Century*, Routledge and Kegan Paul, London, 1963:

> Such an enormous and rapid transfer of land had not been seen since the confiscations and sequestrations of the Civil War, such a permanent transfer not since the dissolution of the monasteries in the sixteenth century. Indeed a transfer on this scale and in such a short space of time had probably not been equalled since the Norman Conquest (pp. 332–333).

7. *Ibid.*, p. 343.
8. Anthony Giddens, 'The rich', *New Society*, 14 October 1976.
9. *Ibid.*, p. 66.
10. P. Haslett, *The World We Have Lost*, Methuen, 1965, p. 26.
11. Hugh Kearney, *Scholars and Gentlemen*, Faber, London, 1970, p. 26.
12. L. Stone, 'Social mobility in England 1500–1700', *Past and Present*, April **1966**, No. 38.
13. R. H. Tawney, 'The rise of the gentry, 1558–1640', *The Economic History Review*, **40** (1941), and 'The rise of the gentry: a postscript', *The Economic History Review*, **7** (1954).
14. L. Stone, 'The Elizabethan aristocracy—a restatement', *The Economic History Review*, **4** (1952). For the decline of the gentry thesis see H. R. Trevor-Roper, 'The Elizabethan aristocracy: an anatomy anatomized', *The Economic History Review*, **3** (1951).
15. Lawrence Stone, *The Crisis of the Aristocracy 1558–1641*, Oxford University Press, London, 1965, p. 13.
16. *Ibid.*, p. 14.
17. See W. L. Guttsman, 'The changing social structure of the British political elite, 1886–1935', *British Journal of Sociology*, **2** (1951).
18. N. Hans, *New Trends in Education in the Eighteenth Century*, Routledge and Kegan Paul, London, 1951. Calculations are based on data in Table III, pp. 26–27.
19. Hugh Kearney, *Scholars and Gentlemen*, Faber, London, 1970, p. 33.
20. N. Hans, *New Trends in Education in the Eighteenth Century*, Routledge and Kegan Paul, 1951, Table V, p. 32.
21. P. E. Razzell, 'Social origins of officers in the Indian and British Home Army: 1758–1962', *British Journal of Sociology*, **14** (1963). The landed-gentry contribution to the Indian Army always exceeded that of the aristocracy but was never as great as their contribution to the Home Army. The same increased contribution occurred in the Indian Army: the English landed gentry contributed 6 per cent. of the officers from 1758 to 1774 and 19 per cent. from 1805 to 1934.
22. C. B. Otley, 'The social origins of British Army officers', *Sociological Review*, **18** (1970).
23. P. E. Razzell, 'Social origins of officers in the Indian and British Home Army: 1758–1962', *British Journal of Sociology*, **14** (1963).
24. C. B. Otley, 'The social origins of British Army officers', *Sociological Review*, **18** (1970).
25. J. A. Schumpeter, *Capitalism, Socialism and Democracy*, George Allen and Unwin, 1976, p. 137.
26. T. W. Bamford, 'Public Schools and social class, 1801–1850', *British Journal of Sociology*, **12** (1961).
27. D. C. Coleman, 'Gentlemen and players', *The Economic History Review*, **26** (1973).
28. T. J. H. Bishop, *Winchester and the Public School Elite*, Faber, London, 1967, Table 5, pp. 104–108.
29. Simon Raven, 'Perish by the sword', *Encounter*, **12** (1959), and Gwyn Harries-Jenkins, *The Army in Victorian Society*, Routledge and Kegan Paul, London, 1977, p. 4.
30. Harries-Jenkins, *ibid.*, p. 100.
31. David C. Itzkowitz, *Peculiar Privilege: A Social History of English Foxhunting, 1753–1885*, Harvester Press, 1977, pp. 20–21.

32. C. B. Otley, 'Militarism and militarization in the Public Schools, 1900–1972, *British Journal of Sociology*, **29** (1978).
33. *Ibid.*
34. T. J. H. Bishop, *Winchester and the Public School Elite*, Faber, 1967, pp. 69–70, 73, 108.
35. Anthony Trollope, *An Autobiography*, Oxford University Press, London, 1974, pp. 33–34.
36. J. M. Compton, 'Open competition and the Indian Civil Service, 1854–1876', *English Historical Review*, **83** (1968).
37. Philip Woodruff, *The Men Who Ruled India · The Guardians*, Jonathan Cape, London, 1954, pp. 180–181.
38. Ralph E. Pumphrey, 'The introduction of industrialists into the British peerage: a study in adaptation of a social institution', *The American Historical Review*, **65** (1959).
39. W. L. Guttsman, 'The changing social structure of the British political elite, 1886–1935', *British Journal of Sociology*, **2** (1951).
40. T. W. Bamford, 'Public Schools and Social Class, 1801–1850', *British Journal of Sociology*, **12** (1961).
41. P. E. Razzell, 'Social origins of officers in the Indian and British Home Army: 1758–1962', *British Journal of Sociology*, **14** (1963).
42. C. B. Otley, 'The social origins of British Army officers', *Sociological Review*, **18** (1970).
43. P. E. Razzell, 'Social origins of officers in the Indian and British Home Army: 1758–1962', *British Journal of Sociology*, **14** (1963).
44. W. L. Guttsman, 'The changing social structure of the British political elite, 1886–1935', *British Journal of Sociology*, **2** (1951).
45. *Ibid.*
46. Ralph E. Pumphrey, 'The introduction of industrialists into the British peerage: a study in adaptation of a social institution', *The American Historical Review*, **65** (1959).
47. See F. M. L. Thompson, 'The end of a great estate', *The Economic History Review*, **8** (1955–56), for a close study of the finances of the second Duke of Buckingham and Chandos between 1839 and his death in 1861.
48. Simon Raven, 'Perish by the sword', *Encounter*, **12** (1959).
49. Correlli Barnett, 'The education of military elites', *Journal of Contemporary History*, **2** (1967).
50. Michael Howard, 'Officers and gentlemen', *Times Literary Supplement*, 5 August 1977.
51. Gwyn Harries-Jenkins, *The Army in Victorian Society*, Routledge and Kegan Paul, 1977, pp. 280–281.
52. F. M. L. Thompson, *English Landed Society in the Nineteenth Century*, Routledge and Kegan Paul, London, 1963, p. 21.
53. D. H. Aldcroft, 'The entrepreneur and the British economy, 1870–1914', *The Economic History Review*, **17** (1964).
54. David Ward, 'The Public Schools and industry in Britain after 1870', *Journal of Contemporary History*, **2** (1967).
55. Charles Wilson, 'Economy and society in late Victorian Britain', *The Economic History Review*, **18** (1965).
56. D. C. Coleman, 'Gentlemen and players', *The Economic History Review*, **26** (1973).
57. David Spring, 'The role of the aristocracy in the late nineteenth century', *Victorian Studies*, **4** (1960–61).
58. S. J. Chapman and F. J. Marquis, 'The recruiting of the employing classes from the ranks of the wage-earners in the cotton industry', *Journal of the Royal Statistical Society*, **75** (1912).
59. Lord Ernle, *English Farming Past and Present*, Heinemann, London, 1961, p. 173.
60. Lawrence Stone, *The Crisis of the Aristocracy 1558–1641* Oxford University Press, London, 1965, pp. 335–344.
61. J. G. Crowther, *Scientists of the Industrial Revolution*, Cressett Press, 1962, p. 318.
62. Hugh Malet, *Bridgewater · The Canal Duke, 1736–1803*, Manchester University Press, 1977, pp. 33, 55, 97–98.

63. *Ibid.*, pp. 16–18.
64. Robert H. Kargon, *Science in Victorian Manchester*, Manchester University Press, 1977, pp. 8–9.
65. A. E. Musson and E. Robinson, 'Science and Industry in the Late Eighteenth Century', *The Economic History Review*, **15** (1960).
66. Mathew Arnold, *Culture and Anarchy*, John Murray, 1949, pp. 63–64.
67. David Newsome, *Godliness and Good Learning*, John Murray, 1961, pp. 195–197.
68. Mary Douglas, *Purity and Danger*, Penguin Books, Harmondsworth, 1970, pp. 54–72.
69. Claude Levi-Strauss, *Totemism*, trans. by Rodney Needham, Penguin Books, Harmondsworth, 1973, p. 174.
70. Brian Harrison, 'Animals and the state in nineteenth-century England', *English Historical Review*, **88** (1973).
71. Brian Harrison, 'Religion and recreation in nineteenth-century England', *Past and Present*, **1967**, No. 38. 'In reality the accusation of class bias ignores the pan-class nature of so much brutal sport at this time.'
72. David C. Itzkowitz, *Peculiar Privilege · A Social History of English Fox-hunting 1753–1885*, Harvester Press, 1977, pp. 25–6, 33–4.
73. *Ibid.*, p. 16.
74. David Newsome, *Godliness and Good Learning*, John Murray, 1961, p. 22.
75. D. C. Itzkowitz, *Peculiar Privilege · A Social History of English Fox-hunting 1753–1885*, Harvester Press, 1977, p. 27.
76. Philip Woodruff, *The Men Who Ruled India · The Guardians*, Jonathan Cape, London, 1954, pp. 180–181.
77. D. C. Itzkowitz, *Peculiar Privilege · A Social History of English Fox-hunting 1753–1885*, Harvester Press, 1977, pp. 21–22.
78. See, for example, Paul Wilkinson, 'English youth movements, 1908–30', *Journal of Contemporary History*, **4** (1969). Wilkinson emphasizes the apolitical character of the youth organizations: 'The interesting thing about the English movements in contrast to the continental, is why they did not become vehicles of overt political protest or instruments of party political manipulation.'
79. Brian Simon, *Education and the Labour Movement 1870–1920*, Lawrence and Wishart, 1965, p. 83.
80. *Ibid.*, p. 272.
81. *Ibid.*, p. 70.
82. Alicia C. Percival, *Youth Will Be Led*, Collins, London, 1951, p. 69.
83. *Ibid.*, p. 90.
84. C. E. B. Russell, *Lads' Clubs*, Black, London, 1932, p. 69. These observations were written by Russell in 1908.
85. *Ibid.*, p. 68.
86. *Ibid.*, p. 233.
87. Calculations based on data in E. J. Dearnaley and Margaret H. Fletcher, 'Cubs and brownies—social class, intelligence and interests', *Educational Research*, **10** (1968).
88. See Paul Wilkinson, 'English youth movements, 1908–30', *Journal of Contemporary History*, **4** (1969), p. 3 n.
89. *Ibid.*, p. 23.
90. See James Joll, *Gramsci*, Fontana/Collins, London, 1977, pp. 88–104, and Gwyn A. Williams, 'The concept of "egemonia" in the thought of Antonio Gramsci', *Journal of the History of Ideas*, **21** (1960).
91. Richard Hofstadter, *Anti-Intellectualism in American Life*, Jonathan Cape, London, 1964, pp. 145–171.
92. Lawrence Stone, *The Crisis of the Aristocracy 1558–1641*, Oxford University Press, London, 1965, p. 16.
93. *Ibid.*, p. 672.
94. S. M. Lipset, *Political Man*, Heinemann, London, 1963, p. 327.

95. Edward Shils, 'The intellectuals. I. Great Britain', *Encounter*, **4** (1955).
96. John Porter, *The Vertical Mosaic*, University of Toronto Press, 1965, p. 492.
97. Hugh Kearney, *Scholars and Gentlemen*, Faber, 1970, p. 22.
98. Thomas Hobbes, *Leviathan*, Michael Oakeshott (Ed.), Basil Blackwell, Oxford, 1964, p. 225.
99. See Anthony Arblaster and Steven Lukes, *The Good Society*, Methuen, London, 1971, pp. 109–113.
100. Quoted in Asa Briggs, 'Development in higher education in the United Kingdom', in W. R. Niblett (Ed.), *Higher Education · Demand and Response*, Tavistock, 1969, p. 109.
101. N. G. Annan, 'The intellectual aristocracy', in J. H. Plumb (Ed.), *Studies in Social History*, Longmans, Green and Co., London, 1955.
102. Richard Hofstadter, *Anti-Intellectualism in American Life*, Jonathan Cape, London, 1964, p. 145.
103. Roy Jenkins, *Asquith*, Collins, 1964, p. 76, and Margot Asquith, *The Autobiography of Margot Asquith*, Eyre and Spottiswoode, 1962, pp. 117 and 142.
104. W. L. Guttsman, 'Aristocracy and the middle class in the British political elite 1886–1916', *British Journal of Sociology*, **5** (1954).
105. M. Asquith, *The Autobiography of Margot Asquith*, Eyre and Spottiswoode, 1962, p. 154.
106. Marcus Cunliffe, 'The intellectuals. II. The United States', *Encounter*, **4** (1955). Cunliffe examines America's intellectuals in terms of 'clerisy' and 'avant-garde'.
107. Lionel Trilling, 'The two environments: reflections on the study of English', in *Beyond Culture*, Penguin Books, Harmondsworth, 1967.
108. S. M. Lipset and R. H. Dobson, 'The intellectual as critic and rebel', *Daedalus*, Summer **1972**.
109. Joseph Schumpeter, *Capitalism, Socialism and Democracy*, George Allen and Unwin, London, 1976, p. 152.
110. Daniel Bell, *The Coming of Post-Industrial Society*, Penguin Books, Harmondsworth, 1976, pp. 150–153, 343–344.
111. C. B. Otley, 'Militarism and militarization in the Public Schools, 1900–1972', *British Journal of Sociology*, **29** (1978).

CHAPTER 8

Progressive Schools, Counter-Cultures, and Black Elites

People in superior social positions sometimes 'step down' or arrange for their sons and daughters to do so. It is partly for this reason that history, as Pareto claimed in a famous phrase, is a graveyard of extinct aristocracies.[1] There is a circulation of elites. Pareto did not refer to the part that education plays in this process, but important subsystems of modern educational services facilitate and regulate these downward movements. These subsystems are the 'progressive' boarding schools (augmented in the past fifteen years or so by an informal 'counter-culture' which expresses similar values and has a similar function).

Formerly, when taxation was low, there was less need of progressive schools: one joined the idle rich. Many who might have been in the running for superior positions in life 'stepped down' in reasonable comfort and idleness on four or five hundred a year.[2] A modest settlement of 10,000 pounds would yield such an income in mid-Victorian England—as much as the local doctor or newspaper editor would earn and twice as much as the grammar school's headmaster. Thus vacancies were left for the deserving poor and elite circulation was enhanced. Abbotsholme was founded in the year that Goschen first introduced death duties, Bedales in the year that Harcourt gave them teeth. For the past eighty years, since taxation really began to bite, very costly educational services have been provided not to help people to go 'up' but to enable them (with reasonable comfort) to go down.

There is no logical reason why, in an expanding economy, with the number of superior jobs increasing and lowly jobs diminishing, there should be any downward intergenerational mobility at all. Anyone who moved could go up. In fact modern industrial societies experience a considerable amount of downward mobility. (Sociologists often point to this fact;[3] few have systematically explored it.) One explanation is in terms of the free and open competition which characterizes meritocratic societies; but downward movement also occurs because this is what some sons (and their fathers) prefer. Pareto recognized this and called it decadence. It is only ambitious and ruthlessly self-driving sociologists—and some old-fashioned economists—who imagine that everyone wants to go to the top, or even that privileged people invariably wish to reproduce themselves.

Elites go soft. (They stop sending their sons to Eton and send them to Bedales or Dartington Hall.) This is the heart of Pareto's argument. He was fully alive to the importance of 'structural' factors in the circulation of elites: the opportunities for ordinary soldiers in war and for ordinary citizens in industrial expansion.[4] But he focused attention on the decline of elites when they became humanitarian in outlook and shrank from the use of force to maintain their power.[5] They failed to instil into their children the qualities that had brought them success. In the language of modern social science, there had been a 'failure of socialization' (translated into Bourdieu's terminology, the 'habitus' had failed to take). These failures are quite common. There is no inevitability about 'the socialization process': 'Which largely explains,' says Andreski, 'why armies suffer defeats, states succumb to conquerors, firms go bankrupt, administrations disintegrate, families break up, and governments collapse.'[6]

Christopher Jencks was surprised to discover, when he began his research on inequality, that most people, even in America, do not especially want high-status jobs.[7] This is partly because they have a shrewd suspicion that they cannot get them. But like Robinson Crusoe's father (who had retired after acquiring 'a good estate by merchandise'), many successful men discourage their sons from aiming too high and recommend an easier position in life than their own. (Defoe drove his point home by making Crusoe suffer the torments of shipwreck as retribution for high ambition and filial disobedience.)

It is perhaps especially men in positions of power and responsibility in industry—senior managerial and administrative staff—who want something easier, more civilized (and perhaps humanitarian) for their sons. This is certainly what the Pahls found when they made a study of industrial managers and their wives. They even concluded that: 'Basically we consider that what we may be detecting is the beginning of a middle-class reaction against competition.'[8] Richardson, in one of the few studies of downward mobility, found managerial staff recommending their sons to learn a trade and find secure, skilled manual jobs. None of those who took father's advice suffered shipwreck; as hydraulic fitters and the like they seemed supremely happy with their lot.[9]

The circulation of elites with which this chapter is concerned is the voluntary stepping down of upper-class whites, and the legally assisted ascent (in America) of educated, though not necessarily very talented, blacks. The ascent of blacks into American elites has been made via the Civil Rights Act of 1964 and the Equal Employment Opportunities Commission. The descent of upper-class whites has been via Kilquhanity House, Summerhill, and Monkton Wyld; the Ranch School at Mendocini, California, and Lewis-Wadhams in New York State; Hare Krishna communes, journeys to the East, and the Baader-Meinhof gang. One of the most remarkable aspects of the 'failure of socialization' in our time is the contempt for capitalism among the sons and daughters of capitalists.

PROGRESSIVE BOARDING SCHOOLS

The 'progressive' boarding schools and the (apolitical) counter-culture of bucolic communes share many key characteristics and both have more in common with the gentry culture than with industrial capitalism. These interconnexions are perhaps most clearly illustrated in the lives and relationships of two men: Sir George Trevelyan (the fourth baronet) and, at an earlier date, Edward Carpenter. These are not the only possible illustrations: a transatlantic parallel might be seen in Paul Goodman, an elderly prophet of the counter-culture (duly celebrated by Theodore Roszak[10]) who was much involved for a time in the progressive Black Mountain College in North Carolina. (The college had recruited in 1942 two notable music teachers, Frederic Cohen and his wife, Elsa Kahl, from Dartington Hall.) Goodman's utopian anarchism was no problem for Black Mountain, but his rather extravagant homosexuality kept him out of the permanent teaching job that he would have liked.[11]

Sir George Trevelyan, bt., is also elderly (born 1906). He was educated at the progressive (Quaker) Sidcot School and Trinity College, Cambridge; he taught in the nineteen-thirties at what Maurice Punch calls a 'marginal', relatively conservative progressive school, Gordonstoun (Punch classifies it with Abbotsholme, Bryanston, and Leighton Park). By the late nineteen-seventies Sir George was a prophet of the 'New Consciousness'. He was growing organic foods; he was into yoga, Tibetan Buddhism, and meditation; he saw the central values of life in stillness rather than action. He was, of course, vegetarian. Everything in his personal history leads naturally to his awareness of the great spiritual awakening of our times.

Edward Carpenter, son of a naval family and Fellow of Trinity Hall, Cambridge, was the first hippie. And he was the co-founder, with Cecil Reddie, of England's first progressive school, Abbotsholme. (Reddie was rather Germanic in his concern for efficiency and hierarchy: Carpenter transferred his affection and support to Badley at the newly-founded Bedales.) Before this he knew Walt Whitman well and lived on a potato patch in the Derbyshire Dales. He was interviewed there in 1889 by the *Pall Mall Gazette*, which described him as 'an exponent of what may be called the Gospel of potato-digging'.

Carpenter was opposed to excessive intellectuality in education and life. He toiled on his Millthorpe small-holding along with his labourers. The *Pall Mall Gazette* highlighted his closeness to nature: 'At Abbotsholme they will mark out the year by seedtime and harvest, the county calendar, as much as by the date when cricket begins and football ends.' He is uncannily like a Victorian version of Paul Goodman. He interested himself in the self-supporting Ruskinian communes at Totley near Sheffield and Norton near Nottingham. He has recently been described as 'the aristocratic simple-life Socialist, who farmed and made sandals, the writer and poet, the admirer of Whitman and the mystical religions of the East, the reformer of sexual attitudes, the advocate of dress reform, manly love and comradeship'.[12] He prefigured the Californian counter-culture by roughly a hundred years.

The twenty independent upper-class progressive boarding schools which were established in England between 1889 and 1940 de-emphasized intellect and competitiveness; they gave a central place to the emotions, to aesthetic experience, to spontaneity, and to cooperation in the education of the young. Curry in his long headmastership at Dartington Hall always clung to a more rationalist and less intuitive approach to education and to life,[13] but in broad outline the enduring ideals of 'progressivism' were stated by Edward Carpenter in 1889. At Abbotsholme boys would learn, above all, 'habits of gentleness and justice'. They would not be crammed and coached for competitive examinations: 'Our daily program obviously disqualifies us from taking places in the cramming competition, but we shall be all the better able to prepare boys for the less exacting examinations, for ordinary honours at the universities, for business, for everyday life.'[14]

Freudian psychology later provided progressivism with a 'legitimating ideology'; in these early days it was sufficient to be reacting, quite explicitly, to the highly pressurized regime of the late-Victorian Public School.[15] In practice, of course, progressive schools (in both England and America) have been used by the upper classes as 'approved schools' for their delinquent children and as therapeutic communities for the emotionally disturbed. In this way, too, they uncannily prefigured the counter-culture of a later date.

At Abbotsholme the sons of what Reddie, the headmaster, called 'the governing classes' worked on the land, went in canoes on the River Dove, and felled trees. A visiting French sociologist, Edmond Demolin, was deeply impressed by both Bedales and Abbotsholme as a way of providing for a young man who in France would probably live off his parents or his wife's dowry. Bedales and Abbotsholme turned them into Empire-builders, not in the exalted sense of holders of high imperial command but in the sense of men capable of roughing it in the outback and surviving in frontier conditions. Edward Carpenter saw the large manual element in the curriculum as 'most useful to the increasing number of boys who are destined for the colonies'. Demolin reached the same conclusion quite independently in his book, *Anglo-Saxon Superiority*. The *Leeds Mercury* endorsed Demolin's interpretation, pointing to upper-class Englishmen who conducted tramcars in New York or opened a lamp store in San Francisco: 'No gentleman would like his sons to do these things at home, but few mind how the "lost legion" that Mr. Kipling writes of, makes its way abroad.'[16]

In fact most of the boys (and girls) who have attended English progressive boarding schools have had perfectly respectable though seldom outstanding careers, often in the professions (especially medicine) at home. The main change has been this: whereas their fathers were typically men of power, they have turned to the 'caring professions' and the arts. They have not 'reproduced' their fathers' positions or wealth; they have turned away from the great bureaucracies (and the Army) and many have turned to nature and the land. As Badley said, looking back over the first thirty years of Bedales, an unusually large proportion of former pupils had chosen either a life on the land or some kind of craft work:

> Such a life may not always be as remunerative as other kinds of work; but if it allows those who follow it to use their best powers to find their happiness in doing so, a system of education which gives these powers free play, instead of crushing them into another mould in which their use and enjoyment will be lost, is surely justified.[17]

There has always been some ambiguity about 'success': while too much would be vulgar, too little would scarcely justify the high fees. And success in terms of 'adjustment' to life and its demands has never been spurned: while the millennial intention has always been to produce a new race of just, caring, peace-loving men and women, there has never been any intention of nurturing real subversives or social misfits. Today Marxists upbraid them for their apolitical innocence.

Badley was delighted to record that in 1896 one of the boys at Bedales gained an Open Scholarship in science at Cambridge after being trained in the school's makeshift laboratories. He hastened to add that the boy was the best darner of socks in the school and also a most promising book-binder. He was properly proud of the 238 Old Boys who served in the First World War: some 80 per cent. were commissioned, one won a Victoria Cross, four the DSO, and twenty-three the Military Cross.[18] Those who went to the universities did well: by 1923, eighty-eight had taken honours degrees and a third of these had gained Firsts. But farming claimed a high proportion in civilian life; architecture, medicine, and teaching were also well represented. Few—only 4 per cent. by 1923—had entered (civil) government departments. But some sons of men of power also became men of power. Ramsey MacDonald, the first Labour Prime Minister, sent two children to Bedales. Malcolm (born 1901) had a spectacular career in politics, serving as Minister of Health (1940–41) and subsequently presiding over the post-war transformation of Empire as Governor-General of Malaya, High Commissioner in India, and Governor-General of Kenya.

The Trustees of Dartington Hall were very concerned that Maurice Punch should interpret the 'success' of Old Boys and Girls by appropriate criteria (and on the basis of proper samples). They wrote a preface to Punch's study of Dartington Hall to record their displeasure with his work and their rejection of his conclusion that: 'Males in particular were handicapped for filling conventional occupational roles.' It is true that his samples leave much to be desired (and the Trustees are properly incensed by the sociological language which does even more to hide the truth than the imperfect statistics), but the picture that comes over—based on sixty Old Boys and Girls who left either in the late nineteen-thirties or early nineteen-fifties—is generally convincing. It is not as replete with orthodox success as Badley's very well documented book on Bedales half a century before.

In an important article on elites and class Giddens used the term elite '... to designate those individuals who occupy formally defined positions of authority at the head of a social organization or institution'.[19] In this sense fathers of boys at progressive boarding schools are mainly members of the elite; the boys themselves in later life are not. (Punch's Dartingtonians also felt it impossible, even when a sociologist pressed them, to place themselves in a 'social class': I'm not trying to be awkward, but I have absolutely no class identity at all. ...') Punch certainly highlights the non-competitiveness of his respondents and their stepping aside from positions of authority. Dartingtonians conscripted into the Army felt they should not take commissions: 'Not only was it irksome to be controlled, but also it was distasteful to exert authority over other people.'[20]

Some of Punch's respondents were quite explicit that Dartington Hall had not prepared them for the competitiveness that is involved even in the 'caring professions' and artistic careers. An actor said: '... in a profession where so much depends upon push and luck, it's possible that the gentleness which perhaps I learnt at Dartington hasn't helped me in obtaining work.' One who had tried schoolteaching discovered that this was not work for gentle people but required 'very strong individuals'. He moved into industry: 'By and large I haven't been happy in industry because of the discipline. That is why I drifted into research and development, because it's very informal, you're not jammed in narrow guide-lines.' Punch sees this as a characteristic relationship to power and authority: 'Whether by accident or design, the Dartington males had avoided situations where they were directly subordinate to someone in a rigid hierarchy of superiority–inferiority.'[21]

Nevertheless, almost a third of the men (nine out of thirty) were 'acceptors'—sales representatives, business managers, and other such conformist organization men. They tended to complain that 'Dartington didn't make people hard enough for business'. The majority were 'rejectors'—people in somewhat unconventional occupations (photographers, musicians) 'who appeared undermotivated in comparison with the competitive values of modern society'. But only two were doing manual jobs (on the fringe of the art world): 'One of them lets his flat for several months of the year and goes to Greece to paint. His jobs are spasmodic and he does not hold a national insurance card.'

This picture is not in essence different from the results of Stewart's postal survey (1963–64) of former pupils of fourteen progressive schools. His 800 respondents did not appear to have had an education that was so unworldly that they had been handicapped in their careers, but the kind of work they did was less well paid than the work normally taken by boys from Public Schools.[22] When they were compared with grammar school leavers (of similar social background) '... service, culture, the arts, science, outdoor pursuits, are leading categories for the progressive schools'.

Their fathers are not to any significant extent Bernstein's (or Parkin's) 'new middle class'. From the very beginning they have tended to be old-fashioned men of power. Badley had not kept detailed records, but he claimed that, especially in its early years, Bedales gained most of its support from manufacturers in the Midlands and the North.[22] It is true they were 'thinking families of Unitarian connection', but they were nonetheless the families of rich and powerful industrialists. Stewart gives us a more statistical picture for the period up to 1963: only half as many sons as fathers were in organizational jobs.[24] Punch found likewise that the largest single category of fathers was 'organizational': 'Dartington fathers had their conventional occupations to a greater extent than we might have expected, such as managers, accountants, company secretaries, a financial controller, and an estate manager.'[25] They also included a Wing Commander, a Naval Commander, and an Admiral.

The working classes have always known that progressive education was a luxury for the upper classes in which they dare not indulge; the risks were too great. Writing of the American scene, Bowles and Gintis underscore the risks of progressivism: 'Young people whose dominant experiences in school have been co-operative, democratic, and substantially participatory, will find integration into the world of work a wrenching experience.' They are likely to find a 'back-to-the-earth or craft solution'.[26] In the inter-war years in America private progressive schools (says their historian, Patricia Albjerg Graham) were supported by '... the prosperous in New York, Boston, Baltimore, Washington, Philadelphia, Cleveland and

Chicago'. Poor immigrant Italian families resisted the downward spread of progressivism; they wanted their children to be efficiently Americanized.[27]

When Bernstein links the 'invisible pedagogy' to the 'new middle class' he is talking not only about state primary schools but quite explicitly about the independent progressive boarding schools. Whereas, he claims, the ideologies of the old middle class were institutionalized in Public Schools and grammar schools: 'The invisible pedagogy was first institutionalized in the private sector for a fraction of the middle class—the new middle class.'[28] He is quite wrong. He is also misguided in playing down the invisible pedagogy as a mere 'interrupter system' which reflects a change of Bourdieu's 'habitus' but somehow does not show Bourdieu's reproduction theory to be wrong.[29] The facts are quite straightforward: an invisible pedagogy has been supported by some of the old middle class for almost a century, precisely to avoid reproducing themselves.

Of course, a significant minority of parents of progressive boarding school children have been from those ancient sectors of the middle class, intellectuals and men of letters. Parents of pupils at Dartington have included Aldous Huxley, Bertrand and Dora Russell, Clough Williams-Ellis, Stephen King-Hall, F. R. Leavis, Geoffrey Grigson, and Richard Crossman. It is also clear that some parents, who are known to have tried orthodox schools first, were not necessarily inspired by the invisible pedagogy; they were less committed than desperate. Commitment has perhaps been highest among Professors of Education. In the middle of this century numerous incumbents of Chairs of Education had been pupils at progressive boarding schools (including progressive Quaker schools) or, more often, had taught in them. Thus Stewart, who occupied the Chair at Keele, Oliver at Manchester, and Joselyn at Aston had taught at Abbotsholme; Arnold, who occupied the Chair at Cambridge, was educated at Sidcot School; Pedley (Southampton) had taught at Great Ayton; and Castle (Hull) had been headmaster of Leighton Park.[30] (The 'professional' connexion with progressivism is also evident in America; thus after his visits to Black Mountain in the mid-nineteen-thirties Dewey became a member of its Advisory Board.) A spell of inter-war involvement with English progressive independent boarding schools was an astute strategic move for an aspiring educationist.

The independent progressive schools, like the later counter-culture, are a transmutation of the gentry culture. Closeness to nature does not necessarily exclude careful estate management, but an undue preoccupation with wealth and careers is at least indelicate and probably immoral. Progressivism (and the counter-culture) are the gentry culture with the blood sports left out.

Edward Carpenter is a fair illustration of this transmutation, but Leonard Elmhirst is much better. With his rich New Yorker wife (the former Mrs. Dorothy Whitney Straight) he bought the Dartington Estate near Totnes in 1925, and from the first the School and the Estate were run side by side, at first in a closely integrated way. Leonard Elmhirst was the son of a Yorkshire parson-landowner, very conscious of his family's six hundred years of landed-gentry status. After Repton, Cambridge, the Guards, and India he turned to Eastern mysticism, crafts, the land, and education. His basic text as an educator was *Scouting for Boys*.

He had previously helped the Bengali poet and philosopher, Rabindranath Tagore, with an Institute for Rural Reconstruction, Sriniketan or Abode of Grace.[31] In the mid-nineteen-thirties Uday Shankar came to Dartington to perform ritual Hindu dances; Walter Gropius restored the fourteenth-century tithe barn; Bernard Leach, the potter, joined the staff; and every evening the adults dressed for dinner at the Hall, 'where the table was resplendent with silverware, shining glass and finger bowls, and where the meal was followed by the circulation of a decanter of port'.[32]

THE COUNTER-CULTURE

The upper-class counter-culture has ranged from the 'Situationists' at Strasbourg in the mid-nineteen-sixties through the Californian hippies to Germany's extremist Baader-Meinhoff movement. We have witnessed a spectacular revolt by upper-class children against being socially 'reproduced'. Marxists find this revolt of the privileged and unoppressed difficult to explain. Sociologists commonly fall back on 'socialization'. In other words, their homes have unfitted some upper-class children for the world into which they were born. The counter-culture is the 'habitus' that failed.

Or perhaps it has really succeeded. Upper-class counter-cultural defectors from the status quo are not inverting but expressing (with a little added emphasis) parental values: they are only doing what their parents did not have the courage to do. There is not only a new middle class, there is a 'new childhood' to go with it. The 'new children' are reared by tolerant 'non-interventionist' parents, and when they meet bureaucracy and technology may experience outrage and shock. This is Peter Berger's argument;[33] Richard Flacks, who studied the parents of student activists at Chicago in the mid-nineteen-sixties, produced evidence which points in the same direction.[34]

But this merely pushes the problem one stage back: why have the upper classes, in significant numbers, failed to support and transmit to their children the values not only of entrepreneurial but of a more cosy corporate capitalism? Whatever its generational base, what we have seen is precisely what Joseph Schumpeter was predicting almost fifty years ago: a widespread distaste for capitalism, not because of its failure, but because of its success—not because it failed to produce wealth, but because it produced it in ever greater abundance.[35]

The attack was first of all directed at consumerism, technology, and bureaucracy rather than the capitalist system as such. (Even now bureaucracy and capitalism are commonly confused.) The 'situationists' took their stand against what they called 'spectacle', the hollowness, sham, and banality of the consumer society. They denounced work. The anarchism of the mid-nineteen-sixties was not specifically Marxist; it harked back to Godwin and Shelley. Marxism at this stage took the curiously eroticized form of Herbert Marcuse's analysis of superabundance and our imminent release from 'surplus repression'. Marcuse attacked work, too. The attack on the productive base of capitalist societies entered the counter-culture as a Marxist afterthought.

The counter-culture has two wings, once very closely related, now moving further apart:[36] a political activist, combative wing (today largely Marxist in its ideology); and a retreatist-expressive-artistic wing. Both have always been minority movements, and as adherents get older they often grow out of them; but good estimates place support for the Baader-Meinhoff movement at 20 per cent. of Germany's student population.[37] There may now be a measure of international specialization in the two emphases: the Welsh mountains appear to be peppered with the sons of British capitalists (Rootes, McVitie, Gilbey) who produce organically grown vegetables and hand-sewn leather-ware. The Hon. Nicholas Rootes (aged twenty-six) was reported in October 1977 from Adfa near Newtown, Powys, as saying: 'I'm not a very competitive person. I wanted to do something I enjoyed. People who are very competitive do not enjoy life. They become so nasty and selfish getting to the top that once they are there, they find it too late to change.'[38] In Germany the sons, and especially, the daughters, of capitalists do not retreat to the Black Forest; they kill capitalists.

From my programme of research in the nineteen-seventies (1971 to 1976) on counter-cultural values among university students, on counter-cultural groups and formations in Manchester,[39] on a Sufi commune of Islamic mystics in the Cotswolds, and a Hare Krishna commune near London,[40] I drew a sharp distinction between the artistic-environmentalist-mystical aspect of the counter-culture (which, in my book *Ecstasy and Holiness*, I labelled the 'Ruskin–Southey' wing) and the political activists (the 'Godwin–Shelley' wing). The former was not very closely related to age—it was certainly not a 'youth culture'; the latter had relatively few supporters over the age of about thirty-six. The independent progressive boarding school fits tidily into the apolitical (Ruskin) wing. The Sufi commune which I investigated (and in which I studied) was strikingly like the conservative end of the progressive schools in its curriculum, organization, and the upper-class background of its members. It also had the difficulty that progressive schools have of reconciling an individualist philosophy with a communal life.[41]

The progressive school movement is interlocked with the counter-culture over the past hundred years as a critical commentary on an industrial civilization based on regimentation, rationality, and a dehumanized technology. The Ruskinian influence on Abbotsholme was clear and explicit from the beginning, and the *Pall Mall Gazette* described the New School as 'Ruskinian to the backbone'. Black Mountain College in North Carolina, which was founded in 1933 and closed in 1956, has been described quite explicitly as an anticipation of the counter-culture which erupted in the late nineteen-sixties. In fact Black Mountain, like other progressive schools, was probably less intuitive and mystical and more intellectual, less contemplative and more given to action (and even assertion) than the later counter-culture; but Martin Duberman's authoritative study of the school came to this conclusion:

> The case can easily be overstated, but I think it's true that Black Mountain
> in its last years prefigured today's emerging 'counter culture'—prefigured
> it both in its life style of a loosely related tribal council, and in a value
> structure that emphasized honesty in human interaction, distaste for an
> ethic of possession and accumulation, and the reserving of highest respect

not for the abstract intellect, but for how it showed itself, was used and useful, in one's life.[42]

And some Faculty wives were already into Tarot cards, dietary reform, and pot.

The map of successful capitalism—from Los Angeles to Hamburg via Amsterdam—is also the map of the late twentieth-century counter-culture; and in America, where independent progressive schools are commonly day schools, it is the map of educational progressivism, too. The counter-culture and progressive schools are not found with failure, poverty, and privation, but with success and great concentrations of wealth. The explosion of upper-class, white, progressive ('free') schools in America between 1967 and 1972—a carefully estimated 600—exactly parallels the spread of the counter-culture and the eruption of communes. These are mainly parent–teacher cooperatives; they are small and often short-lived. More than 50 per cent. appeared in four states: California, New York, Massachusetts, and Illinois. Particular areas of concentration are the San Francisco Bay Area, the Chicago area, the Boston area, Madison-Milwaukee, and Minneapolis-St. Paul:

> There is good reason to think that cosmopolitan urban areas, especially those with high concentrations of university and college-associated people, generate the critical masses of people who share the philosophy of free schools and have the willingness and capability to commit the necessary time, energy, and resources to such efforts.[43]

The counter-culture and the progressive schools are the despair of Marxists. Only circuitous arguments can present these oppositional movements as the outcome of class oppression. Deeply conservative and supremely self-confident working-class 'bike-boys', who stand four-square for the capitalist work ethic (and a white Britain), are more easily presented as victims of class oppression; middle-class hippies, who offer a genuinely radical critique of modern industrial societies (that is why the bike-boys bash them as well as Pakis and queers) are denied real oppositional status.[44] It is a real difficulty that the most strikingly visible (and perhaps even counter-hegemonic) youth culture of our times was cradled not in privation but privilege. The challenge has to be pronounced not merely illusory but even 'profoundly adaptive to the system's productive base'.[45]

The progressive schools are rebuked for their apolitical stance and for not knowing that they are really a profoundly conservative political force. It is by way of rebuke that Jonathan Kozol says (referring to America): 'By and large, Free Schools begun for the children of upper class white people have been not merely non-political, but conspicuously and intentionally anti-political.' It is true that there is not only a cosiness but a depressing uniformity about well-fed white upper-class children in a score of 'free schools' in the Bay Area, all reading Herman Hesse and Tolkien, wearing Mexican sandals, and eating brown rice and mushrooms. Kozol is angry:

> 'Spontaneity' is the magic word among the liberal and genteel men and women I now have in mind, but the ideological antisepsis of the kind of

Free School they inevitably create guarantees well in advance that no child will ever choose spontaneously to learn of things which lie outside the province of privilege, the kingdom of trivia, or the boundaries of self-gratification.[46]

Kozol is dismayed that free schools '... do not suppress the revolutionary instincts of our children; instead they buy them out'. It is no part of the argument of this chapter that progressive schools subvert the social order, but that they sustain it by playing a significant part in the circulation of elites. In doing so, they offer a greater service to the relatively underprivileged than they know.

BLACKS AND THE AMERICAN ELITE

The counter-culture, argues Peter Berger, is a 'sociological windfall'. It benefits those who are relatively disadvantaged in life. It is the kind of windfall that Pareto saw as the very stuff of history. Quite simply: it creates new room at the top.

Exactly contemporaneous with the counter-culture and the spread of progressive 'free schools' for upper-class whites has been the spectacular ascent of Blacks into American elites. They have not gone up simply because some high-status whites have gone down; they have had quite extraordinary Federal help. Nevertheless, as upper-class whites have in effect stood down, this process of elite circulation has been considerably eased.

Writing in 1971 Peter Berger interpreted the mainly upper-class American counter-culture in the following very perceptive passage:

Who is most likely to benefit from this sociological windfall? It will be the newly college-educated children of the lower-middle and working classes. To say this, we need not assume that they remain untouched by their contact with the youth culture during their school years. Their sexual mores, their aesthetic tastes, even their political opinions might become permanently altered as compared with those of their parents. We do assume, though, that they will, now as before, reject the anti-achievement ethos of the cultural revolution. They may take positions in intercourse that are frowned on by Thomas Aquinas, they may continue to listen to hard rock on their hi-fi's and they may have fewer racial prejudices. But all these cultural acquisitions are, as it were, functionally irrelevant to making it in the technocracy. Very few of them will become sandal makers or farmers on communes in Vermont.[47]

Astonishingly, Berger made no reference to Blacks as beneficiaries of the 'green revolution'. And yet by 1971 a remarkable process of displacement was at work, and it was highly visible, especially, perhaps, on university campuses. It is true that effective power was not given to the Equal Employment Opportunities Commission, which greatly accelerated the process, until 1972; but the anti-discriminatory Civil

Rights Act was passed in 1964 (the very year in which the counter-culture first erupted with high drama outside Sproul Hall on the Berkeley plaza).[48]

American Blacks who hold university degrees have moved into American elites on a proportionately massive scale since the mid-nineteen-sixties. Before that they became schoolteachers. Discrimination against Blacks had traditionally been worst at the top. In his authoritative study, *Black Elite*, Richard B. Freeman's favourite adjective in relation to these changes is 'dramatic': '... there was a dramatic collapse in traditional discriminatory patterns in the market for highly qualified black Americans. *Black Elite* is a detailed examination of this remarkable socio-economic development.'[49]

By the nineteen-sixties black Americans were in a better position than ever before to take advantage of opportunities to move to the top. In the previous thirty or forty years great advances had taken place in the quality of their schools. Welch has argued that this improved competitive position of Blacks is sufficient to account for their rapid advance in the last twelve to fifteen years. In the nineteen-twenties and thirties the income of Blacks actually fell as school completion levels rose. 'Recent evidence shows, on the other hand, that returns, as a fraction of earnings, for Blacks schooled in the 1950's and 1960's exceed returns to whites.'[50] Welch's argument rests essentially on the 'vintage effect': that more recently educated Blacks, who have enjoyed high quality schooling, get higher returns from their schooling than older Blacks who were schooled at a time when the quality was poor. But he is cautious in interpreting his data and concedes: 'There are, of course, many alternative explanations of the vintage effects of rising relative black income: a downward drift in market discrimination being the simplest and most obvious.' This is the explanation to which Freeman attaches most weight.

There has been a sharp decline in the proportion of eighteen to nineteen-year-old white Americans enrolled in college (from 43 per cent. in 1970 to 35 per cent. in 1974) and a steep rise in the proportion of eighteen to nineteen-year-old black Americans (from 13 per cent. in 1960 to 17 per cent. in 1970 and 22 per cent. in 1974). There has been an increase of 66 per cent. in the actual number of Blacks enrolled between 1960 and 1974.[51] There have been similar trends among graduate students: as a proportion of the relevant age-groups, white enrolments fell, black enrolments rose. Areas of black concentration were Law and Medicine. (The proportions entering school teaching fell to levels similar to Whites.) Much of the increase occurred in predominantly white universities: 'In prestigious Ivy League schools such as Yale, Brown, and similar institutions like M.I.T., the proportion of freshmen who were black jumped from less than one to six and 10 per cent. between 1960 and 1970.'[52]

College-educated black Americans have now gained entry into formerly 'closed' occupations and even in the depressed early nineteen-seventies more than held their own. Freeman concludes from his thorough and expert analysis of trend data that '... there is no denying the extraordinary improvement in the economic status of black graduates, after decades of severe discrimination in high level markets'.[53] While the proportion of white graduates entering management remained stable in the late nineteen-sixties and early nineteen-seventies, the proportion of black male graduates obtaining jobs in management tripled in the decade after the Civil Rights Act of 1964. Reverse discrimination meant 'minority hiring policies', and this meant that no white executive at IBM, Xerox, or similar corporation could expect promotion unless he had shown appropriate zeal in favouring black applicants for jobs.[54] Selection tests in which Blacks might perform badly have been abandoned. In these circumstances Freeman is able to report 'a remarkable transformation' in the college job market for black Americans which 'represents one of the most striking socio-economic developments in American history'.[55]

Blacks have done particularly well in academic elites: universities have felt the full force of 'affirmative action' and are required to give a detailed racial breakdown of all employees and applicants for jobs.[56] In 1973 black faculty were paid more than white faculty with the same qualifications.[57] Freeman made regression analyses and concluded that 'the quality-adjusted incomes show black faculty earning 6.6 and 8.9 per cent. more than white faculty'.[58] Five published papers yielded for a Black, a remarkably handsome dividend.

While black Americans enjoy this unprecedented and even spectacular movement upward into elite positions, young white middle-class American experience an unprecedented reversal of fortune. The decline in college enrolments among high school graduates has been greatest in high-income families. Freeman observes:

> One consequence of the drop in enrollments from the middle and upper classes is that unprecedented numbers of young persons from advantaged backgrounds appear likely to receive less schooling, and presumably to achieve lower occupational status, than their parents. The long-standing pattern of upward mobility across generations, with children doing better than their parents, may thus be in the process of being replaced by a period of downward generational mobility for a not inconsiderable number of families.[59]

Freeman is describing a very ancient Paretian phenomenon, although the mechanisms are more contrived than Pareto could have imagined and far more artificial than he would have approved.

CONCLUSION

The circulation of elites does not subvert the social order; it sustains it. Normally it promotes efficiency and confers legitimacy. Most people feel that there is genuine opportunity, and the system can be supported because it is fair. But the management of myth is as important as what actually happens. The effective myth is no longer the American myth of opportunity; it is the sociologists' myth of the lack of it. This provides the basic legitimation of the favouritism shown to black people often of indifferent ability. Legitimacy itself is an unequally distributed resource; sociologists have been quite influential in redistributing it.

This chapter has been concerned with quite small minorities: pupils in private progressive schools; adherents of the extremer forms of counter-culture; black

Americans who get into the elite. In each case we are talking about no more than 4 or 5 per cent. of the relevant age–class category. But these minorities have an importance out of all proportion to their numbers. They are located at key positions in the social system; they are highly visible; and they are very good material for myth-makers. It is more than usually important to get the facts right.

The circulation of elites described in this chapter approximates only very roughly to Pareto's model, and, with regard to the escalation of America's Blacks, is likely in the long run to promote neither efficiency nor legitimacy but to subvert both. This very deliberately and powerfully managed circulation is a far cry from the free-market social Darwinism which Pareto described and approved. It makes sense as a very temporary expedient to bring about the take-off of Blacks; it makes no sense as a strategy to sustain them permanently in orbit.

Perceptive American commentators have made very muted protests and ventured timidly to suggest a possible white backlash against the patent unfairness of it all— except, perhaps, as some kind of self-imposed punishment for past wrongs.[60] It is the kind of reverse discrimination that we saw in England on a diminutive scale under Ellis's headship at the William Tyndale School. But the real and deeply corrosive problem is the introduction of a completely new criterion for elite membership. The shift is from achievement (which had a very short run) to ascription. As Daniel Bell has warned, what is now being introduced is a 'new ascriptive principle of corporate identity'.[61] Once you got in (in England) because your uncle was a lord; now you get in (in America) because your skin is black.

The movement is towards quotas and proportional representation with relatively little concern for personal fitness. This, as Daniel Bell says, is a complete reversal of radical and humanist values: 'An entirely new principle of rights has been introduced into the (American) polity.' This is certainly not without precedent in the history of mankind: the Ottoman Turks conscripted Christians from the Balkan states into their civil and military elites. But it is ironic that the principle should be revived and implemented in the country which has enjoyed the most popular, pervasive and ill-founded sociological myth of all—that America prospers under 'contest mobility' while England languishes under an effete and 'improper' system of 'sponsored mobility'.[62] Full-blooded social Darwinism is now very properly out of fashion. The weak need help. But it should not be too readily assumed that the great middle mass of either England or America enjoys any remarkable 'privilege' and can easily look after themselves. They are not especially 'advantaged'; they are highly vulnerable in the face of deliberate policies of reverse discrimination. They may need a little help, too, if elite circulation is not to be quite grotesquely distorted and as enfeebled as it will be discredited.

NOTES

1. S. E. Finer, *Vilfredo Pareto, Sociological Writings*, Pall Mall Press, London, 1966: 'Aristocracies do not last. Whatever be the reason, it is incontestable that, after a time, they disappear. History is a graveyard of aristocracies' (p. 249).
2. See W. D. Rubinstein, 'Men of property', in P. Stanworth and A. Giddens (Eds.), *Elites and Power in British Society*, Cambridge University Press, 1974, pp. 160–164.
3. See Seymour Lipset and Reinhard Bendix, *Social Mobility in Industrial Society*,

University of California Press, 1959, pp. 88–90; John Westergaard and Henrietta Resler, *Class in Capitalist Society*, Penguin Books, Harmondsworth, 1976, pp. 306–307; and S. M. Miller, 'Comparative social mobility: a trend report', *Current Sociology*, **9** (1960).

4. S. E. Finer, *Vilfredo Pareto: Sociological Writings*, Pall Mall Press, 1966, p. 162.
5. *Ibid.*, pp. 135–136, 249.
6. Stanislav Andreski, *Social Sciences as Sorcery*, Penguin Books, Harmondsworth, 1974, p. 175.
7. C. Jencks *et al.*, *Inequality*, Penguin Books, 1975, p. 176.
8. J. M. and R. E. Pahl, *Managers and Their Wives*, Penguin Books, Hamondsworth, 1972, pp. 261–226.
9. C. J. Richardson, *Contemporary Social Mobility*, Frances Pinter, 1977, pp. 119–120.
10. See Theodore Roszak *The Making of a Counter Culture*, Faber, London, 1970, pp. 178–204.
11. Martin Duberman, *Black Mountain*, Dutton, New York, 1972, pp. 329–333.
12. W. A. C. Stewart, *The Educational Innovators. Vol. 2, Progressive Schools 1881–1967*, Macmillan, London, 1968, p. 253.
13. Maurice Punch, 'W. B. Curry (1900–1962): a re-assessment', *New Era*, **51** (1970).
14. See Cecil Reddie, *Abbotsholme*, George Allen, 1900, pp. 48–52.
15. See J. H. Badley, *Bedales*, Methuen, London, 1923. Badley points out that the 'New School Movement' was a mutation of the Public School: 'It arose as a modification of our public school system', with a wider curriculum, less emphasis on organized games, more on creativity and outdoor pursuits (pp. 2–11).
16. *Leeds Mercury*, 22 January 1898.
17. J. H. Badley, *Bedales*, Methuen, 1923, p. 191.
18. *Ibid.*, pp. 224–231.
19. A Giddens, 'Elites in the British class structure', *Sociological Review*, **20** (1972).
20. Maurice Punch, *Progressive Retreat*, Cambridge University Press, 1977, p. 111.
21. *Ibid.*, p. 119.
22. W. A. C. Stewart, *The Educational Innovators. Vol. 2, Progressive Schools 1881–1967*, Macmillan, 1968, p. 336.
23. J. H. Badley, *Bedales*, Methuen, 1923, p. 71.
24. W. A. C. Stewart, *The Educational Innovators. Vol. 2, Progressive Schools 1881–1967*, Macmillan, 1968, p. 333.
25. M. Punch, *Progressive Retreat*, Cambridge University Press, 1977, p. 33.
26. S. Bowles and H. Gintis, *Schooling in Capitalist America*, Routledge and Kegan Paul, London, 1976, p. 254.
27. Patricia Albjerg Graham, *Progressive Education: From Arcady to Academe*, Teachers College Press, New York, 1967, pp. 161–162.
28. B. Bernstein, *Class, Codes and Control: Vol. 3: Towards a Theory of Educational Transmissions*, Routledge and Kegan Paul, London, 1977, p. 124.
29. *Ibid.*, pp. 125–126.
30. These details are merely illustrative: the Quaker-Progressive network of 'educationists' awaits its doctoral student. Other notable Quakers who held post-war Chairs of Education (although they never taught in schools) were Curle (Exeter) and Wilson (Bristol). Tibble (Leicester) had close connexions with Dartington Hall and sent both his children there.
31. Maurice Punch, 'The Elmhirsts and the early Dartington: a neglected experiment', *New Era*, **57** (1976).
32. M. Punch, *Progressive Retreat*, Cambridge University Press, 1977, p. 24.
33. Peter L. Berger and Brigitte Berger, 'The blueing of America', in Brigitte Berger, *Readings in Sociology*, Basic Books, New York, 1974.
34. Richard Flacks, 'The liberated generation: an exploration of the roots of student protest', *Journal of Social Issues*, **23** (1967).
35. Joseph Schumpeter, *Capitalism, Socialism and Democracy*, George Allen and Unwin,

London, 1943, pp. 134–155.

36. Compare K. Westhues, 'Hippiedom 1970: some tentative hypotheses', *Sociological Quarterly*, Winter **1972**.

37. See Robin Smyth, 'Daughters of the gun' and 'A state under siege', *Observer Supplement*, 11 December 1977.

38. See Ian Mather, 'Scions in search of rural peace', *Observer*, 30 October 1977. Sons of the McVitie (biscuit) family, of the Gilbey (gin) family, and of the Rootes (motorcar manufacture) family were among those observed.

39. See F. Musgrove, *Ecstasy and Holiness: Counter Culture and the Open Society*, University of Indiana Press, 1974, pp. 81–100, 125–148.

40. See F. Musgrove, *Margins of the Mind*, Methuen, London, 1977, pp. 168–213.

41. Compare Maurice Punch, 'The sociology of the anti-institution', *British Journal of Sociology*, **25** (1974).

42. Martin Duberman, *Black Mountain*, Dutton, New York, 1972, p. 407.

43. Allen Graubard, 'The free school movement', *Harvard Educational Review*, **42** (1972).

44. For a comparative study of bikeboys and hippies within the framework of Marxist class analysis, see Paul Willis, *Profane Culture*, Routledge and Kegan Paul, London, 1978. It is conceded that hippies were mainly from middle-class homes (p. 8), but both counter-culture and bike-culture are examined as 'oppressed or excluded social groups' (p. 170). For a criticism of recent Marxist interpretations of youth cultures and counter cultures see F. Musgrove, 'Profane Culture' (review), *Research in Education*, **1978**, No. 20 and F. Musgrove, 'Resistance Through Rituals' and 'Working Class Youth Culture' (review), *Sociology*, **12** (1978).

45. John Clarke *et al.*, 'Subcultures, cultures and class', in Stuart Hall and Tony Jefferson (Eds.), *Resistance Through Rituals*, Hutchinson, London, 1975, p. 65.

46. Jonathan Kozol, 'Politics, rage and motivation in the free schools', *Harvard Educational Review*, **42** (1972).

47. Peter L. Berger and Brigitte Berger, 'The blueing of America', in Brigitte Berger, *Readings in Sociology*, Basic Books, New York, 1974, p. 442.

48. See K. E. Gales, 'Campus revolution', *British Journal of Sociology*, **17** (1966); and *Education at Berkeley* (the 'Muscatine Report'), University of California, 1966: 'They (dissident students) condemn the University because it is a factory that turns out the products demanded by society and trains students in the rules of the game. ... They see the University as an agent of the power structure, and they want it to become instead an agent of their moral revolution' (pp. 34–35).

49. Richard B. Freeman, *Black Elite*, McGraw-Hill, New York, 1976, p. xx.

50. Finis Welch, 'Black–white differences in returns to schooling', *American Economic Review*, **63** (1973).

51. R. B. Freeman, *Black Elite*, McGraw-Hill, 1976, Table 22, p. 46.

52. *Ibid.*, pp. 47–48.

53. Richard B. Freeman, *The Over-Educated American*, Academic Press, New York, 1976, p. 147.

54. R. B. Freeman, *Black Elite*, McGraw-Hill, 1976, pp. 136–137.

55. R. B. Freeman, *The Over-Educated American*, Academic Press, 1976, p. 157.

56. See Edward Shils, 'Editorial', *Minerva*, April 1971.

57. R. B. Freeman, *The Over-Educated American*, Academic Press, 1976, p. 146.

58. R. B. Freeman, *Black Elite*, McGraw-Hill, 1976, p. 207.

59. R. B. Freeman, *The Over-Educated American*, Academic Press, 1976, pp. 36–37.

60. R. B. Freeman, *Black Elite*, McGraw-Hill, 1976, p. 224.

61. Daniel Bell, *The Coming of Post-Industrial Society*, Penguin Books, Harmondsworth, 1976, p. 417.

62. Ralph H. Turner, 'Modes of social ascent through education: sponsored and contest mobility', in A. H. Halsey, J. Floud, and C. Arnold Anderson (Eds.), *Education, Economy and Society*, Free Press, New York, 1964.

CHAPTER 9

Final Judgements

DEMORALIZING THE SCHOOL

The kind of education we need is a matter of judgement and its provision a matter of political will. It is not a semi-automatic replication or reproduction of the social state. None of the evidence reviewed in this book supports such a hidden-hand theory of the social order or of social change. The possibilities for education are not socially predetermined and they are enormously wide. There are usually both obvious and more covert ways in which educational systems serve society: there are 'correspondences' which either meet the eye or stand revealed after imaginative analysis. But what is usually more striking is the disjunction, the lack of fit, between schooling and society. For many people involved in education this counter-position (Lionel Trilling called it 'adversary' and David Riesman 'counter-cyclical') may be the very source of their legitimacy.

The judgement that we make about the desirable shape of education will be formed by some grasp of historical context and a sharp awareness of the way the world is different now. Both England and America responded to great historical threats to social order by providing an overwhelmingly moralized education. In England the great threats were the Civil War of the seventeenth century and the Industrial Revolution of the nineteenth; in America it was the massive and sustained bombardment of immigration. In England the problem was to bring first the disruptive upper classes and then the new industrial workers within the social order; in America the problem was to turn polyglot immigrants into citizens.

Both England and America in the late twentieth century are the inheritors of a massive tradition of education as socialization: schools are first and foremost about moulding and shaping people and to only a subsidiary degree about the acquisition of skill, knowledge, and understanding. In 1980 this is not only an irrelevance; it is a gigantic impertinence. The first judgement that I make is that schools should be systematically demoralized.

The secularization of education has generally lagged behind the secularization of society: this is another facet of the same problem. It is true that even Public School headmasters today are not generally parsons and that a somewhat secularized 'personality' has tended to displace character as the centre of educational concern. The educational psychologist and the 'pastoral tutor' have gone some way to displacing the priest. But games are still about moral fibre rather than physical growth, and teachers of all subjects see their job in essentially, though not exclusively, moral terms.[1] Headmasters put 'personality and character' at the top of a long list of educational objectives for school leavers and examination achievement and career advancement at the bottom.[2] Only men teaching in grammar schools (in the nineteen-sixties) gave pride of place to intellectual attainment.[3]

It is doubtful whether pluck and clean living are today more important to society than intelligence; but in 1929 the headmaster of Harrow wrote a large book to rebuke Bertrand Russell for voicing this doubt.[4] Whatever the value of a highly moralized education when the very basis of the social order seemed threatened, by the early twentieth century it was certainly dysfunctional. Correlli Barnett says that it has been our ruin. Public Schools and chapels 'clapped succeeding generations into a spiritual corset, the whalebone of idealism at odds with the flesh of real life'.[5]

In North America Carl Bereiter has been advocating schools without education; and by this he means substantially what I mean by demoralization. His argument is partly based—as indeed was Bertrand Russell's—on the view that schools cannot really mould character anyway. This is not true, although boarding schools will do it more effectively than day schools, and it will not be done overnight. As Correlli Barnett says of upper-class Englishmen in late-Victorian times: 'Except for young Nazis or Communists no class of leaders in modern times has been so subject to prolonged moulding of character, personality and outlook as British public-school boys in this era.' They bore the stigmata for life.

The purposeful moulding of character to predefined ends has to some extent been superseded by the fostering of 'natural development', at least in the early years of elementary (primary) education. In Bereiter's terms, the underlying idea of informal early schooling is 'non-educational': 'It is to provide a suitable environment for children to live and grow in. The child's life and destiny are essentially his own, with the teacher as an adjunct to nature rather than an agent of society charged with making the child turn out the way society wishes.'[6]

Bereiter would give (elementary) schools in North America a custodial role, but primarily would charge them with imparting skills, notably reading and calculating. Their essential concern should be with children's ability to perform. The need for training arises from the incompleteness of normal experience. For Bereiter schools have no business concerning themselves with 'the whole child' (and teachers would have no business assuming the 'diffuse role' that B. R. Wilson has assigned to them).[7] In an impoverished and brutalized society schools properly and necessarily take on such wider tasks; to arrogate these wider tasks in highly sophisticated modern societies is effrontery. As I have argued elsewhere, in modern societies the teacher's job is expert, technical, restricted, and professional in providing an efficient service for clients.[8]

SCHOOL AND COMMUNITY

When we look at the direction that education has taken in recent years we see not the influence of society but of sociologists. Three of the key notions of sociology have been at the centre of the education debate for the past thirty years: class, culture, and community. They have done great harm. They are ideas without much substance or exactness; they have been accorded a high level of reality. They have been employed extensively as 'explanatory variables'. They explain little; their essential function has been ideological. They have been used to legitimate the imprisonment of working-class children in working-class worlds.

When I taught my Banyankole pupils in Western Uganda that the earth was round I did not think then—and I do not think now—that I was committing an epistemologically ethnocentric act. It is true that they responded with complete unbelief, maintaining that the earth was a bowl and Nyakakaikuru, a little old woman, held up the skies. When I offered counter evidence I did not think I was guilty of symbolic violence. But that was thirty years ago, and since that time we have seen a massive shift in sociological and educational though towards cultural relativism.

The strong version of cultural relativism says that one culture is simply not intelligible to another—each has its own logic, its own rationality; the weak version simply says that one culture is no better than another—there are no supracultural criteria by which to evaluate and order them. Class cultures, accordingly, have been invested with an integrity which is unassailable; and the basis of a class culture is a community. The working-class culture rooted in working-class communities must be protected from the imposition of middle-class culture via the school. Curiously, these views have been held most strongly by 'educationalists' in connexion with the education of the seriously disadvantaged and deprived.

Education has been very largely about 'culture' in another sense—works of literature and art. The whole point about culture in this second sense has been to undermine the power of culture in the first—to enable people, as Lionel Trilling says, 'to extricate themselves from the culture into which they were born'.[9] Cultural relativism now defines this as a kind of treason: class cultures must be kept inviolate.

Midwinter has invoked anthropology to argue that the child's conceptual development depends on '... his city, street, gang environment. He will be bombarded in school perhaps by new concepts which are foreign, remote, bizarre, irrelevant and unrealistic in terms of his background. ...'[10] In the Liverpool Educational Priority Area, curricula were to be locality-based and schools were to be community schools. Teachers—even those voluntarily involved in this project—appear to have been very sceptical of the value of such an approach; one inquiry reports that the senior member of the team '... took issue with the environmentally-based syllabus of Midwinter. Perhaps more significantly he was an ex-headmaster of one of the original project schools. ... He felt that teaching the basic skills was the primary consideration, in order to equip children for occupation in future life.'[11]

Of course, there is desperation about getting unintelligent children in poor areas of big cities to learn anything that schools wish to teach. Most of them will acquire skills far beyond the reach of many university graduates—like snooker, running a market stall, and driving lorries and cranes. After the age of twelve they should be able to go to a demoralized educational institution, if they so wish, to acquire one or more out of a range of specific skills. It is absurd to elaborate fraudulent theories of culture to justify the existence of ineffective schools and their failure to achieve the impossible.

The great danger that faces education is the uncertainty as to which of the founding fathers of sociology will be high fashion next. A Tonnies revival is long overdue. His writing would provide an appropriate vocabulary for a movement already discernible (especially in the growth of 'Further Education') which makes sense—a shift in education from emphasis on community to emphasis on association.

The linking of school and community as a desirable end is relatively new, but always tightly tied to the moralized conception of education was the idea of the school *as* a community. The school as a community exacted loyalty and taught the overriding virtue of *esprit de corps*. With the demoralization of schooling must go the death of the school as a community, and on its grave must rise a fundamentally different kind of organization: voluntary in character, sensitive to the needs of clients and consumers, tolerant of diversity, unceremonious and indifferent to tradition, careful of the contractual rights of its members, consultative and participatory in its style of management. It probably will not have a football team; there may be neither school crest nor colours. It will be an association and not a community.

RESTRUCTURING EDUCATION AT THE SECONDARY STAGE

Education matters. Since Christopher Jencks published *Inequality* in 1972 and referred to schools as 'marginal institutions', it has been widely claimed that they are, after all, of little social or personal consequence. Jencks was making a limited and highly specific reference to the influence of schooling on progress towards economic equality ('glacial'); he concedes that in many respects education is crucial (for instance in relation to the job you are likely to get). It does not influence income as much in America as it does in England,[12] but a young man (and his parents) at least in England would be very foolish indeed to discount it in future-planning.

There are, nevertheless, powerful reasons for some measure or form of de-schooling at the secondary (high school) stage. The most powerful of these is the simple one advanced by John Holt, that most schools are 'bad places for children or, for that matter, anyone to be ...'.[13] There is a lot of cruelty in them for one thing, says Holt, and they generally make children less curious, resourceful, and confident than when they started.

But the primary stage (the American elementary stage) is vital and must be more highly developed; and it must be compulsory. It is vital because some abilities are never, or poorly, acquired if they are not learned by a particular age or at a specially critical period of growing up.[14] The sequential nature of many aspects of human development—especially cognitive development—means that growth is in stages, and if an early stage is omitted, future growth is impaired. The six years before the age of ten must not be allowed to suffer from neglect.

Life even in childhood is usually too simple to promote full mental development. Significant learning is unlikely to occur unless the environment is more complex and uncertain than 'normal'; and children may not seek out for themselves the possibly risky real-life situations which would stretch them. It is the job of school to be more difficult than life. It is also its job to be more secure—to present problems in a controlled setting, without the insecurities that real-life difficulties commonly entail.

To de-school the primary (or elementary) stage of education would be catastrophic: it would not equalize experience and opportunity; it would give advantage to upper-class children (who would probably be provided with an appropriate 'learning environment' anyway). It would widen the gap between the rich and the poor. Jencks is quite clear that the research evidence on this score—showing social-class differences in out-of-school and in-school learning—shows that school matters:

> These findings imply that if all elementary schools were closed down, so that growing up became an endless summer, white middle-class children might still learn much of what they now learn. ... But most poor black children would probably not learn to read without schools. The cognitive gap between rich and poor and between black and white would thus be far greater than it is now.[15]

In view of the importance and effectiveness of schools in reducing cognitive inequalities Jencks admonishes: 'Those who propose to abolish schools might ponder this possibility.'

My first main judgement was that schools should be demoralized and reconstituted as associations serving clients and not communities. My second is that the legal or statutory school leaving age should be twelve. There must be compulsory education from four to twelve, but the secondary stage calls for fundamental transformation. Two essential conditions must attach to a school-leaving age of twelve: voluntary attendance at courses from twelve to eighteen, and abundant and appropriately supported opportunities to re-enter the educational system throughout life.

Bereiter has a sense of the impending radical transformation of the North American high school: 'It is not at all certain that the high school will survive as an institution.' He speaks of 'pressures towards disintegration' and with reference to the training needs of adolescents considers that they are 'so diverse that it makes little sense to cram all sorts of training within the same four walls'.[16]

This also applies to the English comprehensive school. My third main judgement is this: that in the voluntary post-twelve schools of the future, there must be more specialization (both within schools and between them) and not less, and there must be more selection (largely as a corollary of this) and not less. Young people must be doing things they are actually capable, with some effort, of doing. Anything else is futility and waste.

But the immediate case against compulsory schools for adolescents is quite simply their barbarity: it is the triangle of hatred, humiliation, and contempt that Rosser and Harre found in the two comprehensive schools they studied;[17] it is the suvival technique of teachers as Peter Woods observed it: 'a tactic deliberately aimed at undermining dignity and producing embarrassment, shame and degradation.'[18] Rosser and Harre and Woods use very strong terms. My own direct continuous professional experience of diverse secondary schools over more than thirty years leads me to a further judgement: their terms are not strong enough.

It is true that for both pupils and teachers degradation and desperation alternate with 'having a laugh': this is the unending dialectic of school life, the 'alternation between laughter and soulless despair'. But this is a civilized calling, a learned profession, that we are talking about: it is not trench warfare. Peter Woods underlines the preoccupation of teachers with 'survival', the heavy and destructive demands that it makes on their time and energies. This is language for describing my own wartime experience of flying with Bomber Command.

The staffroom is a strongly protected enclave, a refuge which offers a passage back to sanity, where (somewhat hysterical) laughter makes the nightmare outside manageable and transforms otherwise intolerable realities. But in the perceptive and entirely convincing account that Woods gives, it is by no means infallible. Laughter does not invariably dissipate the anger and resentment felt and expressed at losing a free period; it had not prevented or healed the rift between two members of staff who had not spoken to each other for eight years; it had not prevented an idealistic young recruit to the staff from resigning within a year.[19]

In the entirely and genuinely voluntary post-twelve high school we shall have students who want to be there and find importance in the work; and teachers who are there only if they are good enough to get students. This is 'adult education' for young adolescents on the model of the WEA and university extramural departments. The contrast between secondary school teaching and this kind of work is dramatic and startling, as anyone who has done both will testify. This is the way forward.

It makes no sense in modern highly sophisticated societies to make all adolescents follow a broad course of study. There will doubtless be a place for the all-purpose (voluntary) comprehensive school with a broad curriculum, but young people today live in an environment which is 'information-rich' and, indeed—in an entirely admirable sense—culture-saturated. Much of the school curriculum, by contrast, is simply a bore: it cannot compete for interest, significance (and even accuracy) with the exposure to knowledge and ideas that comes from television and travel. The broad, balanced curriculum has been overtaken by life; and reading *Twelfth Night* round the class is a trivial, debilitating, and anti-educational experience compared with watching play-of-the-week.

We need specialist high schools for mathematics, art, music, various branches of engineering, and languages; the students will need to show interest, aptitude, and commitment, and although enrolment is voluntary, they will enter a contract to stay for a three- or five-year course and will be expected to honour it. The specialist high school will also take returnees aged about thirty or forty who have discovered an aptitude interest or use for such studies. The 'whole man' who emerges from an education in breadth is commonly an incomplete man; it is the one-sided man who is the fulfilled man. The educational system must be dedicated to producing fulfilled one-sided men.

HOW CAN WORKING-CLASS CHILDREN BE HELPED?

The English grammar school has not disappeared. It has finally become a middle-class institution. It has been handed over to that well-to-do sector of the middle class that can afford day-boy fees (1980) of around a thousand pounds a year. A significant number of direct-grant grammar schools have taken this course in one of the most socially divisive changes in our recent history.

This section will address itself to the question: how can the general run of working-class children be helped by the educational system? But there is a broader, prior question: is there much economic advantage to be gained through education anyway? Has educated labour been proletarianized, and is it the working class in particular that suffers? Christopher Jencks concluded for America that it was excellent economic sense for working-class whites, blacks, and women to drop out of college: 'Dropping out seems in many cases to be the most economically rational decision.'[20] Staying on could be justified only on non-economic grounds.

We almost certainly overestimate the amount of highly educated talent that modern complex societies need, although Daniel Bell is doubtless correct in pointing up the centrality of theoretical knowledge in a post-industrial world. It is not the centrality but the number of theoreticians that is in doubt. Modern societies have large excesses of human talent. Raymond Aron has observed: 'It is useful to recall that all societies, including the wealthiest, continue to train the men they need, but that none, despite its proclaimed objectives, needs to have all men realize their individual potentialities.'[21]

It requires even more education to get the same rewards, but there is no doubt that whatever its 'needs', England still rewards education. This may be a form of irrational economic behaviour that it will eventually correct. But even in America, says Jencks, employers are impressed by a lot of schooling and are prepared to reward it at least with status.

The problem remains the social distribution of rewards. It is not simply that working-class children of high ability and potential may get an inferior education; even when they obtain a superior one they are likely to get less out of it in career terms than upper-class children. This is the twofold problem that the destruction of grammar schools has almost certainly made worse.

My judgement is that there are five basic requirements: no post-twelve school will be a neighbourhood school; there will be roughly the same social-class mix in every school; the profile of teacher qualifications will be the same in every school; strong guidance will be given to working-class children not to apply for subuniversity institutions and general arts and social science degree courses, but to go for the great professional schools of major universities; and there will be massive, means-tested post-educational financial support for the preliminary stages of a wide range of careers and undertakings. Justice has a sixth and final requirement: that the Public Schools be abolished.

There are broad lessons to be learned from the history of segregation and desegregation in education: one is that the 'disadvantaged', whatever their colour, have little to gain from being isolated and kept together. Desegregated American negroes who went to poor-white schools gained no scholastic advantage; those who went to 'good' schools (for middle-class whites) did.[22] It is no doubt dangerous to extrapolate from American experience; it is no less foolish to ignore it. There can be little doubt that the children who are especially penalized by comprehensivization and neighbourhood schools are able children in working-class neighbourhoods who previously would have got a scholarship and got out. Everybody must get out. Everybody must go to school on a bus.

Teachers count. They must be equitably distributed. When their quality is high (in terms of academic attainments) their pupils tend to do well. This is what Ainsworth and Batten found in secondary modern schools in Manchester (in grammar schools the quality was too uniformly good to discriminate).[23] Bowles has reanalysed Coleman's data on equality in American education and reached a similar conclusion. Teacher quality was particularly related to the scholastic performance of negro children.[24]

Kelsall writes about the 'graduate elite' but he knows that this is a misuse of terms and warns his readers to remember 'the conceptual quotation marks'.[25] As we move nearer to mass higher education there is ever less justification for using the term at all. But what we know little or nothing about in England is the social-class background of students in different areas of higher education. My own work shows a technological university recruiting more working-class students than universities generally;[26] but we have no systematic knowledge of the social-class distribution of students in different subject areas.

Daniel Bell has pointed to 'the class divisions within the structure of the "Scientific City" itself' in America;[27] Bourdieu and Passeron have produced substantial trend data for France. It appears that 'the privileged classes' enjoy a 'quasi-monopoly of the scientific grandes ecoles', they are heavily represented in university Faculties of Law and Medicine, and '... the slight improvement in working-class children's chances of entering university has in a sense been offset by a strengthening of the mechanism tending to relegate survivors into certain faculties'.[28] They are being fobbed off with courses which in a career sense lead nowhere.

English universities must not be guilty of exploiting the idealism (and often the ignorance) of working-class boys and girls by luring them into overexpanded Arts departments to maintain staff—student ratios and lecturers' jobs. If your father is a property developer or even a Rear Admiral a History degree will no doubt serve you well; if he is a textile operator in Blackburn it will not. Those who are equal at the finishing post of higher education will not be equal five years later when the lagged effects of class have had time and opportunity to bite.

We are likely to see some specialization among English universities within the next decade with six or seven of them in the big provincial cities—especially Birmingham, Manchester, Sheffield, and Leeds—developing great professional schools of law, medicine, accountancy, architecture, and engineering. It is towards these that working-class boys and girls must be firmly turned; they will be England's equivalents of the French 'grandes ecoles'. Working-class boys and girls must be steered away from the sixty or seventy small-town and parkland universities, polytechnics, and colleges of higher education. These must be reserved for the privileged classes.

Even such determined guidance of working-class students is unlikely to counteract altogether the lagged effects of class. There is commonly a 'starving period' and extended course of training after formal education ends and a

G*

worthwhile career begins which working-class students cannot afford. This is principally why they take the subsidized year of teacher training. There must be at least comparable subsidies for a wide range of careers and callings, so that even the railway porter's son with a degree in Philosophy can go on to qualify as a barrister and embark on a legal career even without a family of lawyer uncles and cousins to support him. And there should be 'legacies' in mid-career in the form of state bursaries and fellowships so that even the farm labourer's son, who has been teaching for fifteen years with his Geography degree or who left school at twelve with nothing, can branch out in new directions or start all over again.

And finally the Public Schools must be abolished. This is not because they are strongholds of privilege; they are in fact highly meritocratic. But the odds are now grotesquely and unfairly stacked against working-class boys and girls in neighbourhood comprehensive schools. We have committed the unspeakable tragedy of abolishing the state grammar schools. Elementary justice and decency demand that we redress the balance.

THE PROBLEMS OF COMPREHENSIVE SCHOOLS

Comprehensive schools, at least as presently organized, are unlikely to promote throughout the nation a random association between parental and filial status. Their influence is likely to be in a contrary direction. Their problem is not comprehensiveness but precisely the lack of it: the social-class bias in any particular comprehensive school reflects the class bias of the neighbourhood it serves. Comprehensive schools are, in the main, 'neighbourhood schools' (it is only in rural areas with thinly scattered populations that they will tend not to be). The social level and the intellectual abilities of pupils in any particular school will be negatively or positively 'skewed'.

The evidence that we have suggests that the influence of 'social class' on children's friendships, aspirations, and perhaps academic achievement is considerable in comprehensive schools and may be greater than under the so-called 'tripartite' system which preceded it. Ford's well-known study of the nineteen-sixties pointed in this direction. She compared three schools in mainly working-class areas of London: a grammar school, a secondary modern school, and a comprehensive school. It was the grammar school which most successfully eliminated 'class' in the choice of friends: 'The evidence from this sample suggests that if any type of schooling diminishes the likelihood of class bias in informal social relations within the classroom this is not the comprehensive but the grammar school.'[29]

The evidence on social class and scholastic attainment in comprehensive schools is as unsatisfactory as evidence on this relationship generally. In any event, what we need is evidence on between-school rather than within-school differences. If there are social-class influences on levels of attainment, are they less in comprehensive than in selective schools?

Holly's study of the London comprehensive school in which he was teaching in the early nineteen-sixties purports to show the influence of 'class' on academic achievement as on other aspects of school life.[30] It fully merits the strictures of

Giddens and Holloway.[31] It is not only inadequate and confusing in its use of 'social class' categories, but unhelpful in its presentation of examination results in social-class terms. As Giddens and Holloway observe:

> Few would wish to claim that the comprehensive school serves to eliminate class differentials in educational success altogether. The problem is to discover whether comprehensive schools are *relatively* more effective in this respect than the tripartite system. What is relevant in the lean statistics which Holly provides on differential examination success is not that there is a statistically significant difference between the examination performance of the middle class and the working class children, but how these statistics compare with similar ones in other types of school.

Giddens and Holloway are too polite. Holly's statistics are not simply 'lean'; they are useless. They are, indeed, outrageously deficient, like so much of the 'statistical evidence' used in the social-class debate. This is not because they tell us nothing about differences between schools of different type; they are wholly unconvincing on social class and academic attainment *within* a particular school. (Holly concedes that there was no significant social-class difference among 'academic' pupils, and combines incommensurate examinations to claim social-class differences among 'non-academic' pupils.) If Holly's pathetic statistics actually meant anything, they would be telling evidence in favour of the comprehensive school and not, as he imagines, against it.[32]

In Ford's study '... there is some indication that "wastage of ability" among bright working-class pupils may be occurring on an even larger scale' at the comprehensive than the grammar school.[33] This is based on the stated leaving intentions of Fourth Year pupils. This pinpoints what is probably the most grievous mischief of comprehensive education: that it is the clever working-class boy and girl who are likely to be its principal victims.

The problem with the comprehensive school is its variability. It is impossible to talk about 'the comprehensive school' even as one could reasonably talk about 'the grammar school'. Comprehensive schools differ principally according to where they are located and the type of school out of which they have been formed. The comprehensive school embedded in a well-to-do middle-class suburb which was formerly an academically successful maintained grammar school is a very different proposition from the comprehensive school in a decaying inner city or on a slum-clearance housing estate which is a transfigured secondary modern. The able working-class boy who now attends the latter would previously have attended the former. The latter is 'negatively skewed' with regard to social class and ability, and it is this 'negative skew' which is likely to be deeply damaging.

King Edward VII School, Sheffield, is a former high-powered grammar school now a comprehensive which is probably 'positively skewed'. It 'went comprehensive' (and coeducational) ten years ago, in 1969, but inherited the grammar school staff (and traditions) and includes in its catchment area a good slice of middle-class Sheffield. There was no direct-grant grammar school in Sheffield to cream off its best pupils either before comprehensivization or since. It is true that in the nineteen-fifties an average of twenty-one pupils a year went on to Oxford or Cambridge, while in the nineteen-seventies only thirteen a year. In the five years from 1964 to 1968 the school obtained fifty-one open scholarships and exhibitions at Oxford and Cambridge; in the five years from 1974 to 1978, only eight. But in spite of elements of continuity, the school today is a different school and direct comparisons are misleading. It probably gives able working-class pupils as good and demanding an education as any other comprehensive school in the land.

The new headmaster was fully committed from the start to the comprehensive idea, and at the same time to high academic standards and success. After the school's first nine years as a comprehensive he warned against premature judgement, but is reported as saying (in 1978):

> We may fail dismally, but I'm quite sure the only way is to have all children in the same school. Either there was a most colossal blunder in deciding schools should be comprehensive, or we're being led towards a new way. We may fail, but at least we've tried.[34]

Strong indications of the damaging consequences of 'negative skew' are to be found in the recently published work not of a sociologist but a psychiatrist—Michael Rutter. His report is based on a study of twelve London inner-city comprehensive schools in the mid-nineteen-seventies. None had been a selective school in the past. The schools varied in their 'outcomes': attendance and delinquency rates, in-school behaviour, and examination success. The variations in 'output' did not simply reflect the variations in 'input': they were systematically related to school characteristics. And crucial among these charateristics were different kinds of 'balance' or lack of it—what I have called 'skew'.

The major defect of this study of 'school effect' is the homogeneous nature of the schools. All of them are negatively skewed or out of balance with regard to social class and ability. Children in all the schools came to an abnormal extent from the homes of unskilled workers living in subsidized local authority housing, and 'none of the schools had a particularly advantaged intake with respect to intellectual ability'.[35]

Nevertheless, there was sufficient variability to permit some statistical analysis of the effects of different school circumstances. Rutter and his colleagues addressed themselves to the question: 'Does a largely disadvantaged intake to a school depress scholastic attainments in some overall way?' Conversely, are there benefits to the school as a whole in having a relatively high concentration of able pupils—benefits, that is to say, on other pupils? The answer to both questions was: 'yes'.

The 'balance' that was most important was in ability; rather less so, but still significant, was social-class balance (in terms of fathers' manual or non-manual occupations).[36] 'When the proportion of less able children becomes too high, this will mean that a *preponderance* of the pupils will fail to achieve examination success. ...' Rutter and his colleagues offer admittedly speculative explanations in terms of the highly fashionable 'anti-school subculture'. There is no need for this flight into sociology; no one with much common sense would imagine that we are likely to get the best out of a bright boy by sending him to school for five years with a collection of dullards.

CONCLUSION

The record of sociology in its application to the study and practice of education since the war is a sorry story. Quite apart from its tragic practical consequences, one wonders at the intellectual shoddiness of it all, the spectacle of people of modest talents on the make. It has been a tawdry, over-hasty but curiously bombastic exercise as reviewed in this book, pretentious and arrogant, often with careless, incompetent, or none-too-scrupulous treatment of evidence either through cowardice in the face of fashion or perhaps unawareness that truth matters.

The affair of the William Tyndale School in the mid-nineteen-seventies was perhaps no more than a little local difficulty; but it illustrates the tragi-comic intellectual muddle that we call 'the Sociology of Education'. The Tyndale affair was not a product of class conflict; it was the product of university-based in-service training. The school under its headmaster, Tony Ellis, who had recently obtained his Diploma in Primary Education (with a thesis on team teaching),[37] implemented a fair selection of the sociologically inspired cliches in the repertoire of advanced diploma courses for serving teachers.[38] The school was a middle-class institution and must be re-oriented to serve the disadvantaged; Ellis and his colleagues claimed to be the champions of the oppressed (but emphatically not the aspiring) working class. The school must have an integrated day, vertical grouping, non-competitive activities, undifferentiated sex roles, all on the open plan. In his application for the headship Ellis had strongly supported the idea of a community school. It is in the day-to-day life in classrooms, as well as in Education's Grand Design, that the indescribable and deeply destructive intellectual muddle of the Sociology of Education will be found.

NOTES

1. See Louis Cohen and Kenneth Boothroyd, 'Community expectations of the teacher's role: some mistaken perceptions of primary school teachers', *Research in Education*, **1972**, No. 7.
2. Schools Council Inquiry I, *Young School Leavers*, HMSO, London, 1968, Fig. 5, p. 42.
3. F. Musgrove and Philip H. Taylor, *Society and the Teacher's Role*, Routledge and Kegan Paul, London, 1969, p. 63.
4. Russell's attack on character training and emphasis on the overriding importance of intellect appeared in the book, *Education*, which was published by Allen & Unwin in 1926; Cyril Norwood's reply is contained in the book, *The English Tradition of Education*, which was published by Murray in 1929.
5. Correlli Barnett, *The Collapse of British Power*, Eyre Methuen, 1972, p. 43.
6. Carl Bereiter, 'Schools without education', *Harvard Educational Review*, **42** (1972).
7. B. R. Wilson, 'The teacher's role—a sociological analysis', *British Journal of Sociology*, **13** (1962).
8. F. Musgrove and P. H. Taylor, *Society and the Teacher's Role*, Routledge and Kegan Paul, 1969, pp. 86–88.
9. Lionel Trilling, *Beyond Culture*, Penguin Books, Hammondsworth, 1967, p. 12.

10. E. Midwinter, 'Teaching with the urban environment', in J. Raynor and J. Harden (Eds.), *Equality and City Schools. Readings in Urban Education*, Vol. 2, Routledge and Kegan Paul, London, 1973.
11. P. S. A. Thomson, *Educational Priority Areas and the National E.P.A. Project 1968–71 : A Study with Special Reference to Liverpool*, Unpublished M.A. thesis, University of Liverpool, 1978, p. 259.
12. See George Psacharopoulos, 'Family background, education and achievement', *British Journal of Sociology*, **28** (1977):

> The crude correlation between earnings and schooling for comparable populations are U.S. 0.330, U.K. 0.400. Although the correlation is higher in the U.K., the difference is not very dramatic. Perhaps the most dramatic difference between Jencks' findings and mine relates to the direct path from earnings to education. If this is adopted as the criterion of importance, then schooling clearly matters—at least in the U.K.

13. John Holt, *The Underachieving School*, Penguin Books, Harmondsworth, 1971, p. 22.
14. B. Bloom, *Stability and Change in Human Characteristics*, Wiley, New York, 1966, pp. 215–216.
15. C. Jencks *et al.*, *Inequality*, Penguin Books, 1975, pp. 87–8.
16. C. Bereiter, 'Schools without education', *Harvard Educational Review*, **42** (197).
17. Elizabeth Rosser and Rom Harre, 'The meaning of trouble', in Martyn Hammersley and Peter Woods (Eds.), *The Process of Schooling*, Routledge and Kegan Paul, London, 1976. See also Elizabeth Rosser and Rom Harre, *Rules of Disorder*, Routledge and Kegan Paul, London, 1978.
18. Peter E. Woods, *Secondary School Realities*, Ph.D. thesis, Open University, 1978, p. 80. See also Peter Woods, *The Divided School*, Routledge and Kegan Paul, London, 1979.
19. Peter Woods, 'Staffroom Humour', in *Secondary School Realities*, Ph.D. thesis, Open University, 1978, pp. 450–501.
20. C. Jencks *et al.*, *Inequality*, Penguin Books, 1975, p. 224.
21. Raymond Aron, *Progress and Disillusion*, Penguin Books, 1972, p. 160.
22. C. Jencks *et al.*, *Inequality*, Penguin Books, 1975, pp. 101–102.
23. Marjorie E. Ainsworth and Eric J. Batten, *The Effects of Environmental Factors on Secondary Educational Attainment in Manchester*, Macmillan, London, 1974, pp. 67–68.
24. Samuel Bowles, 'Towards equality of educational opportunity?', in *Equal Education Opportunity*, Harvard University Press, 1969.
25. R. K. Kelsall, Anne Poole, and Annette Kulin, *Graduates: The Sociology of an Elite*, Methuen, London, 1972, p. 22.
26. F. Musgrove, 'Social class and levels of aspiration in a technological university', *Sociological Review*, **15** (1967).
27. Daniel Bell, *The Coming of Post-Industrial Society*, Penguin Books, 1976, p. 242.
28. Pierre Bourdieu and Jean-Claude Passeron, *Reproduction in Education, Society and Culture*, Sage, London, 1977), pp. 222–230.
29. Julienne Ford, *Social Class and the Comprehensive School*, Routledge and Kegan Paul, London, 1969, p. 103.
30. D. N. Holly, 'Profiting from a comprehensive school: class, sex and ability', *British Journal of Sociology*, **16** (1965).
31. A. Giddens and S. W. F. Holloway, 'Profiting from a comprehensive school: a critical comment', *British Journal of Sociology*, **16** (1965).
32. Holly says that those pupils admitted to the school at eleven-plus 'for an academic education' showed no statistically significant difference with regard to social class in their General Certificate examinations. But the numbers, he says, were small. He does not tell us what they were. His case for social-class differences in academic achievement rests on the performance in public examinations of the remainder (the number again is

unspecified but a table of percentages is provided). That is to say, the case rests on those non-academic pupils who stayed on for five years and took some public examinations. They sat either General Certificate or Royal Society of Arts examinations (or perhaps both). Holly does not distinguish between these two examinations in his analysis but combines them. This is indefensible. 'Success' means gaining one or more GCE or RSA pass. In these terms 66 per cent. of the middle-class non-academic pupils were 'successful', 32 per cent. of the skilled working class, and 53 per cent. of the 'less-skilled working class'. It is on the basis of these remarkable statistics that Holly claims that middle-class pupils derive more scholastic benefit from the comprehensive school than the working-class pupils. In fact, at least among these non-academic residuals, unskilled workers' children seem to be doing far better, relative to other social classes, than was ever the case in the tripartite system.

33. J. Ford, *Social Class and the Comprehensive School*, Routledge and Kegan Paul, 1969, p. 40.
34. Graham Turner, 'Two schools, two worlds: who wins?', *The Sunday Telegraph*, 2 July 1978.
35. Michael Rutter, Barbara Maughan, Peter Mortimore, and Janet Ouston, *Fifteen Thousand Hours. Secondary Schools and their Effects on Children*, Open Books, 1979, p. 159 n.
36. *Ibid.*, pp. 152–161.
37. The Auld Report, *William Tyndale Junior and Infants Schools Public Inquiry*, ILEA, 1976, paras. 163–164, p. 51.
38. See John Gretton and Mark Jackson, *William Tyndale: Collapse of a School—or a System?*, George Allen and Unwin, London, 1976, pp. 52–53; and Terry Ellis *et al.*, *William Tyndale: The Teachers' Story*, Writers and Readers Publishing Cooperative, London, 1976, pp. 45–46.

Author Index

Subject Index